THE A

CARLO BONINI has spent the pa
organised crime in Italy and internatio....,
Woodward of Italian journalism'. He started working as a journalist age
his native Rome as a city reporter with *Il Manifesto*. Since then he has worked for
Newsweek magazine in New York and *Il Corriere della Sera* in Milan before joining
La Repubblica in Rome in 2001. His bestselling *Suburra* has been made into a film
and a successful Netflix series.

MANUEL DELIA started dabbling in journalism a few months before the death of
Daphne Caruana Galizia. In life, she encouraged him to write, and after her death,
he resolved to try and keep her legacy going. He spent his early years in student
politics and journalism before reading politics at the London School of Economics
and Political Science on a Chevening scholarship. Between 1999 and 2013, he
held several civil service appointments including press secretary to Prime Minister
Eddie Fenech Adami and head of policy in several government ministries. He
unsuccessfully contested the 2013 general election on the PN ticket and thought
he had left politics for good until the writing bug bit him again in 2017. He blogs
on *Truth Be Told* (manueldelia.com) and writes a regular column on politics for *The
Sunday Times of Malta*. This is his first book.

JOHN SWEENEY is an old-school reporter who used to work for *BBC Panorama*
and *Newsnight*. His interview with Malta's prime minister ended with him accusing
Joseph Muscat of being Europe's 'Artful Dodger' – a charge the PM denied. He
has covered trouble around the world, gone undercover to make films in Mugabe's
Zimbabwe, Chechnya, and North Korea and challenged Donald Trump over his
links to organised crime and Vladimir Putin over the shooting down of MH17.
But he is probably best known for shouting at the Church of Scientology. He
has written 10 books including the best-selling novel *Elephant Moon*. He loves a
limoncello.

To
Daphne

To
Peter, Matthew, Andrew, and Paul

To
Michael, Rose, Corinne, Mandy, and Helene

To
Rose Daphne Caruana Galizia born on 21 December 2018

ACKNOWLEDGEMENTS

The authors wish to thank the Justice for Journalists Foundation for funding and supporting this book.

Although the three authors have written this work on the life and murder of Daphne Caruana Galizia, dozens of journalists from Malta and around the world have unearthed much of the information that has found its way into this publication.

It is impossible to mention all the journalists who worked and are still working on this case. We are grateful to all of them. There are no silver linings in this story. But there are important lessons for us, and for those who think that they can kill a journalist and get away with it. When a journalist is killed, a dozen, a hundred, a thousand will step in to continue their work.

It is right that we thank colleagues from the Daphne Project and Forbidden Stories and the journalists working for international news organisations who wrote about this case. But it is also right that we thank the Maltese journalists working the beat who have documented the drama: the court reporters, the newsroom staffers, the investigators and the editors at *The Times of Malta*, *The Malta Independent*, *Malta Today*, *Lovin Malta*, *Newsbook*, and *The Shift News*. We would not have been able to put this story together without constantly referring back to their work.

The authors are grateful to the international free speech community's efforts to promote the cause for truth and justice for Daphne Caruana Galizia and want to single out Rebecca Vincent of RSF Reporters Without Borders, Tom Gibson of the Committee to Protect Journalists, Flutura Kusari of the European Centre for Press and Media Freedom, Sarah Clarke of Article 19, and others from PEN International, the European Federation of Journalists, IFEX, and the International Press Institute.

Thanks, also, to the editor and staff of *BBC Newsnight* who produced three films reported by co-author John Sweeney – one on Joseph Mifsud, the mystery professor, and two on the murder of Daphne Caruana Galizia and its aftermath, including an interview with Prime Minister Joseph Muscat.

In Malta, the cause for truth and justice for Daphne Caruana Galizia has been taken up by Occupy Justice, Repubblika, and Il-Kenniesa whose work we salute.

The sleeve of this book was designed by Faye Paris.

The authors also acknowledge the kind support of Maria Orzhonikidze, Andrew Borg Cardona, Sharon Spiteri, Valeria Chudarova, Godfrey Leone Ganado, Kurt Scerri, Aarthi Rajaraman, Ellen Trapp, Clémence Dujardin, Jon Wertheim, Stelios Orphanides, Louiselle Vassallo, Alessandra Molinari, Celia Borg Cardona, David Turcan, Johnny Galvin, and Giuliano Foschini.

Alleghe, Italy
September 2019

CONTENTS

This is a very, very dark, black-hearted joke. A joke that's been played on all of us. It's a crime which is not without victims. And many of the victims are journalists. The reason the Panama Papers were exported to the world was because of the work of over 300 investigative journalists who got the word of John Doe, the whistleblower from Mossack Fonseca — or who knows from where — out into the world.

And some people died for it. Daphne Caruana Galizia, the Maltese journalist who was investigating someone at the top in government in Malta and his connection to the Panama Papers was blown up in her car in front of her home.

People died. And people die still if you get the word out.

Actress **Meryl Streep**
at the Venice Biennale press conference
launching Steven Soderbergh's film
The Laundromat, about the Panama Papers
on 1 September 2019

MURDER ON THE MALTA EXPRESS

If we are judged by the nature of our enemies, then Daphne Caruana Galizia should be remembered as a hero of our time. Her murder matters, and it is of concern not just to the people of Malta, but to the world. It speaks to the great problem of today, dirty money's erosion of democracy and the rule of law. Gangsters and their smooth-talking lawyers, fixers, and PR truth-twisters are using crooked microstates to wash their ill-gotten gains from Angola to Azerbaijan so that their money ends up in London, Miami, Rome, or New York. Daphne took them on because she was disgusted at the lies told by her government to enable the money laundering process. Her blog, read by more people than Malta counts as citizens, was a daily whistle-blast, calling out the government and the opposition, the shadowy foreign money men and their cronies for their dodgy deeds. The Panama Papers was just one example of Malta doing precisely nothing to bring to book blatant dishonesty in public office.

Her assassination presents the sleuth with a series of plot twists akin to an Agatha Christie murder mystery for the 21st century. Malta's most fearless journalist was driven by a passionate belief in the truth but she also had a sharp tongue and a nose for a story. She was the living embodiment of Gustave Flaubert's observation that 'when fighting for truth and justice, it is never a good idea to wear one's best trousers'. She fought like a tiger and this earned her so many enemies that one inevitably loses count of the people who wished her harm. Living under threat became a fact of life for an investigative journalist on a small island with a new-found reputation as an international luxury locomotive for dirty money.

Once better known for its history and natural beauty, Malta was the base from which she challenged corruption head on without fear or favour. In a blog post shortly before her death, she wrote:

There is something else I should say before I go: when people taunt you or criticise you for being 'negative' or for failing to go with their flow, for not adopting an attitude of benign tolerance to their excesses, bear in mind always that they, and not you, are the ones who are in the wrong.

Her reward was death by car bomb.

Three men have been formally charged with the killing. They deny it. It seems likely that they are merely the executioners since she never wrote about them. And so, the critical question remains unanswered. Who sent them? Who ordered her death?

Daphne described Malta as a dirty money train hurtling through the night with a cast of dodgy characters on board. Daphne cast herself in the role of Miss Marple and Hercule Poirot joined together at the hip. The other characters are:

- the island's prime minister, branded by some as the Artful Dodger of Europe;
- the woman alleged by Daphne to be the recipient of a million dollar bung who happens to be the prime minister's wife;
- the leader of the opposition, whose claim to fame is Daphne's description of him as a money launderer for brothels in London's Soho;
- the prime minister's duo of creepy consiglieri, both named in the Panama Papers;
- the government minister accused by Daphne of skipping a boring conference to visit a brothel;
- the Iranian boss of a money-laundering bank;
- the Maltese EU commissioner who was asked to resign amid a flurry of bribery allegations;
- the suave and super-smooth Swiss lawyer known as The Passport King for selling citizenships to the fabulously wealthy;

- the daughter of a tyrant currently ruling a fabulously corrupt oil-rich nation;
- the billionaire boss with two passions: casinos and gas power stations;
- the globe-trotting professor named as a bit player in the Trump-Russia inquiry;
- sundry gangsters;
- fuel smugglers; and
- other dubious types.

All concerned deny any wrongdoing.

A Council of Europe report by Dutch MP Pieter Omtzigt in 2019 sets out the failings of the rule of law in Malta. Omtzigt found that the Maltese prime minister hires and fires his police chiefs on a whim. Prime Minister Joseph Muscat is now on his fifth commissioner of police in six years. Too many of Malta's judges are political appointees, reports Omtzigt, a state of affairs 'fundamentally incompatible with the idea of judicial independence'. And the country has a 'culture of impunity', says the man from the Council of Europe.

The picture that emerges is of monstrous corruption, its greatest enemy slain.

Daphne's loss was most brutal for her husband Peter, her three sons, Matthew, Andrew, and Paul, and her close relatives and friends, but it was a huge blow to all decent Maltese people. The outrage echoed around the world.

In the annual report of the Group of States Against Corruption (GRECO) in 2017, Daphne's sons wrote:

> ... *in countries where there's no will or capacity to prosecute the corrupt figures they expose, journalists often become the targets themselves. The state's full force is brought down not on the corrupt, but on the journalists and whistleblowers who bring their corruption to light. When the first Panama Papers reports broke in some countries... journalists working on the Panama Papers were hit with vexatious lawsuits, financial threats, targeted tax investigations, and physical harassment... Some of those journalists are likely to be murdered: since 1992 two-thirds of all murdered journalists were covering politics and corruption. This statistic shows us that a journalist is murdered when institutions fail to*

investigate corruption, when they fail to prosecute it, and when they fail to deter it in the first place. The murder of journalists betrays institutional failure and extreme levels of corruption.

The international community of journalists reacted to her death by creating the Daphne Project, a cleverly effective response bringing together reporters from multiple news organisations around the world, pooling resources to continue her investigations.

This book aspires to be a continuation of the spirit of the Daphne Project. It is written by three journalists, Carlo Bonini, Manuel Delia, and John Sweeney. Bonini is a reporter for Italy's *La Repubblica* who specialises in covering organised crime and is one of the 45 journalists on the Daphne Project. Delia is a Maltese blogger who unwittingly found himself trying – as if anyone could – to fill Daphne's shoes after her assassination. Sweeney was the reporter on *BBC Newsnight* who took Prime Minister Joseph Muscat to task over Malta's culture of impunity.

The reason we have written this book is because the Maltese state seems unwilling to lift stones for fear of what it may find beneath. To take just one example, at the time of writing, the three men accused of her murder have yet to be tried although the evidence against them appears to be overwhelming. The state appears to have ruled out any form of plea bargaining. The former head of Europol has publicly complained about the Maltese state dragging its feet in the investigation. It is almost as if the Maltese powers that be do not want to know who sent the executioners. After all, no one has been ruled out as a suspect. Not even the prime minister.

This is our attempt to pay tribute to Daphne Caruana Galizia, to keep the light of her journalism burning and to set out why the main suspects have not been held to account. The person or persons who ordered Daphne's assassination will not enjoy the contents of this book. This is exactly why we urge you to read it.

Carlo Bonini
Manuel Delia
John Sweeney

EXECUTION

Daphne Caruana Galizia was killed just as the shadows started to lengthen, a few seconds before 3pm on a warm autumn day. Malta is one of the most densely-populated and built-up countries in the world but Daphne lived with her husband Peter in a country house towards the north of the island: green fields running down to the sea, chequered by stone walls and outcrops of barren rock. The family home lies on the northern slope of a valley, hidden by trees. She did not know it at the time, but she was being watched and had been for some time.

The three men charged with her murder are George Degiorgio known by his nickname 'the Chinaman' (*iċ-Ċiniż*) and his younger brother Alfred 'the Bean' (*il-Fulu*) and their friend Vincent Muscat. His nickname in Maltese is *il-Koħħu* which is untranslatable. Vincent Muscat is no relation to prime minister Joseph Muscat. All three are pleading not guilty. They deny any wrongdoing.

A pre-trial hearing has heard evidence from a police inspector that Daphne had been under surveillance for weeks before her death on Monday 16 October 2017. The three men were allegedly trying to identify a pattern to her movements. Mostly, she stayed indoors working on her blog, *Running Commentary*, the most widely-read news source on the island, sometimes reaching 400,000 readers in a single day. It was a must-read; a bitter, sometimes vitriolic account of the waves of dirty money crashing over her island nation.

When she did go out, it was mostly on brief errands. The day before, a Sunday, Daphne and Peter went to lunch in a nearby town, Naxxar. Some time later, they were joined by Matthew, their eldest son, driving the white Peugeot she had rented some months previously. The couple returned home and Matthew took the Peugeot and went to the beach for a swim.

On the Sunday Daphne bought some saplings for her beloved garden from a street market. Incredibly, photographs of her shopping were taken by a government official and posted on Facebook. The peeping tom who took the snaps was called Neville Gafà. It is hard to imagine why anyone would do that. A middle-aged woman and her husband buying plants at a market: why would anyone want to see that?

This seemingly trivial move was part of a concerted campaign of harassment against Daphne. She often published photos taken by her readers, of public figures in a semi-public context: a magistrate partying with politicians whose libel complaints she was deciding, a disgraced judge sentenced to prison for corruption having a business meeting in a restaurant, a government minister having lunch with a lawyer sacked from the police force or the same minister on a pub crawl during office hours in an advanced stage of inebriation.

Her enemies considered her photos an invasion of privacy and in a campaign codenamed 'Taste your own medicine' they sought to retaliate, encouraging anyone who saw Daphne out in the street to take her photograph.

Neville Gafà had reason to dislike Daphne, but more of that in the chapter *A Panama Hat and Caesar's Wife*.

For Daphne, the harassment was worth putting up with. She loved her garden, the place where she sought respite from the death threats and the libel suits.

The court cases had been piling up. At the time of her death, she was facing 42 civil libel actions and 5 cases of criminal defamation, most from figures within the ruling Labour Party (PL) led by prime minister Joseph Muscat. Earlier that year, Daphne had published a story on her blog claiming that Minister for the Economy Chris Cardona had been spotted in a brothel in Germany during an official business trip. Cardona denied the claim and sued for libel. In the process, he obtained a garnishee order freezing her bank accounts. Daphne countered by requesting the court to order Cardona's mobile phone service provider to produce his phone data. These, she argued, would pinpoint his exact location and establish whether he had really been sleeping peacefully in his hotel, as he claimed, or in a brothel called the FKK Acapulco several kilometres away. The service provider complied with the court order but the data was not made public because Cardona repeatedly failed to turn up in court to press his suit even after she had been murdered. In Malta, libel suits can be pursued after death. Eventually, in 2018, the court threw out the case because of Cardona's failure to attend court. Cardona is still, at the time of writing, the economy minister.

More threats of libel action came from British law firm Mishcon de Reya on behalf of Henley & Partners, a Jersey-registered company which likes to nestle up to microstates such as Malta and Saint Kitts and Nevis in the Caribbean and cut a deal with their governments to sell passports to high-value bidders. These buyers tend to be publicity-shy oligarchs or autocratic multimillionaires from Russia, China, Africa, or the Middle East who want a second passport without too many questions asked.

After starting in the Caribbean, Henley & Partners moved to Malta and procured a willing partner in Joseph Muscat's Labour Party when it came to power in 2013. The beauty of a Maltese passport is that it provides free movement within the European Union and easy passage to the United States. Malta charges around €650,000 for a passport but, with the additional requirements, the cost is likely to get close to €1 million. Henley & Partners takes a cut before handing the rest to Malta. The sale of Maltese passports has gone from strength to strength in the past few years and is believed to have hit the €2.5 billion mark, boosting the government's finances, enriching Henley & Partners but also introducing a shed-load of shifty, shadowy scoundrels to the island.

Daphne, with her long dark hair and dark eyes, had something of the sorceress about her. Her enemies called her 'The Witch of

Bidnija' after the hamlet where she lived. It was not magic though, but good old-fashioned journalism that led her to obtain a chain of emails between the prime minister, his chief of staff and wheeler-dealer Keith Schembri, and the chairman of Henley & Partners Christian Kälin also known as 'The Passport King'. In the email chain, the three sanctioned a libel attack on Daphne because she dared to question their activities. Daphne had written an open letter to Kälin in May 2017 in her customary acerbic style:

> *I do not appreciate your threat to sue me in London. The reason you are doing it is not because 'most of your business is there'. Most of your business comes from shady people in Russia and the Middle East, with the occasional Vietnamese MP thrown in. The reason you are threatening to sue me in London is because you imagine that I am somebody from the sticks who is frightened of the words 'London', 'UK courts', and 'high costs'.*

The legal menaces were by no means the gravest dangers. Daphne was no fool. She knew the risks she was taking. One time, in the middle of the night, tyres had been stacked against the back of her house, packed with bottles of petrol and set on fire – but one of her boys spotted the fire and raised the alarm. But she also knew the risks of shutting up, of letting the scandals continue unchallenged and, for her, that was the greater danger.

Daphne and her husband Peter had three sons, Matthew, Andrew, and Paul. All three boys often worked abroad, but on that fateful weekend in October 2017, Matthew was in Malta. After Sunday lunch with his parents, an afternoon swim, and an evening drink with friends, he drove back home in the rented Peugeot in the early hours of Monday morning. He could have opened the gate and driven the car right inside his parents' driveway. But it was late and he was tired. So he parked the car just outside the house. This was not a particularly rare occurrence. The car was left outside just as often as it was driven inside.

It would have made little difference if Matthew had driven the car into the driveway. The perimeter wall of the property is too low to be a serious deterrent and Daphne had lost the two guard dogs she kept to alert her of intruders. Santino, Daphne's loyal

Neapolitan mastiff, had died in 2016. Tony, her Staffordshire bull terrier had been poisoned three months previously and was so sick he was no longer an effective guard dog. The yelp of Hanno, the puppy Daphne got that summer, was no replacement for the barking of fully-grown guard dogs. Daphne's house that October 2017 was as vulnerable to intrusion as it had ever been.

The assassins got to the car while the family slept. They used a device to trick the central locking system into unlocking the doors and then placed a small bomb underneath the driver's seat, hidden from view. The trigger would be a text message to a mobile phone attached to the bomb. The burner phone, a disposable device purposefully not registered in anyone's name, was turned on just after 2am, and 13 hours later it would receive its one and only message.

Evidence in pre-trial hearings under Malta's legal system can be reported. The magistrate heard that either Alfred Degiorgio or Vincent Muscat were watching Daphne's home at 2.30pm on Monday afternoon. The spotter is believed to have been on a bluff overlooking the road down which Daphne was most likely to drive. As she drove her rented grey Peugeot onto the road, the spotter warned the triggerman.

— She is out. No, wait a minute, she's gone back inside.

Daphne had forgotten the cheques signed by Peter which she had to take to the bank to exchange for cash. She needed to pay the monthly car rental bill and her bank accounts had been frozen as a result of the court order obtained by Economy Minister Chris 'I wasn't at the brothel' Cardona and his aide in their libel action. So she was using signed cheques from her husband's account and cashing them in personally. It was the best solution to her state of legally-enforced financial penury. She said goodbye to her eldest son and drove off again.

— She's coming back out. It's time.

The spotter's signal went out to sea, several hundred metres beyond the mouth of Valletta's harbour. There, bobbing up and down on his fishing boat, was the triggerman, reportedly George

Degiorgio. He stayed just within range of the mobile phone antennae to be able to send and receive messages. Malta is a crowded place. The open sea was the only place you could act without being seen.

His job was simple. Send a message by SMS to a number. The number would detonate the bomb in the witch's white car.

As assassins go, the alleged triggerman was a moron, if the evidence against him is to be believed. Or a man who believed he could act with impunity. That morning he had taken his brother's boat, the *Maya*, and had spent the day out at sea. He had three phones with him. His own, a second 'walkie-talkie' burner phone he used exclusively to talk to his brother Alfred and his associate, Vincent Muscat, and a third burner phone he would only use to send the text that would trigger the bomb. The three 'walkie-talkie' phones they used to talk to each other were all bought on 19 August 2017 along with their SIM cards.

Was the order to kill Daphne given on that date?

On 16 October 2017, while out at sea, George Degiorgio realised he had run out of credit on the second 'walkie-talkie' burner phone. So he used his personal phone to call a friend to top it up. The friend was out hunting and could not help so, at 9.01am, George called a second friend who could. The phone was topped up with €5 and George could talk to his brother and Vincent Muscat on their own secret 'walkie-talkie' network. At 2.59pm George sent a message from the the third burner phone, or kill phone, to a SIM card which went off signal instantly. That SIM card went up in the explosion which killed Daphne Caruana Galizia.

The explosion was loud. Matthew and some of Daphne's neighbours in the hamlet heard it. On the *Maya*, George Degiorgio was listening in on the 'walkie-talkie' phone held by Alfred Degiorgio or Vincent Muscat on the bluff overlooking the murder scene. He would have heard the bomb go off.

At 3.30pm George Degiorgio sent another text to his wife. It was later retrieved by police and said:

— Open a bottle of wine for me, baby.

Moron.

What the three did not know was that George Degiorgio was being investigated by Malta's security service who suspected him of other, unrelated criminal activities. His personal mobile phone was being tapped. His two calls requesting a top-up to the 'walkie-talkie' phone were recorded. Those calls alerted the Maltese intelligence service to the 'walkie-talkie' network. Malta appealed to Europol who got in touch with the Finnish police. Thanks to the existence of Nokia, the Finns are world experts at reading phone data. Using the phone company's data, they established that at the time the trigger text was sent, the phone was on a boat somewhere near the Siege Bell war memorial in Valletta. There are CCTV cameras by the Siege Bell looking out to sea. On the CCTV cameras, the police saw the *Maya*. The boat was not moving because George Degiorgio could not steer the boat and listen to his brother on the 'walkie-talkie' phone at the same time. And it was important that he hear his brother give the order to send the text message which would kill Daphne.

The 'walkie-talkie' phone data for the previous night places George Degiorgio in Bidnija, the hamlet where Daphne lived. At 1.30am, George was at his house but 10 minutes later he was in Bidnija again, along with Alfred Degioergio and Vincent Muscat. So the 'walkie-talkie' phone data places all three in Daphne's hamlet around the time the bomb was planted and the phone to detonate the bomb switched on. This, coupled with the timing of George's text to his wife later that afternoon, creates a compelling case against the three men.

Meanwhile, back in Valletta harbour after the explosion was triggered, George Degiorgio docked the boat and tossed the burner phones into the water. One of this book's authors, Carlo Bonini, wrote in *La Repubblica* that Maltese army divers had found eight such burner phones in the shallows beneath the Siege Bell memorial, suggesting that George had done this before. Officially, George was unemployed but he drove a Corvette and an Audi Q7. He was reportedly known to the Maltese criminal underworld as a hitman. His brother Alfred was also known to the police.

Vincent Muscat was a suspect in the failed heist of the HSBC's Malta headquarters in 2010 which ended in a shootout with the police. He has been charged but not tried in connection with this robbery. His defence lawyer in 2010 was Chris Cardona, now the infamous brothel-creeping minister. In 2014, someone shot Vincent Muscat in the head while he was sitting in his car. He survived, but was blinded in one eye and a bullet fragment left in his head. The man who allegedly tried to kill Muscat was later murdered in a shower of bullets. No one was charged, still less convicted for his murder.

All three men insist on their innocence. They have not yet been tried and the authors recognise that they are, of course, presumed innocent until proven guilty.

Daphne had not written about George Degiorgio, Alfred Degiorgio, or Vincent Muscat. It is hard to think that they had any reason to kill her, bar the fact that they had presumably been commissioned to carry out the killing by someone with a lot of money.

Who could that be?

Around the time the bomb went off, one of Daphne's neighbours was driving up Triq il-Bidnija (*triq* is Maltese for road or street), heading in the direction of his house. He heard a noise that made him brake. This was, most likely, the detonator firing. He saw a woman inside a car and could see she was in trouble. He did not recognise Daphne. She appeared to be wounded and was panicking. Then there was a second loud explosion, the bomb igniting, followed by a third explosion as the petrol tank blew up. The Peugeot became a ball of fire.

The road goes downhill, kinking to the left, but the burning Peugeot ploughed straight on, propelled by its speed and the force of gravity into a muddy field. The witness was in shock and did not process what was happening until later. All he could say was that when he stepped out of his car he saw body parts scattered across the road. And that he stood guard until the police came, to stop anyone driving over them.

Matthew heard the explosions from inside the house. His mother had just driven away. He ran out barefoot over the unmade road and saw the black smoke rising from the field below. He ran to the car, as close as he could get. He was trying not to think it would be hopeless. He was trying not to think. He just screamed for his mother, refusing to accept she could not hear him.

Out of the corner of his eye, he saw two uniformed policemen rushing up to the car. They carried a pitifully small fire extinguisher, the one they routinely carried in their police car. 'Do something!' he screamed at them. They told him there was nothing they could do.

The field was strewn with his mother's limbs. When the flames started abating, he could see his mother's torso inside the car on the passenger's side, between the seat and the door. There was no part of her he could touch to say goodbye. It was an obscene way for a human being to die.

As he looked about him, a neighbour he vaguely recognised stood at the edge of the field holding up his phone to capture the carnage. He pointed out the neighbour to the policemen. Frustrated by their hesitation, he ran up to the man, grabbed the phone and threw it to the ground. 'You cannot take pictures of my mother in this state,' he roared.

The neighbour, indignant about the damage to his phone and not quite appreciating the full horror of the situation, punched him in the face. The police held back the neighbour but eventually sent him on his way.

Matthew got on his phone and tried to reach his father. Peter was in chambers at a small law firm in Valletta where he was a partner. The lawyer was with clients and did not pick up. So Matthew called his brother Andrew, who was working at the Foreign Office in Valletta, some 500 metres from his father's office. Andrew was a diplomat who had spent most of his time working in Maltese embassies abroad but he had inexplicably just been recalled early from his posting in India to sit in a Valletta office doing not very much – a move the family believed was in retaliation for his mother's journalism. Peter saw Andrew rush in to his office, his face ashen. 'Matthew says something happened to mum. We have to go.'

During the 15-kilometre journey, Andrew found a story on *timesofmalta.com*, the website of Malta's newspaper of record. It broke the news that a car bomb had exploded in Bidnija.

Daphne Caruana Galizia was not the first Maltese person to be killed by car bomb. From the beginning of 2011 to the day before her death in 2017 six cars had been blown up. No one had been arrested, let alone charged, in connection with any of these car bombs. Had the police pulled their finger out, Daphne's assassination may not have happened. Since coming to power in 2013, prime minister Joseph Muscat had burned his way through four police commissioners and by 2017 was on his fifth. It is hard to see how a police force that loses four bosses in as many years can perform its role. In Malta, it barely functions at all.

By the time Peter and Andrew arrived, the police had already cordoned off the murder scene. The senior officer had been expecting Peter and was watching out for the car to try and spare him the scene. As he walked towards the officer, Peter had only one question. 'Is she dead?'

The family home was just 300 metres from the crime scene, so there was little refuge from its realities, with police and scene of crime officers collecting evidence and the press cars and cameras. At home, they were joined by Daphne's elderly parents Michael and Rose Vella, both well into their 70s, and Daphne's younger sisters Corinne, Mandy, and Helene.

The close-knit family was only missing Paul, Daphne's youngest son, who was in England and who, on hearing the news, drove straight to a London airport with his fiancée and flew to Malta that evening.

Malta's criminal justice system is a confusing concoction of laws adapted over time from Roman, Napoleonic, and British law, reflecting the island's chequered history. Magistrates act as judges of first instance and moonlight as crime scene investigators. 'Investigation' is a big word. Their job is to oversee the different stages of the compilation of evidence in serious crimes before they go to trial. The initial process known in Maltese as '*inkjesta*' and somewhat misleadingly translated as 'inquiry' does not lead to a verdict but a series of recommendations to the prosecution. A magistrate can sometimes recommend prosecution against named individuals and even indicate which charges should be brought against whom, but both the police (who lead the criminal prosecution in the first instance) and the attorney general (who heads the prosecution service) are not bound to follow these recommendations.

The initial work of the magistrate during the magisterial inquiry is vital if a prosecution is to be successful. Magistrates – Malta has about 20 – take it in turns to be on call for days at a time and any serious crimes taking place on their watch will fall within their caseload of magisterial inquiries.

There are some aspects of journalism in Malta which are somewhat particular to the fact that, on a small island, everyone knows everyone else. There are some unspoken boundaries few have the courage to overstep, and one of these is the private life of people in authority. Daphne's reputation as a fearless tiger was not unearned. She had no qualms stepping over these invisible lines and calling out judges and magistrates when their behaviour, even in private, was in conflict with their role as upholders of justice.

It was bitterly ironic then that the magistrate she had singled out for particular scorn and reproof was the woman on duty on the afternoon of her death. Magistrate Consuelo Scerri Herrera's private life had attracted Daphne's ire. And although her reporting of the magistrate's private dalliances may have been unsparing, it was right on the money.

The acrimony between the two spilled into the public domain in 2011, when Daphne wrote a series of posts on her blog.

The fact is this, Consuelo: the law is the law. Being a magistrate, you should know that. But you also know that you shouldn't be socialising with plaintiffs and defendants in cases you're hearing, and still you do it. You know that you shouldn't preside over a criminal case in which the defendant is the brother of the man you're secretly sleeping with (though not secretly enough), and still you did it. You know that as a magistrate, you shouldn't have had secret sex (though not secret enough) with a police inspector, and still you did it.

The man she had been sleeping with was Robert Musumeci, a former Nationalist Party (PN) mayor who switched sides and made his career as a senior advisor to Joseph Muscat's government. The relationship was not so secret. Musumeci also ran an online campaign hash-tagged *galiziabarra*, Maltese for 'Galizia Out'. Even after Daphne's death, Musumeci did not relent and campaigned against protesters seeking truth and justice in Daphne's case, branding them 'holier than thou'.

Daphne wrote about Scerri Herrera's wild parties, her indiscriminate choice of friendships and sex partners, and her closeness to the Labour Party leadership. Daphne's relentless scrutiny of the magistrate's private life delayed Consuelo Scerri Herrera's promotion to a judgeship. When the government first nominated her to be a judge, she was rejected by the judicial appointments committee, who were put under pressure to rethink their decision. Scerri Herrera is now a judge, having been appointed by prime minister Joseph Muscat nine months after Daphne's death. At her swearing-in, he made it clear that he thought her appointment was long overdue.

Scerri Herrera's brother was a criminal lawyer and a Labour member of parliament. But that alone did not explain her superiors' resistance to her rise in the ranks before 2013 when the Nationalist Party was in government and may have been reluctant to promote a known Labour sympathiser. In 2010, three years before Joseph Muscat became prime minister, she had been relieved of the job of deciding libel suits involving politicians because it was thought she could not be relied upon to decide fairly in matters of political bias. And she had also been admonished by the judiciary's disciplinary body for private behaviour that had brought her public role into disrepute.

So when Daphne's sons learnt that Scerri Herrera was the magistrate on duty and would be conducting the magisterial inquiry into their mother's death, they wanted Scerri Herrera off the case. They felt she was the last person who could be trusted to be impartial in Daphne's case. Peter called Jason Azzopardi, a lawyer who was also the shadow justice minister. Azzopardi asked the magistrate to recuse herself from the inquiry.

Meanwhile, Scerri Herrera had arrived at the scene of the crime and took in the smoking car wreck, the scorched earth, and the Bidnija field and road littered with body parts. She looked up at Daphne's house nearby, knowing that her family were inside, but did not make any attempt to visit them. There was no communication, no information, and no message of sympathy.

When the magistrate returned to her chambers in Valletta, she sent for the family, making them travel the 40-minute journey to wait in the corridor of the law courts at her pleasure. In court the family met the last people they wanted to see, Chris Cardona and Keith Schembri. The magistrate had the power to call in potential suspects, and both men had been at the receiving end of Daphne's piercing pen. Cardona had a grudge to bear over her reporting of the German brothel story and was suing her. Schembri, the prime minister's chief of staff, was separately suing Daphne for libel over corruption allegations made in the Panama Papers.

Daphne was no small-time island scribe. She had scooped the Panama Papers by a month in 2016 when she had reported that Schembri owned a secret company in Panama, a tax haven. This was behaviour at odds with Schembri's position as a politically exposed person (PEP). He denies wrongdoing but it is hard to see why Schembri needed a shell company in Panama controlled by a shell trust in New Zealand other than to hide the proceeds of corruption. Everywhere else in the democratic world, a politician or senior government official accused of owning a shell company in Panama would have been forced to resign. But not in Malta.

So Magistrate Scerri Herrera (as she was then) brought the family face to face with two of the men she seemed to think might have had reason to want Daphne dead.

For four hours.

At 10pm, she sent one of her minions to hand the family a copy of her decision to step down 'for the sake of appearances'. She could have recused herself instantly. She could have chosen to walk the few metres to the family home and speak to them there. She could have seen them as soon as they arrived in court, sparing them the four-hour wait alongside some suspects. She did not do that.

Meanwhile, the investigation was delayed until a new magistrate could be appointed, and the scene of the crime had to remain untouched, which meant Daphne's family had to walk by her exposed remains every time they went to and from the house.

When Magistrate Anthony Vella was appointed as the inquiring magistrate, he would periodically reassure Peter Caruana Galizia, Daphne's widower, on the progress of the investigation and ask the family about the events leading up to Daphne's murder.

The police were less informative. No family liaison officer was ever appointed, something that could be expected from the police in such a high-profile murder case.

The head of Malta's criminal investigation department (CID) at the time was Silvio Valletta. He is married to Justyne Caruana, a minister in Joseph Muscat's cabinet, well known on the island for an angry speech in which she branded anyone who was not a Labour supporter 'a snake who does not belong'.

Silvio Valletta is no Sherlock Holmes. On his watch, the CID did not make a single arrest in connection with a series of car bombs, five fatal, in the six years leading up to Daphne's murder. Valletta was one of the senior detectives on all these cases and no one has been brought to book.

The 2016 car bombing of 'Soapy' Camilleri is particularly intriguing because he was the estranged business partner of George 'the Chinaman' Degiorgio, one of the men accused of carrying out Daphne's execution. Soapy and the Chinaman had fallen out over

€50,000 in a big way. Two days after Daphne's murder – but long before he was arrested for it – the Chinaman was in court, sued by Soapy's heirs. If only the previous car bombs had been properly investigated, Daphne's killers may not have been at large to strike again. Once again, the three men deny murdering Daphne.

Four days after Daphne's murder, Silvio Valletta sat next to police commissioner Lawrence 'Number Five' Cutajar as they held the first and last press conference on the investigation. Reporters asked a series of questions but the police chief and his top crime-buster claimed they were legally unable to answer any questions which might compromise the magisterial inquiry. What was the point of calling a press conference if no questions about the investigation were going to be answered, asked a brave reporter. Would those people targeted by Caruana Galizia in her writing be questioned? Everyone relevant to the investigation would be spoken to, replied Valletta. That has turned out not to be quite true.

The grandly-titled 'crime conference' conducted four days after the assassination would be the last time the Maltese police made an official statement on the case. All press requests since then have been ignored or dismissed.

The international press needed answers from the police about the investigation into Daphne's death. They also needed answers from the Maltese government. Why had she been killed? Who was behind it?

This was a line of questioning Malta's government was not prepared to entertain. From the outset, government ministers and spokespeople avoided roving microphones. But journalists were not about to let the matter rest. After all, this was the killing of one of their own, in a European country to boot.

Joseph Muscat sat down to a live split-screen interview with CNN's Christiane Amanpour the day after the murder. He offered thoughts and prayers and promised he would personally ensure not to offer cover to anyone linked to the murder, even if they were in politics. There would be no impunity, he said. That also turned out not to be quite true.

But the prime minister was not the first to mention the word impunity. Matthew Caruana Galizia had beaten him to it in an eloquent Facebook post earlier that morning. Matthew is very much his mother's son, a journalist and a member of the team from the International Consortium of Investigative Journalists (ICIJ) who won a Pulitzer prize for their work on the Panama Papers.

My mother was assassinated because she stood between the rule of law and those who sought to violate it, like many strong journalists. But she was also targeted because she was the only person doing so. This is what happens when the institutions of the state are incapacitated: the last person left standing is often a journalist. Which makes her the first person left dead.

I am never going to forget, running around the inferno in the field, trying to figure out a way to open the door, the horn of the car still blaring, screaming at two policemen who turned up with a single fire extinguisher to use it. They stared at me. 'I'm sorry, there is nothing we can do,' one of them said. I looked down and there were my mother's body parts all around me. I realised they were right, it was hopeless. 'Who is in the car?' they asked me. 'My mother is in the car. She is dead. She is dead because of your incompetence.' Yes, incompetence and negligence that resulted in a failure to prevent this from happening.

I am sorry for being graphic, but this is what war looks like, and you need to know. This was no ordinary murder and it was not tragic. Tragic is someone being run over by a bus. When there is blood and fire all around you, that's war. We are a people at war against the state and organised crime, which have become indistinguishable.

A few hours later, while that clown of a Prime Minister was making statements to parliament about a journalist he spent over a decade demonising and harassing, one of the police sergeants who is supposed to be investigating her murder, Ramon Mifsud, posted on Facebook, 'Everyone gets what they deserve, cow dung! Feeling happy :)'

Yes, this is where we are: a mafia state where you can now change your gender on your ID card (thank God for that!) but where you will be blown to pieces for exercising your basic freedoms. Only for the people who are supposed to have protected you to instead be celebrating it. How did we get here?

A culture of impunity has been allowed to flourish by the government in

Malta. It is of little comfort for the Prime Minister of this country to say that he will 'not rest' until the perpetrators are found, when he heads a government that encouraged that same impunity. First he filled his office with crooks, then he filled the police with crooks and imbeciles, then he filled the courts with crooks and incompetents. If the institutions were already working, there would be no assassination to investigate – and my brothers and I would still have a mother.

Joseph Muscat, Keith Schembri, Chris Cardona, Konrad Mizzi, the Attorney General, and the long list of police commissioners who took no action: you are complicit. You are responsible for this.

In her interview Christiane Amanpour put the point made by Matthew to the prime minister. Muscat gave her his trademark rictus smile and dismissed it, as gently as he could, as the grief-stricken thoughts of someone who had just lost his mother. He did not address Matthew's point.

The interview with CNN was the last he gave for months.

Three days after the murder he went on a scheduled trip. It was business as usual.

In January 2015, when the *Charlie Hebdo* massacre took place in France, Joseph Muscat was one of the heads of government who accepted an invitation from the French president to join him on the streets of Paris in a march of solidarity and defiance, in defence of a world order where speech was free.

But when a journalist was killed in his own country, Joseph Muscat did not take to the streets to protest against the murder.

Instead, he flew to Dubai to meet potential passport buyers, wealthy punters tempted by the Henley & Partners package designed by Christian Kälin. The Passport King's scheme has been described by the Organisation for Economic Cooperation and Development (OECD) as a backdoor for money-laundering. It was the subject of one of Daphne Caruana Galizia's most blistering investigations.

Muscat appeared to be saying all the right things, expressing his condolences and assuring international journalists that a proper investigation was being pursued. But, at the same time, he did not chide some of his supporters who continued to drum their narrative of hatred, particularly since Daphne was causing their dear leader more political harm in her death than she had when she was still alive.

When Matthew wrote his Facebook post hours after his mother's death, he had already had a taste of the vitriol. A serving police officer crowed at Daphne's murder and describe her as *'demel'*, meaning dung. The implication was that Daphne had got exactly what she deserved. Many expressed their delight at her death openly, mocked her family in mourning, and expressed their sympathy for the 'real victim', the prime minister.

Muscat himself had set the tone when he sat down with Amanpour. After expressing his condolences, he said he had been the person 'most harshly criticised' by Daphne Caruana Galizia.

So the most fluent and effective Maltese journalist in living memory would be cast as an embarrassment and her work as treason, sedition, even witchcraft. Her death became a very partisan matter. And because the groundwork had been laid months and years earlier, people were so conditioned to hate her that there was no pause, no shock at the inhumanity, the brutality, the utterly misplaced *schadenfreude*. This is what Matthew meant when he described his mother's death as 'war'. Only in war are people conditioned to take satisfaction in death.

Matthew speaks of a decade of harassment and demonisation of his mother led by the prime minister in his party's media. Before he entered politics, Joseph Muscat was himself a journalist and a television producer for the Labour Party media. He learned the ropes campaigning against Malta's EU membership in the years leading up to a 2003 EU referendum in which he was the face of the 'No' campaign.

Daphne Caruana Galizia was on the pro-EU side of the debate. She was a true cosmopolitan with a liberal mindset and encouraged her children to study and work away from Malta. She was horrified by the backward, inward-looking isolationism and her detractors took this as an opportunity to cast her as a member of the elite who was out of touch with the people.

In the context of Malta's postcolonial culture, the notion of treason, or collaboration with 'the foreigner', was a capital charge. And in the context of a misogynistic macho culture in the Mediterranean, the charge of witchcraft was the ultimate insult.

Many thousands of Malta's Labour Party supporters could not read English and got their 'Daphne' translated and mediated by the party. They did not actually read her words but lapped up the myths started by her detractors which acquired a life of their own. To this day, there are people who believe she once wrote that she hoped the prime minister's children would die of cancer. She did not.

What made things worse for Daphne when she was alive was that she believed compromise to be a dirty word. Certainly, she was a career critic of the Labour Party but the Nationalist Party, the other main political party in the Maltese democratic duopoly, was also at the sharp end of her stick many times.

Her mistrust of the Labour Party is rooted in the excesses of the 1970s and 1980s culminating in its crusade against the Catholic Church and the party's attempts to close down Catholic schools in the 1980s. Those two decades in Malta were full of political drama.

The then Labour government nationalised a bank whilst threatening its shareholders, cosied up to Libya's Mu'ammar Ghaddafi, kept a stranglehold on the economy, and ran the country as a personal fiefdom of the party bigshots.

In 1984, students of Catholic schools were forced to receive their education secretly in the cellars of private homes while their school gates were locked. The scenes were reminiscent of a latter-day Tudor clampdown.

Back then, a teenage Daphne, herself an alumna of a Catholic school, joined in the protest marches in her hometown of Sliema which faces Valletta across a harbour.

In the early 1980s, the government took a dim view of street protests. While Daphne had already left secondary school at 19, she marched in support of her younger sisters and friends. Her presence at the protest led to her arrest. The arresting officer was none other than Anġlu Farrugia, who would go on to change careers a few times, first becoming a lawyer, then a Labour MP, and eventually became the Speaker of the House of Representatives.

Years later when Anġlu Farrugia made a bid for the leadership of the PL, Daphne wrote:

I was one of three 19-year-old girls Anġlu Farrugia had arrested on 11 trumped-up charges, including that of assaulting a very large police officer. He had us locked in dark and dirty cells for almost two days. He refused to contact our parents. He refused us access to a lawyer. He threatened me during interrogations. He lied to me. He told me that he had photographs of me attacking police officers and I told him innocently that he must be mistaken because I hadn't attacked anyone, and the photographs must be of somebody who looks like me.

He had me dragged out of my cell in the small hours of the night, put in front of me a statement that he had written, and told me to sign it.

The statement was full of lies, a confession to crimes so absurd that, if I hadn't been so frightened and worried, I would have laughed out loud in his face. He told me that he would only let me go if I signed it, so I did.

In those days, you didn't cite chapter and verse of the law, because one man had already come out of there dead in the boot of a car, and others had been so badly beaten they had to be hospitalised.

Outside the then dreaded gates of the Floriana lock-up I found my father, who had been there day and night asking for me, ageing 10 years in the process. Somewhere in a cupboard, there is an 11-page judgement handed down by Magistrate David Scicluna, condemning in the harshest terms possible the actions of Anġlu Farrugia and his colleagues, the methods they used to obtain my 'confession' (which Inspector Farrugia had invented and written himself) and declaring it invalid and worthless – this after I testified in great detail as to what had happened.

I mention this case because it is my own, and I can speak about it with absolute certainty as to the facts. There are newspaper cuttings and court documents that record it. There are probably others who underwent similar ordeals, and who are now looking at the posturing of the would-be Labour leader and thinking to themselves 'Him as leader? Him as prime minister? Come off it! How low can this country possibly sink!'

A man cannot become prime minister when on public record there is a magisterial condemnation of him for the ill-treatment of a 19-year-old girl illegally kept in police custody, and for threatening her into signing a false 'confession', full of absurd lies, that he himself had written.

Forget it, Dr Farrugia, you're history already. It may be a case of anything goes in today's Labour Party, but on a nationwide scale, the situation is not quite the same.

Daphne's funeral took place two weeks after her death. It took so long because her remains were held as evidence as is routine in any violent death. They were eventually released to her family for burial. The formal identification of her remains was completed in a laboratory. There was nothing left for anyone to recognise.

The funeral itself was a grim political event in its own right. The president of Malta, Marie Louise Coleiro Preca, was a Labour Party veteran and herself the subject of several critical pieces written by Daphne. Within hours of Daphne's assassination, Joseph Muscat was using the president as a messenger. Muscat offered a reward of €1m to anyone providing information on the circumstances of the murder 'if the family would accept that' and the president tried to persuade Daphne's sons that this was the sort of gesture from the government they should welcome. Daphne's family responded that their endorsement either way was irrelevant. The family refused to 'welcome' the government's reward and all mention of it appears to have been quietly dropped. The family also made it clear that they did not wish the president to attend the funeral.

The Caruana Galizias were not about to waste their time watching others wipe crocodile tears at their mother's funeral, their last chance to pay their respects. Joseph Muscat publicly acknowledged that he would not be attending the funeral as he had got the message. And the Speaker of the House of Representatives – the former police officer who had treated her so badly in custody – did not attend but sent a wreath.

The leader of the opposition, Adrian Delia, had also been held to account by Daphne for his connections to the sex trade in London's Soho and his mounting debts. He also stayed away. All the former living leaders of the Nationalist Party (PN) attended. The TV station owned by the PN, Net Television, omitted to mention their presence in its report so as not to make the incumbent look too bad by comparison.

With most civic leaders staying away from the funeral, the community at the Mosta church was led by two improvised replacements. The leading figure was Antonio Tajani, President of the European Parliament, who flew to Malta for the funeral after paying tribute to Daphne at the parliament in Strasbourg a few days earlier.

Before he was a politician, Antonio Tajani had been a journalist in Italy. He had personal experience of the killing of journalists, magistrates, and state officials at the hands of organised crime. He knew intuitively that Malta needed to cut through the fog and rhetoric and ask itself some very clear questions: Who killed Daphne? Who paid them? Why? They are questions the local authorities still shy away from.

The other leader was Malta's Archbishop Charles J. Scicluna, a close confidant of popes and a senior lawyer of the Church in his own right. He did not mince words. From the pulpit, the archbishop's voice rang a clear warning. The killing of a journalist was the killing of democracy. Journalists must be protected. They must not be made to feel afraid. Their duty to discover and reveal the truth should not be compromised by the fear of personal consequences.

Without using the word, Archbishop Scicluna declared Daphne Caruana Galizia a martyr for democracy.

Daphne's son Matthew took to the altar to read her favourite passage from the Book of Ecclesiastes: 'a time to tear and a time to mend, a time to be silent and a time to speak, a time to love and a time to hate, a time for war and a time for peace ...'

As Matthew returned to his seat, he saw the wreath bearing a ribbon with the words 'The Speaker' in Maltese. This was the man who had kept his mother as a young girl in a cell overnight. Matthew pounced on the wreath and tore the ribbon to shreds.

Like his mother before him, Matthew was consumed with a righteous anger.

MALTA THE BRAVE

Daphne Caruana Galizia did not study journalism. She only went to university after her sons were old enough to go to nursery and she chose to study archaeology which she loved and found very rewarding. She also minored in anthropology, and both sciences would give her an unorthodox but incisive perception into the realities of her country.

After all, looking under the surface is what archaeology is about. Knowledge comes in layers and it is hidden in places the uninitiated would think unlikely. In her journalism Daphne would often cite the sceptic's aphorism that 'absence of evidence is not evidence of absence'. That principle is as useful in good journalism as it is in archaeology. On the other hand, the anthropologist finds meaning in the behaviour and organisation of a community, interprets the patterns of deference, the cleavages of hostility, and the profound, though often buried, links of solidarity that define a group of people.

Malta is a treasure trove for archaeologists and anthropologists alike.

The archipelago's history is enviably long and fascinatingly intricate. People have lived in its caves for 9,000 years, probably first coming here on boats or improvised rafts from Sicily, the only other land from which Malta is sometimes visible.

The link to its much larger neighbour, only 60 miles distant, is deeper than most people in Malta are wont to admit.

For thousands of years, the history of the two islands was inseparable and indistinguishable. Before recorded history, however, was the Temple Culture of the large megaliths, sophisticated complexes of temples dotted throughout the Maltese islands, dwarfing the pyramids in age and much else in the Western world.

But the cultures that built those temples left nothing but stones. Historical memory in the rising and falling spheres of Phoenicians, Carthaginians, Romans, and Byzantines placed Malta as a provincial but dignified heir to Western Mediterranean antiquity.

The defining era for both Sicily and Malta was the Arab expansion of the 9th century. If the Arabs had not totally repopulated a desert island when they came to Malta from Sicily, they would not have found much when they got there.

The language spoken by the Maltese, *il-Malti*, is based on a cousin of Arabic as spoken a thousand years ago, but it is written in Roman script. Arabic speakers can sometimes work out the gist when they hear Maltese spoken. It is a Semitic language built on the dialect brought here in the 9th century and evolving in its isolation from Arabic from the 13th century onwards. There is no remnant in the Maltese language of any other language spoken on the island before the arrival of the Arabs.

The agricultural landscape was formed in that era; the names of towns and villages in use today are reminiscent of the Arabic lexicon with town names such as *Sliema* (peaceful), *Ħaż-Żebbuġ* (olive village), *iż-Żejtun* (the olive-pressing village), and *l-Imdina* (the city), a daily reminder that the deepest concepts of the Maltese vocabulary are rooted in Arabic.

The very few Maltese who are Muslim are recent immigrants rather than native descendants. But the Islam that founded the mediaeval Arab expansions was Christianised here when the Normans landed in Sicily, and by extension, Malta in the 12th century. Lent in Malta is known as *Randan*, a corruption of the term for the month of Muslim fasting, Ramadan. And the Maltese word for God is *Alla*, a crisper, stunted pronunciation of the more languid Arabic *Allah*.

Sicily and Malta were both returned to Christianity from the 13th century onwards when the Normans settled definitively on the islands. They were subsequently taken by the Angevins (French) and Aragonese (Spanish). Throughout these times Malta was something of a backwater fiefdom gifted by European kings to a succession of largely absentee landlords.

That changed when the first heir of the unified kingdom of Spain found a strategic use for this small foothold in his enormous portfolio of territories. King Charles V of Spain was the heir of Ferdinand of Castille and Isabella of Aragon who joined forces in battle, as well as in marriage, to oust the last Muslim emir from Spain.

But the rivalry between Christianity, militarily led from Spain, and Islam, from the Sublime Porte in what was then called Constinople (now Istanbul), was nowhere near over.

A small front of that battle was the island of Rhodes, just off the coast of what is now Turkey. For over 200 years, it had been the base of the Knights of St John of Jerusalem. They used their base to continue, as best they could, their crusading mission, harassing the Ottoman navy as glorified corsairs, all in the name of the one true Holy Catholic Church.

The Knights of St John were founded during the brief rule of the Latin Kingdom of Jerusalem in the 11th century, originally to man the pilgrims' hospital of St John, but soon to take up arms in the 'holy' war against Muslims. They retained the moniker 'knights hospitallers', keeping their medical and religious missions alongside their military vocation. They existed in parallel to the Knights Templar founded at around the same period but headquartered in the ruins of the Temple of Solomon after which they were named.

After the Latin kingdom of Jerusalem was abolished and the Christian armies were cast out from the cities of Palestine, the two Orders wandered around Europe and the Mediterranean. The Knights Templar would meet their end in a massacre in 1312. The Knights of St John would outlive them, cocking a snook at the sultan's navy.

In 1522, they were thrown out of Rhodes after a siege ordered by Suleiman the Magnificent. After seven years of homelessness,

Charles V of Spain handed Malta to the Knights of St John in the hope it would be of some use in his struggle with the sultan's might. The yearly rent in exchange: one Maltese falcon.

The year 1530 is the point where the political history of Malta is detached from that of Sicily. The archipelago becomes a distinct political entity with a decidedly international outlook. Though technically a theocracy governed by monks, Malta's government by the Knights was run by an international, polyglot oligarchy of aristocratic European second sons.

Its rulers came from Italy, France, Spain, Germany, and Portugal, each vying to compensate for the peripherality of their castle in the European scheme of things with opulent expenditure in architecture, decoration, costume, and culture.

The Knights' resources were depleted after the loss of Rhodes. Their mission was in doubt as crusading faded from the priority list of many Catholic monarchs. Protestant monarchs ignored the issue completely. The Knights' toehold on Malta and their own very survival became precarious.

The Ottomans understood this and pressed their advantage when they launched their siege of the island in 1565.

This date is at the heart of a romanticised Maltese identity. The local population was dragooned into supporting the Knights of St John, besieged in the pocket-sized fortresses around the harbour. The siege started when almost 200 vessels sailed from Constantinople, the biggest invasion fleet since antiquity. A key position was St Elmo's Fort which guarded the entrance to Grand Harbour. The Turks finally captured St Elmo, but at the cost of 6,000 men. The Ottoman commander cut off the heads of the surviving knights and had their bodies floated across the bay on mock crucifixes. By way of an answer, the leader of the knights, Jean de Valette beheaded all his Turkish prisoners and fired the heads as human cannonballs at the Turks. De Valette was a 70-year old war veteran, a one-time galley-slave, who would today be described as a religious fanatic. Battle was cruel and merciless.

After the fall of St Elmo, the Christian powers started to fear an Ottoman victory. Queen Elizabeth I of England summed up the panic: 'If the Turks should prevail against the Isle of Malta, it is uncertain what further peril might follow to the rest of Christendom.'

The Turks now ringed the Knights' citadel with more than 60 siege guns and began one of the most sustained artillery bombardments of the time. One of the defenders reckoned that 130,000 cannonballs were fired during the siege. In August 1565, the Turks breached the town's walls but fell back in alarm when they thought a Christian relief army had landed on the island from Sicily. They were wrong. The Knights' cavalry leader, Captain Vincenzo Anastagi had attacked the unprotected Turkish field hospital, putting everyone to the sword. The panic in the Turkish camp bought precious time. The Christian relief force turned up in September and the Turks fled with their tails between their legs.

The Siege of Malta was a turning point in European history, the moment when the might of the Ottoman Empire, fielding forces numbering around 40,000, was broken by 6,000 defending soldiers. It was a perfect storm of stubborn resistance, the hubristic attitude of the invaders, and a weak supply chain which forced the Ottomans to abandon their siege before the onset of winter.

Valette followed up his military victory by founding a city from scratch. Malta's capital city, named after its founder, is a masterpiece of the late Baroque. The palaces of political power and influence used today by the government were built by European aristocrats who fancied themselves princes and would eventually take to placing on their escutcheons the closed crown of a sovereign.

The 1789 French Revolution struck at the heart of the Knights of St John. When revolutionary France nationalised property owned by religious Orders, the Knights' revenue from France, a third of their income, was lost. As the revolutionary wars expanded the Republic's control on ever more European territory, the fate of the Knights was sealed.

Napoleon Bonaparte himself stopped in Malta on his way to near glory in Egypt and annexed Malta to the Directorate in 1798, giving the islands an early draft of his secular law-making.

He left a garrison that would soon be besieged from the sea by the Royal Navy and from the land by a Maltese rebellion as unsympathetic to their new French masters as they had been to their old masters. Perhaps more.

There were a few intellectual revolutionary sympathisers among the Maltese. They were branded 'Gakbini', originally a corruption of the political affiliation Jacobin, but eventually acquiring the meaning of 'traitor' or 'backstabber', as all sympathisers with the French cause came to be labelled.

It is said history is written by the victors. There was hardly any time for the Francophiles to write it up. The French were locked up inside the walled towns within three months of Napoleon's departure and just over a year later they surrendered to Horatio Nelson's fleet.

When the British landed in Malta in 1800 they did not know what to do with it. Perhaps because they did not seem too keen, a group of local leaders wrote to King George III asking him to accept the sovereignty of Malta as a conditional gift from a sovereign people adult enough to make their choices.

The British were not altogether impressed and, in the 1802 Amiens settlement with Bonaparte, they promised to hand the islands back to the Knights of St John.

But Britain was not finished with Napoleon and soon Malta would be the pretext for another war. They professed interest in the island and, being a sea-going nation that wanted to rule the waves, the idea of a safe harbour in the middle of the Mediterranean grew on them.

Malta formally became a British colony under the Treaty of Paris of 1814.

'Colony' is perhaps a misleading term. Malta had no metals in the ground, did not grow much food, and was hardly a powerhouse of human resources, slave or free. The small, poor, isolated population was not an obvious market for goods manufactured in the English workshop either.

The value of Malta was its physical location, a harbour that guards the facing doors of the East and West Mediterranean. Britain considered the possession of Malta, firstly to deny it to the French, then the Russians, aggressively seeking warm water harbours to extend their influence on the world.

The island would become a strategic pivot in the resistance against Russian expansion and would be used as an outreach station to support the British campaign to support the Ottomans (ironic, given Malta's history) in the Crimean War (1853-56) against Russia.

With the opening of the Suez Canal in 1869 and the shortening of the seaway to the Raj, Malta's strategic value increased manifold. The Maltese harbour became a coaling and repair station concentrating the entire value of the economy away from subsistence farming to the servicing of British military and maritime demands.

Times of war in the British period were, for Malta, times of economic boom. While the men repaired and supplied ships going to war, women tended to the wounded brought back from Crimea or Gallipoli in the First World War. The island became known as 'the nurse of the Mediterranean'.

In peacetime, however, the British had little interest beyond keeping up their 'fortress colony' that inconveniently housed a native population that kept getting in the way. An economy dedicated to war withers when the sword is turned into the ploughshare.

As these extreme boom-and-bust cycles rocked the island, its closest neighbour was fighting a heady war for its own identity. Italy, until the mid-19th century 'merely a geographical expression', was fighting a civil war of liberation inspired by Mazzini's romantic notions of nation and liberty but driven by Cavour's cold and calculated Realpolitik of a legacy kingdom and realised through the military genius of Garibaldi who, unusually, had no personal political ambitions.

Thanks to these three, a country of disjointed histories, mutually unrecognisable dialects, alien cultures, disparate economies, inconsistent norms and customs, and conflicting interests gradually took shape as a political entity founded in 1861. But the forging of Italy took a long time. The young leaders of the Risorgimento had to flee the displeasure of the Kingdom of the Two Sicilies between 1820 and 1860. They took up house in Malta, sheltered by the British pleased to host the rebels challenging French influence on the peninsula.

But rebels cannot be relied on. Their conversations in Malta would recall the shared history of thousands of years between Malta and Sicily. Italian was the informal lingua franca of the Knights of St John, Italian the natural language of trade and business in Malta.

Local community leaders would argue that a nation was forming around Malta and the British occupation was hindering the completion of that project much as the Austrians held back Milan and the French blocked the liberation of Rome.

Malta became '*terra irridenta*', an unredeemed province of the new Italian kingdom waiting for political circumstances to allow it to come home.

The notion was popular with lawyers, intellectuals, and a professional middle class for whom Italian – language, law, culture, political sympathy – was their Sunday best, the formal front of the native, humdrum life of islanders governed by a barely interested, alien race of colonisers.

But it was still a controversial idea among the local population. For the farmers and the poor, Italy was just as unconnected to their everyday lives as England. Perhaps more. Some of them were earning salaries as port workers, ship chandlers, even civil servants with the small but dignified colonial administration.

The Catholic Church too was not keen on allowing Malta to join a kingdom that realised its own existence by stripping the pope of his temporal powers and making him 'a prisoner in the Vatican'.

And the British had treated the Church kindly enough.

One big motivation for the Maltese rebellion against the French was that the Republic's army felt entitled to use property requisitioned from the church to finance the war in Egypt. The local counter-revolutionaries were partly led by clergymen distinctly unimpressed by this strategy.

When the British stepped in they knew better than to repeat the mistake of placing themselves on the wrong side of the Catholic Church. So they used the bishop's influence with the native population and in exchange, they protected his authority as a local prince.

The local British authorities resisted pressure from Anglican missionaries to convert the Knights' grand 16th century church of St John, which the state had inherited from the Knights' civilian government of Malta, into a white-washed Anglican church. Instead in the 1820s they invited Malta's Catholic bishop to bring down half of his cathedral chapter from Mdina and sit on a throne in Valletta's state-owned 'co-cathedral' of St John.

That was far more authority than the local bishop had ever enjoyed during the days of the Knights. In effect the British made the Catholic Church the established religion in Malta after the fashion of the Protestant Church of England. It was a clever scheme.

Whether you were pro-British or pro-Italian became the fundamental fissure of politics in Malta, at least until suffrage was extended to the industrial working class. The workers were less interested in cultural conflicts than bread and money, but the 'Language Question' remained the divisive issue right up to the 1930s. The British had left Malta's established legal tradition, inherited centuries earlier, to run its affairs in the Italian language. But was it still acceptable? Should English be the language of compulsory learning instead, as the first universal schooling system was being introduced?

Malta's traditional political parties coagulated around these divides. Malta's Partit Nazzjonalista, or Nationalist Party (PN), was formally founded in 1880, a cadre party with a secular attitude but identifying Catholicism as key to Maltese national identity.

In Hobsbawmian terms, their 'invented tradition' for Malta was firstly that it was European, white, and Christian. This implied that the 'white man's burden' of colonialism as a civilising influence on backward people from other races did not apply. Also, Malta was Catholic rather than just Christian, and while this was more of a cultural mindset than a matter of orthodox theology, it created an otherness from the British Protestant rulers, or 'the English' as the colonisers were collectively known. The Italians, on the other hand, were closer and shared the island's Catholic identity.

The PN remained vague on the idea of a political and legal unification with Italy. But it was reasonable for the Anglophiles to suspect that such an outcome would not be unlikely if the Nationalists held sway.

The PN's opposite number was the pro-British Constitutional Party led by an Anglo-Maltese, Gerald Strickland. His party was essentially a vehicle for his personal charisma. He was born of a marriage between a British naval officer with an ancient aristocratic pedigree and an heiress of equally ancient Maltese nobility who gave him the title of Count della Catena.

Gerald Strickland was a classically Victorian scion of the Empire. He served the British administration as Governor of the Leeward Islands, Tasmania, Western Australia, and New South Wales. He sat as a member of the House of Commons and was later elevated to the British peerage. He mobilised politics in Malta around loyalty to the British crown and the concept of modernisation and Westernisation to promote Malta as a successful part of the Empire.

In times of plenty, that politics found broad support.

There were moments of deep crisis, however. The end of the First World War brought about massive redundancies with cuts in military and naval services leaving many homeless and destitute. The price of bread, the survival staple of the island, increased heavily, making unemployment a hungry state of affairs.

When a protest was called on 7 June 1919 in Valletta in the square facing the headquarters of the British government, troops were ordered to keep the crowd in line. Shots were fired and four men, some of them innocent bystanders, were killed on the spot. Two others died of their wounds in the following few days.

The events of the 7 June (known locally in Italian as *Sette Giugno*) were Malta's own mini-Amritsar massacre when the British lost their moral authority over the country.

Sette Giugno became the platform for demands of political autonomy and attempts to bring about self-government that would plan for Malta's economic needs in the absence of British military spending.

The British response came in 1921 when Malta was granted 'dominion status', ostensibly modelled on Canadian and Australian autonomy. But the devil was in the detail. The British retained the option to cancel constitutional rights and revert to colony status.

Fairly quickly, the British pulled the plug on Maltese autonomy.

The biggest crisis of all came with the onset of Fascism in Italy and the conversion of romantic, cultural irredentism to an official policy of territorial enlargement. Benito Mussolini's Italy claimed the right to dominance of the Mediterranean Sea which they called *mare nostrum* or 'our sea'. Malta was described as *l'estremo lembo del nido italico* or 'the furthest tip of the Italian nest'.

When Benito Mussolini declared war on Britain on 10 June 1940 in a speech from his balcony in Palazzo Venezia, the Maltese were listening on the radio. They knew precisely which part of the vast British Empire was within flying range of Italian bombers. The next day the first bombs were dropped on Malta and the first casualties suffered.

So began the Second Siege of Malta. The story is best told by Nicholas Monsarrat, a Royal Naval officer, in his novel *The Kappillan of Malta*. *Kappillan* means 'chaplain' or 'parish priest'. The book is a must read for anyone visiting the island.

Received British military doctrine in the 1930s was that Malta was indefensible, so only six obsolete Gloster Gladiator biplanes were on the island when Mussolini declared war. No more than three of the biplanes flew at once. The islanders nicknamed them Faith, Hope, and Charity. Early on, one of the biplanes was shot down but the other two, astonishingly, managed to knock out some of the Italian aircraft. The indefensible island could, it turned out, be defended. Winston Churchill, newly installed at Number Ten, reversed British policy and set out to defend the island come what may.

The best German general knew the strategic importance of Malta. Erwin Rommel, the leader of the *Afrika Korps*, said 'without Malta, the Axis will end by losing control of North Africa'. The bombing campaign against Malta was brutal, probably the most terrible across all the allied territories. Italian bombers had only to fly 60 miles to a sitting duck in clear blue skies. London was being blitzed at the same time and it took an age before the Royal Navy was able to set up successful convoys carrying Spitfires to organise a fightback.

Those British naval officers who at the dawn of the 18th century argued for holding on to Malta were proved right a century-and-a-half later. Malta was heroically described as 'an unsinkable aircraft carrier' from which the RAF and the Royal Navy could harass the supply lines supporting Rommel's *Afrika Korps* in North Africa. The cost in Maltese casualties was high.

The war against Malta ebbed and flowed. In the first stage the enemy was Italian but in the spring of 1941 the *Luftwaffe* arrived in Sicily and the bombing grew heavier. When Adolf Hitler attacked Russia, many of the aircraft targeted at Malta flew east. Then, as the Russian winter set in and flying became virtually impossible in the East, the *Luftwaffe* returned to Sicily to hit Malta once again. In 1941 and 1942, the island suffered more than 3,000 bombing raids, and the worst hit were the heavily-crowded streets surrounding Valletta's harbour. In the first six months of 1942 there was only one day without an air raid. As Monserrat describes so powerfully in *The Kappillan of Malta*, people took sanctuary underground, even among the dead in the catacombs. But living in these grim conditions led to dreadful sanitation problems and eventually a typhoid epidemic. 1,493 civilians died and 3,674 were wounded. As ever in war, the very young and the very old suffered the most.

The assault from the air was only part of the story. Italian and German submarines sank dozens of naval and supply ships approaching from the British base of Gibraltar so that supplies of food were under massive pressure. Axis minefields and enemy aircraft added to the toll. Between 1940 and 1942, 31 ships were lost. By the early summer of 1942, the island was cut off and ordinary people were suffering from malnutrition.

The pivot of the siege was in August 1942. By then, the fortnightly ration on Malta for one person was 14oz (400g) sugar, 7oz (200g) fats, 10.5oz (300g) bread, and 14oz (400g) of corned beef. An adult male worker had a daily intake of 1,690 calories and women and children received 1,500 calories. Such was the desperation of the authorities that a mass slaughter of livestock began on the island. A convoy from Alexandria bringing food made it through, and the near-starving civilian population could eat. From the West came the tanker SS *Ohio* and, although it was bombed repeatedly, it managed to make it to Valletta and with it precious fuel supplies for Malta's Spitfires. Without these supplies, Malta would have fallen.

In the autumn, the *Luftwaffe* were back but by then the war was turning and by the following summer the Axis had been booted out of northern Africa and the siege was lifted.

Such was the courage and defiance of the people of Malta that King George VI awarded the George Cross to the Maltese nation, an honour borne on the country's flag to this day.

The war put paid to any sympathy to the Italian cause in mainstream opinion. Italy had made itself the enemy and any sympathisers became traitors and enemies.

During the war, leaders of the Nationalist Party (PN) were rounded up and imprisoned in a low security internment camp. Eventually they were deported to Uganda to wait out the war fought over the skies of their country. They were presumed traitors and enemy collaborators despite there being no evidence that they were sympathetic to the Fascist cause.

But there was evidence aplenty against Carmelo Borg Pisani. He was Maltese but a believer in Italian Fascism. In May 1942 he was smuggled to the island but bad weather wrecked his plans and he ended up in a naval hospital. There, Pisani was recognised by one of his childhood friends, Captain Tom Warrington. In November 1942 he was tried, sentenced to death for treason, and executed.

Malta's experience of the war is particular to its own circumstances. The Maltese people perceive it as a collateral incident of their colonial experience and believe they would not have been dragged into the conflict were it not for the fact that they were part of the British Empire.

The heroism of a generation is not remembered in the same vein as people in Italy think of the *partigiani* or the French of the *résistance*. Nor did they experience the mortifying heritage of collaboration, whether with the strategic interests of the enemy or, for example, with the denunciation of the Jews or 'degenerates'.

Like Britain, Malta was never occupied by the enemy, though it came close. But, unlike Britain, Malta did not quite see itself as a valiant defender of democracy because it had none it could call its own.

Instead it could pride itself on its endurance and a quasi-fanatical and certainly religious belief in patience being rewarded.

At least in good part, because of the planes flown from Malta to sink ships supplying the *Afrika Korps*, the Axis forces ran aground in North Africa and that front was abandoned. The tide would turn and, from a defensive outpost held in extremis, Malta would become a platform for the invasion of Sicily and the beginning of the end of Italian fascism.

Within months of the end of the war, Britain had to rethink its global role as colonial master. The leaders of the PN came limping back from Uganda and slowly regrouped, promoting an explicit agenda for independence. Unification with Italy was no longer on the cards. The Italian language was dropped from the public space and replaced with English, no longer the language of the philistine colonial masters but rather the language of the victorious side of the war, and alongside it Maltese, a language spoken since the Arab invasion but codified as part of the 'invented tradition' of Maltese identity in the 19th and 20th centuries.

As Britain adopted a formal policy of decolonisation and the dismantling of Empire, the vocation of the pro-British party in Malta, now led by Gerald Strickland's daughter, Mabel, became unclear.

Some of its traditional support, the urban middle and upper classes, flocked to the PN not because they were particularly attracted to it but more because of the fear of the alternative.

The Malta Labour Party, originally the 'Malta Workers Party', grew out of industrial trade unionism in the harbour districts that employed thousands of people in the shipyards and ancillary ship-repair industries. Its leadership was inspired by British Fabianism and as such was culturally, if not socially, closer to the Anglophile Constitutionalists than to the decidedly bourgeois Nationalists.

The Labour Party (PL) would, by the end of the Second World War, absorb the remaining support formerly enjoyed by the Constitutionalists. They won three-fourths of all votes in the first post-war election of 1947 which the Nationalists, still dazed from their years of exile in Uganda, did not contest with any vigour.

Labour established itself as the party of the masses, adept by design at universal suffrage.

A young ideologue, Dominic Mintoff, emerged from the labour movement, and challenged its urbane, moderate leader by founding the Labour Party, a paradoxical mix of mass support, mobilisation machine, and para-religious cult built around his personal charisma.

Dom Mintoff designed his image around the decolonisation moulds of the time – Kenyatta, Nasser, Tito, and Nehru. He projected the image of a strong man, ambivalent in his allegiance to either West or East in a Cold War context but professing willingness to stand shoulder to shoulder with friendly countries that would support his revolution.

He first became prime minister in 1955 and held office for three years until he fell foul of the Catholic Church. Dom Mintoff led the opposition to Malta's independence negotiated by the Nationalist government of 1962-1971 of prime minister George Borg Olivier. His objections were unspecific and mostly irrational, apparently grounded in the frustration that he was not the one in the pictures. He sat out independence but finally returned as prime minister in 1971. Mintoff was energetic, clever – he'd been educated at Oxford – and radical. Under his rule, Malta was the first country to recognise Chairman Mao as the leader of the legitimate government of China, a switching of sides that would prove visionary. But that was from the same vein of foreign policy that would replace Malta's long-standing affiliation with NATO and the West with the tight embrace of Libyan strongman Mu'ammar Ghaddafi.

When Mintoff took over power in 1971, he extended the lease the Nationalists had agreed with NATO for military forces' bases in Malta that was due to expire in 1974. When that extension expired again in 1979 and the British forces left for good, their departure was celebrated by Mintoff as the day Malta truly became independent, rebranding the Italianate term for Malta's sovereignty to the more semitic *Helsien* or 'Freedom'. His guest of honour at the freedom ceremony was Mu'ammar Ghaddafi.

By now Malta had become a two-party country. The PN and the PL fought fiercely to get the few thousand votes either party needed to exceed the 50% support threshold and secure exclusive and unassailable political power for five years.

No MP has been elected to Malta's parliament since 1962 unless they ran on the ticket of one of the two main parties. Independent candidates were and are seen as a loony footnote, comic relief for profoundly confrontational politics.

As the 1970s wore on, politics became violent. Beatings of protesters were an expected outcome of any anti-government manifestation. Discrimination and industrial scale clientilism were mainstream. Things came to a head in 1981 when a close election returned the PL with a majority of parliamentary seats despite gaining fewer votes than the losing PN.

In the early 1980s, Malta's constitutional court was not convened so that the government could avoid answering legal challenges. Armed gangs of the PL would tour PN clubs on Sunday afternoons, shooting in the air, sometimes at the door. A fatality was recorded. The Catholic Church was forced to shut down its schools and its pupils were driven into underground classes in their teachers' homes as the Labour government forced a choice between closure or the abolition of school fees. Malta's economy was pushed into iron-curtain isolationism that created scarcities and discontent.

The PN won the 1987 election by 5,000 votes. It campaigned on the Europeanisation of Malta, normalising its politics, and applying for membership of the then EEC, the predecessor organisation of the European Union.

The programme of reforms that started in 1987 was overtaken by the collapse of the Berlin Wall and Malta was suddenly at the back of the queue of other countries desperate to join the EU. Eddie Fenech Adami, the PN leader through the violent 1980s and reforming 1990s, left the premiership on the eve of accession to the EU in 2004.

Securing EU membership was no straightforward political task. Labour had resisted independence in 1964 for no clear reason. Resistance to EU membership came in a very similar vein. Dom Mintoff and his successors as PL leaders, Karmenu Mifsud Bonnici and Alfred Sant, all forcefully argued that the EU was an immoral, capitalist behemoth which would gobble up a small country like Malta for breakfast.

It was for Alfred Sant, prime minister 1996-98, PL leader 1992-2008, to lead the charge against EU membership, mouthing arguments about absorbed national sovereignty, uncontrolled and overwhelming immigration, and an inescapable European army returning Maltese soldiers in body bags.

His right-hand man was Joseph Muscat, a young propagandist of the PL who became a prominent 'No' campaigner, hosting a prime TV slot on the PL's TV station called, with little irony, *Made in Brussels*.

Joseph Muscat's campaign for Alfred Sant was very nearly victorious. Of the 10 accession countries that joined the EU in 2004, Malta was the first to run a referendum on the matter and the majority supporting membership was the slimmest, barely 54%.

As it happened, a general election immediately following the referendum elected the PN and EU membership followed.

Joseph Muscat started moving away from his leader's coat tails after the referendum. He contested the first European Parliament elections, winning resounding support from Labour followers of his TV appearances.

Aged 33, Muscat was becoming Labour's most prominent politician. He married Alfred Sant's personal secretary, Michelle Tanti. Putting love aside, observers noted the marriage was also strategic, if not dynastic in the classical sense. He used his time in Brussels to make friends on the scene and sat on the European Parliament's joint commission with the Azerbaijan government developing a keen interest in the affairs of the fabulously corrupt Caucasus republic.

Above all, he lay low, fully expecting Alfred Sant to lose yet another election in 2008, his third electoral loss in a row. Alfred Sant was close to winning that election and lost by fewer than 2,000 votes, the narrowest gap between winners and losers in a Maltese election.

Alfred Sant had got close, but not close enough. His overdue departure from the leadership of the PL was now universally accepted, even by him.

It was time for Joseph Muscat, TV star *extraordinaire*, to fly back to Malta from Brussels and save the PL from its losing streak.

Five years later he would be prime minister.

'JOHNNY CASH'

Silvio Zammit asked for the bung on the eve of Valentine's Day 2012. Swedish Match, a tobacco company, had been trying to overturn a European Union (EU) ban on snus, a smokeless tobacco held in the mouth between the gum and the upper lip. It was popular in Sweden but banned in the rest of the EU. Silvio Zammit was a small-time bit player. In Malta he owned a waterside burger joint called Peppi's Kiosk. In Brussels he was of no consequence.

But the man who was then European Health Commissioner, John Dalli, was also Maltese and he and Zammit were good friends. Dalli had the power to overturn the ban. So when Zammit met Johan Gabrielsson, the director of public affairs at Swedish Match, at Peppi's Kiosk, he told him that Dalli might be able to intervene in the snus matter but such 'an operation would [have] a cost'.

The price tag? €60 million.

The Swede said it was not his call to make but thought his company would not go for it. He was right. Swedish Match instructed Gabrielsson to cut contact with Zammit.

Zammit did not give up that easily. The following week he made contact with the lobby group ESTOC, the European Smokeless Tobacco Council. The following is a transcript (edited for clarity by the authors) of a telephone conversation which took place on 29 March 2012 between Zammit and Inge Delfosse, Secretary General of ESTOC. Delfosse recorded the call and eventually handed over the recording to OLAF, the EU's anti-fraud squad:

DELFOSSE: Hi, Silvio.

ZAMMIT: Now. Ah, listen, Inge. What is the best thing that I can offer you … a package of lobbying services, right?

DELFOSSE: Yeah.

ZAMMIT: What I can guarantee … proposal to lift the ban.

DELFOSSE: You can guarantee a lift of the ban. Is that what you said?

ZAMMIT: The proposal.

DELFOSSE: Aha.

ZAMMIT: OK? Er and what I can make you as well … high-level meetings…

DELFOSSE: Aha.

ZAMMIT: Aah, to end the rumours, sort rumours. And … obviously, aah, this is as soon as I give you the guarantee that lifting can be proposed, OK?

DELFOSSE: OK …

ZAMMIT: Aah, regarding the price. For sure, it will start after the first, high-level, meeting …

DELFOSSE: Yeah …

ZAMMIT: Once your boss and my boss are together, obviously, they will be discussing the issue to how you finalise or further materialise this, this issue. You understand?

DELFOSSE: Yeah.

ZAMMIT: So for after that, after that meeting, to carry on after, first payment of ten million.

DELFOSSE: Ten million?

ZAMMIT: Yeah.

DELFOSSE: I am sorry, ah. I'm a poor blonde, aah, I'm a bit shocked here.

ZAMMIT: Well, are you sitting down?

DELFOSSE: Yeah, I am almost lying down now …

The phone recordings and a mass of other evidence were set out in a leaked report by OLAF into John Dalli. The investigation was headed by Giovanni Kessler, OLAF's then head and a former Italian anti-mafia investigator in Sicily. Critical to OLAF's findings were a series of meetings, phone calls, texts, and emails between the Swedish tobacco lobbyists, Zammit, and a Maltese lawyer called Gayle Kimberley.

OLAF had hard evidence of meetings and phone calls between Dalli and Zammit and also a handwritten note of a conversation between Dalli and Zammit made by Zammit himself. The note said Dalli was 'ready to meet the chief executive' of Swedish Match and that Dalli's response to the big question was 'suggest to no ban'. Zammit told OLAF investigators that his notes were 'meaningless scribbles on a piece of paper'. OLAF said this explanation '[could not] be considered credible'.

Both Swedish Match and ESTOC behaved entirely properly by telling OLAF what the Maltese fixer was suggesting. OLAF's investigation led to a prickly meeting on 16 October 2012 at 3pm, when the then head of the EU Commission, José Manuel Barroso, all but fired John Dalli.

By an extraordinarily strange coincidence, five years later, on the same day at the same time, Daphne Caruana Galizia was assassinated.

John Dalli hated and still hates Daphne with a passion, calling her a 'terrorist', 'a poison pen', a 'megalomaniac who brainwashes the people' and so on. Daphne thought Dalli was a crook, a liar, and a conman. The difference between them was that she had a mass of evidence to back up her claims. So did OLAF. Dalli had nothing to show for his description of Daphne as a 'terrorist', never mind the rest.

In May 2015, Daphne gave an interview to two Danish journalists, Mads Brugger and Mikael Bertelsen, for a documentary called 'The Great European Cigarette Mystery'. It was shown as part of the BBC's Storyville strand in July 2017, three months before Daphne was assassinated. The camera shows a stone patio, then the inside of her beautiful home in Malta, a black Staffordshire bull terrier called Tony barking a few friendly woof-woofs and then Daphne speaks. She is considered, mesmerising, lethal.

John Dalli, Daphne told the Danes, *was originally quite a well-respected politician. I'm talking way back in 1987. He won the respect of a lot of people because he took decisive action at a time when Malta's economy was a real mess. And then slowly there began to be whisperings, private conversations, about how corrupt he is. He was the minister responsible for the privatisation of state entities in Malta, including the banks, the airport and there were undercurrents about his involvement, about his maybe taking a cut. The Opposition at the time, the Labour Party, used to call him Johnny Cash because he had such a reputation for going after money.*

Brugger asked: 'But there was no smoking gun?'

No, she agreed, there was no smoking gun. Eventually the Nationalist prime minister made what I and many people considered to be a fatal error, which was to nominate him as Malta's candidate for the European Commission, to get him off his own back and off the island. He exported the problem and inflicted it on a European-wide level.

Dalli lost his job in Brussels because he had been caught red-handed in one of the biggest corruption scandals ever to dog the European Union. Officially, he resigned. Unofficially he was told that if he did not, he would be fired.

Barroso had never liked his underling. Dalli had been the nominee of Malta's prime minister Lawrence Gonzi (PN) when Barroso was forming his Commission after the 2009 elections. Dalli was moody, uncooperative, and clearly not committed to his job. He would fly out of Brussels without warning, going AWOL often to Malta, sometimes to odd destinations in the Caribbean. There was always a feeling that he was up to something. Word in Brussels at the time was that Dalli was bound to blow up.

What had also been worrying Barroso was that, while the people of Libya were doing their utmost to overthrow the four-decade long rule of the Botox tyrant Mu'ammar Ghaddafi, his Commission included someone with a long history of supping with that particular devil.

The articulated policy of the EU was that they were happy to see the back of Ghaddafi. He had been a cruel tyrant, had gone through trigger-happy phases and was a kleptomaniac of the first order, syphoning wealth that properly belonged to the Libyan state but which under his regime became indistinguishable from his person.

Dalli, however, had reasons to regret the downfall of the old colonel or 'brother leader' as Ghaddafi preferred to be known. And he gave voice using his platform of Health Commissioner, departing from the line set by Barroso. While Barroso declared that it was time for Ghaddafi to go, Dalli insisted Ghaddafi should 'make his own decisions'.

In 2004 Dalli had set up a consultancy firm advising businesses that wanted to set up in Libya. He offered access to the Libyan regime, some of which he secured during his tenure as a government minister in Malta. Between 1987 and 1996 and 1998 and 2004, as a government minister, he sat on the Libya-Malta joint commission, securing contacts with decision-makers in Ghaddafi's regime.

He was also director of Azizia Glass Manufacturing Company (AGMC), a multi-million-euro factory in Libya.

In a 2007 speech in Valletta John Dalli said:

Malta had served as a gateway between Libya and the outside world during the days of international sanctions ... Business with Libya means business in Libya and face-to-face contact is essential.

For years he had been that face, and his legacy was falling apart while he was 'serving a sentence' – that is how he described his Brussels job, as some sort of punishment in exile inflicted on him by Gonzi. If Ghaddafi fell, Dalli knew he would be unlikely to see his house in Tripoli for some time. Nor would he have access to his money-making schemes in Libya.

Barroso complained to Gonzi about Dalli but there was nothing much either man could do. Frankly, Gonzi thought that by nominating Dalli to the Commission, he would be rid of a major problem back home.

That would prove to be short-sighted.

OLAF completed their report on 15 October 2012 and

found that the Maltese entrepreneur [Zammit] had approached the company using his contacts with Mr Dalli and sought to gain financial advantages in exchange for influence over a possible future legislative proposal on snus. No transaction was concluded between the company and the entrepreneur and no payment was made.

One last piece of the puzzle was the role of Gayle Kimberley, the second figure who tried to broker a deal between the tobacco lobby and Dalli. In 2012, Daphne drew attention to a report in *The Times of Malta* which quoted a police officer giving evidence before a Maltese court. The officer claimed Kimberley had been blackmailed by her then lover, Iosif Galea, over what to say in court. When OLAF interviewed Kimberley in Portugal that year, Galea was with her. OLAF asked her not to tell anyone about their investigation. OLAF discovered that Galea phoned Dalli from Portugal and met him on his return to Malta. Daphne had previously published a photograph of three men holidaying in Italy: Dalli, Zammit, and Galea. Daphne told the Danish journalists: 'Gayle Kimberley's involvement is tangential. Later she was subject to blackmail. OLAF would not have known that she was sleeping with Galea.'

When the Danes asked Dalli about his friendship with Galea, he dismissed the issue. When Brugger tried to talk to Kimberley, she ended the call quickly. Brugger told Dalli that she sounded afraid. Zammit showed the Danes his bulging file of evidence. The Great European Cigarette Mystery documentary shows Brugger leafing through the file and coming across a nude photo of a woman.

"What is that?" asks Brugger.

"You're not going to... er... do not... er..." stammers Zammit.

"It's a naked woman," says Brugger.

"It is she," says Zammit.

"It's Gayle Kimberley?" asks Brugger.

"What was that?" asks Bertelsen, who was sitting on the other side of the table and could not see the photo.

'It's a nude photograph of Gayle Kimberley,' says Brugger to Bertelsen in Danish.

'Don't say nothing,' says Zammit '... it's illegal... it's my evidence for the court.'

One can only conclude from watching this extraordinarily powerful film, which itself stands on the shoulders of Daphne's journalism, that the rule of law in Malta is as good as dead.

The OLAF report did not find conclusive evidence of the direct participation of Mr Dalli but concluded that 'he was aware of these events.' OLAF does not have policing powers. The EU Commission could fire its employees for wrongdoing, but it could not put them in handcuffs.

'The final OLAF report and its recommendations are being sent by OLAF to the Attorney General of Malta. It will now be for the Maltese judiciary to decide how to follow up,' said a Commission statement at the time.

That must have given Dalli some comfort. He had been suspected of corruption in Malta before, but it had never come to handcuffs. But he needed to be smart. Malta's police chief, John Rizzo, was notoriously effective in fighting corruption. He cracked fake boating licence rackets and prosecuted public officers for soliciting bribes for services. The episodes caused considerable embarrassment to his political bosses.

But his greatest feat was nabbing two Maltese judges for accepting bribes to reduce a drug lord's jail sentence on appeal.

When Rizzo, an appointee of then prime minister Eddie Fenech Adami (PN), arrested Chief Justice Noel Arrigo in 2002, also a Fenech Adami appointee, the glaring weakness of Malta's institutional design did not prevent justice from taking its course. The chief justice was prosecuted, convicted in 2009, and served his sentence in disgrace. Rizzo had done his job and there was no fear that the prime minister of the time would use his powers to fire the police commissioner to avoid the political embarrassment of having appointed a crook to the bench.

Everyone took it on the chin. The show went on.

Dalli could not afford to risk Rizzo's determination to get to the bottom of things. Neither could he count on Gonzi to look after him.

Eight years earlier, in 2004, Gonzi and Dalli had been the final two PN candidates competing to replace Fenech Adami who had been party leader since 1977 and a hard act to follow. In 1981 he won the popular vote for the PN and finally became prime minister in 1987. He then went on to win every subsequent election but one, right up to 2003 when he secured his main objective: EU membership for Malta.

Dalli came up the ranks in the Fenech Adami administration, serving as finance minister for 10 years and earning himself the moniker 'Johnny Cash'. He was a favourite target of the PL, not least because as finance minister he often had to be the harbinger of bad news – new taxes, higher costs, currency devaluation. But he also presided over the transformation of Malta's economy from a controlled Soviet-style state-owned protectionist model to an open economy based on services and aligned with EU laws and standards. That was no mean feat.

But finance minister is never the best job to nurture the grassroots support one needs to make prime minister. Dalli found his aspirations frustrated by Gonzi, a suave lawyer who became Fenech Adami's anointed heir.

The party's grassroots took their cue and voted Gonzi over Dalli two to one. Dalli did not hide his bitterness at the outcome. Gonzi made Dalli a government minister but scandals would emerge that forced his dismissal. Dalli had barely survived allegations circulated by a businessman in the late 1990s that he had hidden money offshore. But in 2004 a fresh scandal led to his resignation. His daughter had set up a travel agency and, not only had his ministry switched its business to her firm, but he had also persuaded a state-owned Iranian shipping company to take their business away from their local agents and use his daughter's firm.

Dalli, in other words, stank of dead fish.

He resigned, protesting his innocence and claiming his downfall was the result of a conspiracy between his enemies within the PN and some journalists, chief among them, Daphne.

Daphne had certainly reported in detail on the scandals that had consumed Dalli. Until then her entire writing career had been under PN administrations, save for a two-year blip between 1996 and 1998 when Alfred Sant (PL) was prime minister. She openly took sides, condemning Labour's core policy against EU membership which dominated the politics of the period. She was also particularly suspicious of Labour politicians from the Mintoff (PL) and Mifsud Bonnici (PL) eras, before 1987, when successive Labour governments were marked by their Iron Curtain politics and institutionalised corruption.

But, Daphne being Daphne, she would not 'close an eye' to the misdeeds of the PN. She was just as outspoken in her criticism, unusually so in the Maltese context as each party buried their scandals, fearing giving the other undue advantage.

Dalli made his anger and bitterness personal. His remarks verged on the unhinged, and with time he would only become worse.

While supposedly directing the European Union's policy on health, John Dalli had been busy with other things. He approached Gonzi's government with plans for an energy project that would use liquid natural gas (LNG) fired up on an onshore power station to provide part of the energy supply for the country.

Dalli's proposals, grouping together an undefined consortium of private interests he was somehow representing, came at a time when the Maltese government needed to take some strategic decisions on upgrading its electricity infrastructure.

Demand had grown but what had really rubbed salt into the wounds was the 2008 oil crisis when Malta's complete reliance on imported fuel oil for its electricity had exposed a huge economic vulnerability. Most of Malta's fresh water supply came from desalinated seawater, using a great volume of electricity, all of it then powered by oil.

Malta's competitiveness in industry and tourism was hamstrung by electricity rates several times those charged in competing European countries. Producers for the domestic market, but also retailers and distributors, passed the inflationary impact on to customers. The same end-users were forced during the longer, hotter summers to use power-hungry air-conditioning and found that their electricity bills had become objects of constant anxiety.

Politically, this was extremely damaging to the Nationalist government. Solutions could not come in the short term. Switching to renewables would have only had a cosmetic impact on cost. Switching to gas would have transferred to a fuel that was consistently cheaper than oil but would have still meant replacing one vulnerability with another.

The Nationalists decided to lay an undersea cable to Sicily which would connect Malta to the European electricity grid and allow locals to use electricity generated elsewhere in Europe for the best price and the lowest carbon footprint that could be secured. They preferred this option over isolated systems, even if possibly cleaner and cheaper such as gas, thereby frustrating Dalli's hopes of brokering a deal for his 'clients' or 'partners'.

Dalli did not give up. He crossed over to the PL in opposition, a party that for years had made him the subject of mockery, criticism, and what can only be described as enmity. He presented his project to Joseph Muscat, who was already being touted as the next prime minister and was in a position to procure Dalli's proposed project.

Dalli did not keep his intentions under wraps. He appeared on the PL's TV station – a surprising move any day – to promote his project and explain why Malta's government policy was wrong and his project was the right solution for the country. His interference in local politics at a time when he was in post as EU commissioner was hugely inappropriate.

When he walked out of Barroso's cabinet, Dalli had 10 minutes to leave the building. During that time he made one phone call, to the then leader of the opposition Joseph Muscat (PL). OLAF communicated its findings to Peter Grech, the attorney general in Malta who, in turn, passed the report to Malta's police chief.

After reviewing the facts, the commissioner of police said there was enough evidence to warrant a conversation with Dalli at police headquarters. But Dalli claimed he was too unwell to travel to Malta and presented a series of medical certificates signed by a German doctor from Mettlach-Wehringen, a village in Saarland. Doctor Michael Scholten certified John Dalli unfit to travel. He is a gynaecologist.

At a parliamentary hearing some time later, Rizzo said he had intended to charge Dalli with trading in influence, legalese for corruption and abuse of power. But something got in the way of that aim. Muscat, having won the election, was sworn in as prime minister on the 10 March 2013 and a month later Rizzo was summarily dismissed.

Around this time Dalli made a miraculous recovery from his condition and flew back to Malta. He knew he was safe. Rizzo was replaced as chief of police by PL patsy Peter Paul Zammit. Zammit was a former police officer turned lawyer who had left the force some time previously and so was an outside appointee.

Within six weeks of taking office, Zammit announced that Dalli had no case to answer, and in November 2013 Dalli was appointed chief advisor to the government on health matters by Muscat.

Meanwhile Dalli lambasted Barroso for firing him 'unjustly' at every opportunity in an absurd campaign unencumbered by any real evidence. He told *The Malta Independent* that Barroso should be arrested if he ever set foot in Malta:

> This is nothing but a media campaign organised by the Commission and OLAF to slander and intimidate me. Another conclusion that I arrive at is that Dr BS is part of this campaign. I am considering publishing the correspondence that I have with OLAF and part of which has not yet been replied to by OLAF and to take further appropriate action.

'Dr BS' was John Dalli's way of referring to the Nationalist leader of the opposition Simon Busuttil, who was leading John Dalli's former party.

Daphne Caruana Galizia wrote in reaction:

> ... the man is obviously not all there. Some crisis must have been triggered off by the catastrophe of the 2004 PN leadership election and he has been left undiagnosed and untreated all this time, becoming progressively worse and more paranoid and delusional.
>
> Unfortunately, in Malta we are so accustomed to abnormal behaviour that we treat it as normal or think of it as unremarkable, and it is only when we come face to face with the astonishment of outsiders that we are brought up short. The fact of the matter is that Dalli's behaviour indicates he is in need of psychiatric help.

Daphne's words must have stung.

And then she went on to break the story of yet another Dalli scandal.

In 2015 Daphne reported that Dalli and his two daughters, Claire Gauci Borda and Louisa Dalli, were embroiled in a Ponzi scheme in the United States. The three Dallis and an American confidence trickster called Elouise Marie Corbin Klein who used various aliases such as Lady Bird, Mary Swann, and Eloisa Chihan, had allegedly cheated an evangelical Christian community called Joy Ministries out of their life savings. The depositors in the schemes, a group of elderly Americans, believed they were paying seed money that would go into ethical gold mines which would fund improvements for the lives of their employees.

The victims were told the money would go to poor miners in Africa and the Philippines who were not be able to get bank loans to start their businesses. But the money, conservatively estimated at around $600,000 but probably a lot more than that, flowed into financial structures set up by Dalli's daughters. Daphne's source had told her that the margin on the currency conversion alone amounted to $2m.

Daphne published a photo showing John and Louisa Dalli with Corbin Klein also known as Lady Bird in the Bahamas in 2012. At the time, John Dalli was still an EU commissioner and had flown to the Bahamas and back from an EU meeting in Cyprus. He tried claiming his flight ticket expenses from the European Commission but got caught.

Daphne showed the picture to the two Danish journalists, Brugger and Bertelman.

Dalli, she said, *was at an EU Commission meeting in Cyprus. He made his excuses and left, he wasn't present for one of the most important dinners, he told his EU Commission colleagues that he was going back to Malta because he had family problems. But he didn't go back to Malta at all. He went to the Bahamas. I know why he went because I spoke to the Americans who were there in the Bahamas who met him.*

The film cuts to the photo. Daphne explains: 'That is Elouise Marie Corbin Klein, also known as the fraudster Lady Bird, that is

John Dalli, that is his daughter, Louisa Dalli. So this man standing at the back, in the blue shirt, he represents a Christian organisation.' The organisation was the Joy Ministries, whose adherents say they were defrauded by the Dallis.

Daphne claimed Lady Bird had multiple identities, including one on a Filipino passport. Although the woman in the Filipino passport photograph had blonde hair and looked Caucasian, the name on the passport was Filipino. It was an obvious fraud.

Brugger asked Daphne whether the Dallis would have known that she was a fraudster. Daphne said Lady Bird had arrived in Malta after being released from a prison in Thailand. Dalli told the Danes that he knew about the prison sentence in Thailand but thought she'd had a problem with her passport.

'Because of her fake identities?' asked Brugger.

'I don't know about that,' said Dalli.

When the Danish journalists confronted Dalli with evidence of the fraud committed by Lady Bird, with his help, Dalli countered that the Joy Ministries victim 'had been contacted by Daphne Caruana Galizia and brainwashed by her'.

One of the investors from the Joy Ministries was a woman who invested her lifetime pension, sending $400,000 to an account in Malta. The money was supposedly destined for a gold mine in Africa; the profits rolled over. Eventually she received a letter saying that the whole thing was a scam. The investor now believes that she was conned by Corbin Klein, also known as Lady Bird.

Dalli claimed the investor had been brainwashed by Giovanni Kessler, then boss of the European anti-fraud office OLAF, and Daphne.

Why would the American Christian pensioners want to hurt you, Brugger asked him.

'Because they were roped in by Kessler and Daphne Caruana Galizia, who is one of my arch enemies in Malta,' he replied. The fraud victims have evidence that they sent money to bank accounts in Malta and that some of the money ended up in entities run by Dalli's daughters and registered at his home address. There is no credible evidence to support Dalli's version of events or his allegations about Kessler or Daphne.

No charges were filed against Dalli in this case either. Daphne had been dead for a year when her story about the Joy Ministries Ponzi scheme led to action in court. Criminal charges were filed in Malta in November 2018 against the Dalli sisters, Corbin Klein also known as Lady Bird, and others for money laundering, misappropriation, and fraud. The defendants deny the charges and the case is still ongoing.

The Americans, who see themselves as victims of a swindle, told authorities they were given instructions on where and how to transfer funds directly from Dalli's daughter Claire.

Brugger told the authors of this book:

I consider Daphne to be one of the most courageous human beings I have ever encountered. It was basically her against the entire gangster state of Malta. In my mind she was the embodiment of what a real journalist should be: relentlessly in pursuit of truth, no matter what the cost might be.

In December 2016, Dalli's lawyers wrote to Daphne, warning her they believed she was writing with the 'premeditated intent to embarrass him, ridicule him, instigate people against him, ruin him financially, and destroy the respect which he has won with such hard work and effort for the country over decades.' The letter said Dalli felt harassed by her undue interest in him and asked her to remove all references to him on her blog and not to write about him ever again. Otherwise he would request the police to prosecute her for a series of crimes he believed she had committed against him.

Daphne responded in the way she always did in these situations: by publishing the letter and reminding her readers that:

now you have some understanding of why journalists in this country buckle under so quickly, when people in a position of great power on an island with few to no institutional safeguards, use the threat of prosecution so abusively. And note that he speaks about prosecution for harassment – the police – and nowhere does he mention a civil suit for libel.

Ten months later Daphne Caruana Galizia was dead. But for Dalli, that was not the end.

'Do not speak ill of the dead' is a wisdom not followed by John Dalli. Two weeks after her death, he wrote a letter to *The Times of Malta* headlined 'Resilience conquers poison pens – John Dalli'. There was a lot of guff in it about Mother Theresa and the primacy of life and godliness. But the nub of it was appalling.

Life is life, fight for it. Destroy this and it is as much of a murder as if a person's heart was pierced with a dagger. Poison pens do just that.

For his Maltese readership, Dalli's phrase 'poison pens' was a clear reference to Daphne. Dalli continued:

This concept was affirmed by Pope Francis when he addressed about 400 journalists in September 2016. He also defined poison pens as terrorists. The life of a person unjustly defamed can be destroyed forever.

John Dalli goes on to quote Pope Francis:

'I have often spoken of rumours as terrorism, of how you can kill a person with the tongue. If this is valid for the individual person, in the family, or at work, so much more is it valid for journalists because their voice can reach everyone and this is a very powerful weapon...'

And then John Dalli goes on with his very specific breed of logic:

Journalism in Malta has strayed a good deal from the papal standard. A poison pen is not a sporadic, individualistic initiative. It is usually an organised activity controlled and manipulated by a megalomaniac who knows that brainwashing the people through the media to demonise his adversaries or those whom he considers a threat to his ambitions is vital to achieve his aims.

Recognising this, Pope Francis, in the same address to journalists, said: 'It is important to always reflect on the fact that, across history, dictatorships – of any orientation or colour – have always tried to not only take control of the media but also to impose new rules to the profession.' This is what is happening in Malta.

And then the one key phrase in Dalli's letter:

No one has the right to take life. Except to preserve life. Likewise in self-defence.

Behind the mumbo jumbo and references to saints dead and living, there's a thinly-veiled and chilling justification that those who have been 'killed by a poison pen' may be excused for retaliating by killing the writer in self-defence.

The letter to *The Times of Malta* does not amount to a confession. But like a rag-tag band of terrorists that claims responsibility for an atrocity because they wish they'd carried it out in the first place, John Dalli seems to want us to believe he had Daphne Caruana Galizia assassinated.

Or that at least he wished he had.

THE ARTFUL DODGER

It is one of the many quirks of Maltese law that libel suits are classed like all other civil debt recovery suits. By nature they seek damages, and liability is inherited if the defendant dies. So, in Malta, you can sue the dead for libel.

Daphne Caruana Galizia died intestate which meant her husband and three sons automatically inherited her estate. At the time of her death, 42 civil libel suits were part of that estate and they had to accept liability for the suits or give up their claim to her legacy altogether.

Defending libel suits essentially amounts to proving the truth of the claims, which becomes very difficult for the heirs of libel suits if their late loved one has not shared the evidence with them in the first place.

Daphne's family, however, had every intention of defending the suits. The day after her death, the father and sons were in court, in place of the mother who had been due to attend a hearing in one of the many suits she was facing. They acknowledged that they would take on responsibility and new dates were set for the cases to continue.

The building which houses the law courts in Valletta can be found on the main street of the city known as Triq ir-Repubblika or Republic Street. As you leave the building through a pair of oversized Doric columns, you step right into the city centre, a busy pedestrian area. Across the street is a bronze memorial on a marble plinth installed in 1927. The memorial consists of three bronze figures. A tall man stands in the centre, bare-chested and square-jawed, grasping the haft of a downturned longsword in his left hand and a shield in his right. He is flanked by two modestly-clad women, one holding the head of the goddess Minerva and the other a papal tiara.

The three figures represent valour, faith, and civilisation. The artist presumably identified these characteristics as European and stood to remind Malta's colonial masters that Maltese people were also white, Christian, and European and did not require saving by the British.

This proud group of figures stand stoutly on an inscription MDLXV, or 1565, the year of the Great Siege when an invasion of Ottoman Turks had been rebuffed by the combined resistance of Knights of the Order of St John and mercenaries and volunteers.

The memorial was created by the legendary local sculptor Antonio Sciortino and the language spoken by its design is self-conscious and unambiguously political.

That first day after Daphne's murder schoolchildren from the San Anton School where the Caruana Galizia boys used to be students reached gingerly over the two-foot perimeter of soil that surrounds the memorial's plinth, and rested a small A4-sized photo of Daphne against the base of the statue. In front of it, they placed flowers and touching messages on cards addressed to Daphne and her family. It is unlikely the children were thinking of the siege of 1565 as they did this.

At lunchtime the next day, around 80 journalists congregated at one end of Triq ir-Repubblika holding up the front pages of local newspapers. The editors of the media houses in Malta, including the state broadcaster, had agreed to forgo content on their front pages, main stories, and websites and carry the sentence 'The Pen Conquers Fear' in white on black.

The journalists, co-author Manuel Delia among them, walked down Triq ir-Repubblika until they reached the law courts and addressed international reporters. They then filed a judicial protest requesting the court to ensure that Daphne's electronic devices, computers, phones, etc, would be held securely and protected from the prying eyes of police officers trying to identify her anonymous sources.

At the end of their short march, they left their posters and flowers against the Great Siege Monument, unwittingly turning it into that most dangerous of symbols to an authoritarian government: a shrine to a martyr. Over the next few days, other groups followed suit.

Daphne's remains were still with the forensic investigators. Without a funeral and a grave, the Great Siege Memorial became the focal point for mourners. The sculpture had become 'the Daphne memorial'. It was makeshift, spontaneous, and colourful. But no less sincere for that.

It became habitual for groups of people to visit the Valletta memorial daily and leave messages, flowers, candles or photos of Daphne. The messages were mainly calls for investigation, justice, and punishment to the perpetrators, and a continuation of her work so that the criminals she was exposing would not get away with their crimes.

But this behaviour did not suit the Labour government, which had already started signalling that after Daphne's death the country was going about its business as usual. The government sends city cleaners to clear the monument as often as Daphne's supporters fill it with flowers, candles and photos. The shrine has turned into something of a battleground.

At every opportunity Muscat did two things: express deep condolences to Daphne's family and cast himself as the victim, repeatedly bringing up the 'harshness' of Daphne's criticism of him and his wife.

Daphne had been the first to report the allegations that his wife had received bribes from the Azerbaijani president's family and had hidden the money in illegal offshore structures.

Daphne's report came in April 2017, although Muscat had been widely suspected of links to the Panama Papers scandal for some time. Muscat denied the story and set up a magisterial inquiry into himself and his wife. He claimed the affair put into question the political stability of the country and called an early general election which he won convincingly three months later.

As he climbed the steps of the Auberge de Castille – the seat of the prime minister in Valletta – he claimed that popular support had wiped his slate clean. Stability had been restored by popular acclamation.

And so Daphne's questions remained unanswered and her death put a stop to her relentless journalism. Most of the country behaved as if the questions were not worth the bother. Muscat presided over a period of undoubted economic well-being. Few wanted to think too hard about the honesty of their prime minister when the country's economic prosperity could not be doubted.

On the eve of Daphne Caruana Galizia's killing, Muscat was at his most popular. He had barely known a time without general adulation. His easy charm landed him his first political job in his 20s, as an anchor for the TV station owned by the PL.

In Malta, political parties are allowed to own and operate broadcast media outlets and take a considerable share of the newspaper business as well. That fact alone is perhaps the most convincing explanation for the extreme polarisation within the country.

It started out innocently enough. Until 1987, the PL administration of the time imposed a strict state monopoly on broadcast media. Even owning walkie-talkies or an amateur radio set could land you in jail. This allowed the government to exploit the state broadcasting monopoly to the hilt. To illustrate the point, for several years the very name of the leader of the opposition – Eddie Fenech Adami – was banned from state radio and TV. He was, quite literally, unmentionable.

In order to make their voice heard on the airwaves in the 1980s, the Nationalists (PN) used contacts in Sicily to set up their own amateur TV station and broadcast their message. The host, Richard Muscat, was warned he would be arrested if he returned to Malta and effectively ended up in exile, waiting for a change in administration.

That came in 1987. One of the first political initiatives of the new PN administration was to ensure that 'never again' would there be a repeat of its banishment from the broadcast media. It opened its own radio and TV stations but also passed a law opening up broadcasting to pluralism and symbolically, but very significantly, handed over to the opposition its first broadcast licences.

They created a monster. The people of Malta have been given mutually exclusive and contradictory renditions of reality for 30 years. The public broadcaster continues to be dominated by government party control, while the parties own a TV station each and employ 'journalists' who act, more often than not, as propagandists.

Maltese audiences effectively get Pravda and Izvestia and, since they cannot reconcile the factual contradictions between the different versions they receive, many simply choose to believe the party line.

In 1991, Malta applied to join the EU. The process of accession proved drawn out as geo-political circumstances changed dramatically during the 90s. With the collapse of the Soviet military block, formerly neutral countries such as Sweden, Finland, and Austria were given precedence over Malta, joining the block in 1995.

Malta and Cyprus were then pinned to the new democracies of Eastern Europe and had to wait for the latter to be ready to be allowed in.

This gave the PL plenty of space to excite suspicions of foreign interference which came intuitively to an island people with a history of colonisation. PL warned of all sorts of catastrophic consequences of EU membership: compulsory military service in European wars, an unbridled invasion of Sicilian hairdressers, the shut-down of local manufacturing, even an increase in AIDS patients.

In the run, up to the referendum on EU accession in 2003, Joseph Muscat hosted the flagship TV programme which warned of the Armageddon that would inescapably follow EU accession.

He was one of the faces of the No vote, perhaps second only to Alfred Sant (PL).

The people of Malta voted 52-48 to join the EU, a loss for the PL which had campaigned against. Notwithstanding, PL supporters celebrated in the streets, as the party line was that, taking into account the number of eligible voters who had abstained, the tally showed that the Yes vote was in reality a minority of total voters.

The matter was settled definitively by snap elections in 2003 that elected the Nationalist Party. Malta joined the EU in 2004 and the Labour Party, now stripped of the overriding mission that had dominated its politics since the 1970s, went into an existential crisis.

It did not rally until 2008 when Alfred Sant, having lost his third general election in a row, finally decided to call it a day, creating a vacancy in the party leadership.

Between 2004 and 2008, Joseph Muscat was no wallflower. In 2004, facing the irreversible reality of Malta's EU membership, the eurosceptic campaigner contested and resoundingly won a seat as a Member of the European Parliament (MEP).

Contesting general elections in Malta is a parochial affair. Malta is split into 13 constituencies, each electing five MPs. This focuses contact with voters to the local level, even for the most prominent and nationally significant politicians.

But Malta is a single constituency that elects six representatives to the European Parliament. This means that candidates have to have a countrywide profile, considerable brand recognition, and a substantial war chest to finance a national campaign.

Joseph Muscat's TV past prepared him for the job like nothing else could.

It is no coincidence that the most successful candidate in the 2004 MEP elections was Simon Busuttil, the most recognisable TV-friendly face of the Yes vote and the architect of the PN government's 'let's convince you with the facts' pro-EU effort.

Joseph Muscat used his European Parliament platform to make the transition from rabid fearmonger and forecaster of doom to a mainstream, youthful, fresh social democrat, the Maltese version of a young Tony Blair.

It worked. In 2008, with the resignation of Alfred Sant, the PL's leadership was his for the taking. The PL would no longer have to tacitly apologise for having been on the wrong side of the EU membership debate. Muscat would simply make everyone forget it ever had a problem with it.

In one of his earliest interviews as party leader, Muscat acknowledged that 'with hindsight' those in favour of EU membership had won the 2003 referendum. That, in itself, was a reversal of PL dogma and no less dramatic for the listeners who had known the truth all along.

That reversal signalled that the PL was no longer hostile to EU membership and, since there was no longer any danger of reversing membership, it could now be trusted with government.

Needless to say, Daphne, who had started her blog *Running Commentary* in 2008, fulminated against what she considered manifest hypocrisy. During the EU membership campaign, Daphne wrote a newspaper column in which she had adopted principally cultural arguments for membership. She understood that what would sway most people would be the amount of money the EU would pay Malta to join. But she found that approach crass and vulgar.

She did, however, see EU membership as a form of guarantee to prevent Malta from falling back to the Iron Curtain-flavoured excesses of the 1970s and 1980s. She was also a champion of freedom of movement, thinking it would help the younger population, including her children, grow if they could be given the opportunity to study and work abroad. She was particularly sensitive to this topic, because she felt she had been trapped in Malta when a PL government shut down her sisters' school and arrested her for daring to protest the schools closure.

But she saw no conviction in the new found euro-enthusiasm of Joseph Muscat and the PL after 2008, merely political convenience.

In 2008, the PN won the election by a whisker. Fewer than 2,000 votes separated the two parties. In Parliament, prime minister Lawrence Gonzi (PN) presided over a single-seat majority.

A small majority stuck with the PN in 2008 because they were still concerned Alfred Sant could take Malta out of the EU. When Sant stood down and his successor shelved euro-scepticism, voters remembered all the reasons they had grown bored of or annoyed with the PN which had been in government since 1987, save for a 22-month hiatus in 1996-98.

No one had any illusion that the 2008-13 legislature would not be the PN's last in government. But not everyone in the PN was ready to go down with the ship.

By his own account, PN malcontent-in-chief John Dalli had grown close to Muscat and became the 'father confessor' of PN backbenchers who could extract promises of reward from a future PL government in exchange for causing trouble for Gonzi.

Jesmond Mugliett (PN) was left out of the cabinet after the 2008 election because, as transport minister previously, he had been tainted by a series of bribery scandals in his department. The PL, until now his harshest critics, charmed him into rubbishing Gonzi's government. After 2013, when the PL was returned to power, his architecture firm would be rewarded with significant government contracts.

Jeffrey Pullicino Orlando (PN) felt entitled to a post in the cabinet but was left out because his character was deemed erratic. He voted against his own government on a series of bills, exposing the weakness of Lawrence Gonzi's government. He then joined forces with the PL, successfully campaigning for a referendum introducing divorce that exposed the vulnerability of the Catholic-liberal coalition that forms the PN. After 2013, he was rewarded by being allowed to keep his post as executive chairman of the Malta Council for Science and Technology.

Franco Debono (PN) was surprised at being left out of cabinet, although his lack of skill and talent made it a surprise to no one else. He voted with the Opposition on several bills including, in

2013, on a finance bill that forced the government out. He was appointed law commissioner by the PL government in 2013, and entrusted with revising laws and leading constitutional reform, none of which he achieved.

All these characters took turns to cripple Gonzi's government in a death by a thousand cuts and all of them felt the heat of Daphne's fiery criticism. She dug into their character flaws.

Often, the criticism became rather personal. Having campaigned for divorce, Pullicino Orlando found himself having to marry his long-term girlfriend. Predictably, the very public, political marriage proved to be a disaster and Daphne documented Pullicino Orlando's extra-marital affairs and public bouts of alcohol abuse.

Muscat knew just what buttons to press in order to ensnare MPs from the PN and ensure that the party languished in political limbo for a long time to come. A combination of flattery, charm, and the promise of great rewards worked on just enough people for word to spread.

Joseph Muscat became someone 'you could do business with'. Business interests lined up at the PL's headquarters to meet him. This raised the hackles of more ideological PL politicians, the old timers who were slowly eased away from the levers of the party machine.

Anġlu Farrugia, the man who as police inspector had unlawfully detained the young Daphne, became deputy leader of the PL in 2008. After Muscat pushed him out in 2012, Farrugia told newspapers he was worried about the secret deals his party leader was making with business interests.

As the prospect of a PL win in 2013 became ever more certain, the PN's donors dried up. It was being increasingly seen as a poor investment, whereas the PL was a sure bet.

In 2008 the PL could barely finance its electoral campaign. As 2013 approached, its fortunes were reversed. The PL's campaigning was lavish, using resources never before seen in previous electioneering in the country.

Public events, advertising, audio-visual productions, social media campaigning: all seemed to be paid for from a bottomless warchest.

As the 2013 confrontation approached, the resources on the two sides could not have been more imbalanced.

Lawrence Gonzi's government had been undermined and had limped through its last five years of tenure. His party was poorly resourced and every euro spent on propaganda dug deeper into its overdraft. People were generally unhappy with the PN. They had been in power for nearly 25 years and had made some bad decisions. The fact that Gonzi had steered an economy dependant on banking and finance through the 2008 financial crisis to the extent that the domestic impact was virtually imperceptible did not win him any points.

Meanwhile, Muscat had spent the five years before the 2013 election, reaping the rewards of Gonzi's weaknesses. His party was endowed by seemingly unlimited funding. And he was the new kid on the block.

At one point, the PL ran two sets of billboard campaigns. The first campaign showed a smiling Muscat on a series of brightly colourful backdrops. The other showed the PN figures who had earned the ire of the general populace in stark black and white. Daphne was included among them, as the PL presented her as part of the PN machine.

The decision to include her was not merely spiteful or convenient. It was strategic.

Placing Daphne in the mix was an example of the kind of reward Muscat could deliver the disgruntled PN politicians she had gone after: Mugliett for incompetence, Pullicino Orlando for hypocrisy, Debono for megalomania, and Dalli for corruption.

It allowed those PN politicians who had fallen from favour to present themselves as victims of the PN party machine. Daphne was habitually lampooned on PL media, called a witch, and described as hatching evil plans to bolster her friends in the PN and destroy their enemies.

The billboard campaign, which hung a journalist alongside politicians, showed how the PL intended to 'manage' Daphne.

At the 2013 election Muscat secured the biggest electoral majority in 60 years. The PL had lost to the PN in 2008 by 1,800 votes. In 2013, it won by 36,000 votes.

The PN was on its knees. Its leader announced his resignation. The party would need to rediscover its sense of purpose and would need to face the reality of a financial situation that for any other business would mean bankruptcy.

Daphne had no such distractions. On Monday morning, Joseph Muscat's first day as prime minister, she got to work on a new mission. Her five-year-old website would become the hub of opposition to the government. She would scrutinise each of their decisions, documenting their every move.

One of those first decisions was to write off a debt of €4.5 million that the operators of a downtown Valletta cafe owed the government in rent. What was effectively a cash grant was authorised directly by the prime minister who intervened in the interests of a party donor.

It would be the first of a long series of scandals that would have rocked any government that did not enjoy Muscat's majority.

Daphne documented each of these scandals. There would be a new shocker weekly, sometimes several times a week. The new government abandoned established practices in favour of methods of dubious legality.

In its first days in office it went through every civil service department and fired its permanent secretary, replacing them with the party faithful. It launched a campaign to employ 'persons of trust' in key positions, effectively transferring the PL's salary bill to the government by placing favoured staffers on the state payroll. The established civil service recruitment process was bypassed.

It unilaterally changed the terms of lease on government properties rented to the PL so that the party could profit from the properties.

It changed the rules to allow its supporters to gain rapid promotions. For example, PL supporters in the armed forces could jump four ranks in one promotion after the government abolished the minimum number of ranks a single promotion could skip.

It placed every single PL MP who was not in the cabinet on the state payroll, supplementing their parliamentary income with retainers or contracts as government advisers. In some cases, it employed MPs directly as staffers in the prime minister's office in direct breach of constitutional rules.

The new government fired the heads of regulatory bodies with legal powers to overrule government decisions, appointing in their place party apparatchiks often with no discernible competence or experience in the area.

The police chief was not the only officer to be fired and replaced by a party loyalist. The team at the top of the police force was rapidly replaced by officers chosen for their political allegiance, squeezing out most career officers.

Daphne closely followed each outrageous move, warning against normalisation and desensitisation. She made it clear that a party in government had to be held to objective standards of decency and public propriety, and there could be no excuses for exceptions.

She also documented in detail how the Muscat government's take-over of institutions was effectively shifting policy-making away from objective rule-setting to a method of overt favouritism for those willing to hop on board the PL train.

In a country the size of Malta, the most valuable currency is land and its development. By 2013, Malta had already started to suffer serious consequences of over-development. To the north of the capital Valletta, the land has sprouted tall concrete edifices. With weak public transport, the build-up of traffic jams has become a way of life.

Critical to good governance is the proper maintenance of local planning laws, to limit building and to defend open, green spaces against predatory developers.

The '70s and '80s had seen widespread corrupt practices in the granting of building permits, which could not be issued without the signature of a government minister. It was not unusual for a landowner to consider making a government minister a silent partner in the development project so that the building permit would go through.

When the PN came to power, it was keen to find a way to stop these practices. In 1992, it set up a planning authority to try and implement a fair and balanced process. Unfortunately the general populace was so accustomed to the practice that it could obtain the desired outcome with a backhander that the new authority failed to meet the expectations of the PN supporters who felt that it was now their turn to benefit.

Under pressure to appease landowners, the PN government extended the zones where building could be permitted in 2009, thinking that this would help moderate demand.

This measure backfired and Muscat's government exploited the hunger for construction and the related short-term benefits to the economy of feeding it. When it came to power, the PL government gave free rein to 'development', a misnomer if ever there was one.

Local plans, the yardstick by which land use was defined and the limits of development set, were in practice shelved. The legal status of the structure plan was rescinded and, with the dismissal of planning authority heads and their replacement with party agents, the building permits became a transactional activity.

The 'sack of Malta' ensued, a series of events reminiscent of the 'sack of Palermo' when political ineptitude and complicity with crime allowed the laundering of Mafia money through a 'construction boom' that spoilt the once-beautiful landscape of the Sicilian capital. Protection of historical buildings was observed in the breach and they were replaced by countless characterless buildings that stuffed as many dwellings as could reasonably (and sometimes unreasonably) be squeezed into the footprint.

The value of the transformation of a two-storey townhouse into a block of 12 flats made many home-owners minor entrepreneurs and property speculators overnight. But it was the big developers who greatly benefited from this building spree. Some of them, those particularly close to political power, were aided by procuring government-owned land on prime real estate for a fraction of the market cost.

One case in particular, the development of a hotel and a tower block of flats in St George's Bay, on a tract of land previously occupied by a state school in Malta's entertainment heartland, was documented by Daphne and the developer filed no fewer than 19 libel suits against her.

Another ploy was to change the conditions of lease for land given to the private sector at subsidised rates. This had taken place at a time when the tourism industry was still growing and they had been encouraged to build hotels on the land. The changes made it permissible for the owners to knock down the hotels and replace them with more profitable luxury apartments. This meant they could benefit from state aid to line their pockets, a moral if not legal transgression.

The environmental cost of this plunder is enormous. But since a lot of people are benefiting from the boom in construction, political disaffection is rare. Increased need of labourers on construction sites has led to consistent reports of exploitation and an increase in site accidents, several of them fatal, due to a lack of health and safety standards.

Enforcement is lax. The health and safety authority is run by a PL MP, Manuel Mallia. Originally given a post as cabinet minister, he lost his seat when his chauffer used his side arm to shoot at a car which had the temerity to drive too close to the minister's car.

Soon after, Mallia was compensated for the loss of his ministerial position with a new political appointment as the regulator of laws unpopular with the funders of his political party.

Daphne was particularly enraged by the fact that the new government did not even attempt to hide its wrongdoing. Documenting these scandals did not require special investigative skills. These were not hidden secrets revealed by strategically placed moles or whistleblowers.

What was required was scrutiny, integrity, and courage and she had all of those traits.

But there was much else that was hidden from public view.

In their first week in office, just outside the prime minister's study at the Auberge de Castille, three men had set up their new desks: Keith Schembri, Konrad Mizzi, and Brian Tonna. Their first move was to get in touch with a law-firm in Panama, Mossack Fonseca.

A PANAMA HAT AND CAESAR'S WIFE

On 22 February, 2016, five weeks before Easter, Daphne wrote a cryptic post with an obscure reference to the tradition of cooking lamb for Easter.

It's traditional to eat lamb on Easter Sunday, so Konrad Mizzi and his estranged wife Sai Mizzi Liang will be getting theirs from New Zealand, courtesy of their fixer Brian Tonna, who has a desk at the Auberge de Castille. When I say that I have an international worldwide network of spies, I'm not quite joking. But sadly, I can't say more for now though I'm bursting to. Lots of things will fall into place and lots of other things will suddenly look very trivial indeed.

Another cryptic post made jokes about Panama hats, written when Panama had no political significance whatsoever in Malta's consciousness.

A few days later the country would work out what she was getting at.

Konrad Mizzi (PL) was fairly new to Maltese politics in 2013 when he became minister for energy and was given a desk inside the prime minister's office. Muscat had presented Mizzi as a 'star candidate' recruited from the private sector to provide a new energy package for Malta that would lower the cost of electricity to consumers.

During its campaign, the PL said it had a plan that would lead to lower electricity costs. The plan would turn out to be remarkably reminiscent of the pitch Dalli had made to the PN government while he was EU commissioner.

Famously, Konrad Mizzi had given assurances that his 'plan was costed' and he was confident prices would go down within two years of a new PL government. If not, Muscat said, he would resign.

Two years later, in February 2016, the new power station had not yet come on line. But fortune favours the brave, and international oil prices had stabilised, giving the government room to bridge the cost of lower tariffs.

Meanwhile, a group of journalists working for the International Consortium of Investigative Journalists (ICIJ) was combing through thousands of pages leaked from the computer servers at a law firm in Panama that was to become infamous worldwide: Mossack Fonseca.

The Panama Papers contained heaps of evidence of wrongdoing by clients of the law firm all over the world. They had used Mossack Fonseca to set up anonymously-owned shell companies through which they could pass money beneath the radar of tax and law enforcement authorities worldwide.

Daphne's son Matthew worked in the core team of the ICIJ, combining his technology skills with his journalistic intuition. He was, in this case, a priceless protagonist in his mother's 'international network of spies'.

He searched through the list and, heavens to Betsy, prominent Maltese names showed up. Most of them were in business, using Panama to avoid paying tax on their earnings to the Maltese authorities.

But two names stood out: Konrad Mizzi, then the energy minister and Keith Schembri, the prime minister's chief of staff, a shrewd and cunning businessman in his own right and credited with being the mastermind behind Muscat's political success.

A third figure was Brian Tonna, an accountant and owner of Malta's franchise for Nexia International. Nexia is a second-tier international accounting brand which is reportedly the ninth largest global accounting network. Tonna's business in Malta was called Nexia BT, using his initials. Although he was not a public servant, he too had a desk in the prime minister's office alongside Mizzi, Schembri, and Muscat.

Tonna also ran the Maltese franchise of another international brand. He was the owner of a company called Mossack Fonseca (Malta) Ltd and together with his junior partner, Karl Cini, he offered to tax dodgers the secret services of the Panama mother company.

One of the services Tonna offered was the possibility of folding companies into trusts that would allow 'investors' to access their funds without revealing their identity. In the jargon, this is called 'layering' or hiding the true ownership of secret companies under layer upon layer of complexity and opacity.

Mizzi and Schembri's new Panama companies would be owned by trusts that Tonna had set up for them in New Zealand. The cryptic Easter lamb joke on Daphne's blog now became clear.

When Daphne revealed that Mizzi and Schembri had set up Panama companies and New Zealand trusts, their first instinct was to deny it. Daphne had been making things up they said. Mizzi was particularly vehement. Schembri, never loquacious in any case, was considerably more circumspect.

The news broke as Mizzi was campaigning for promotion. The PL deputy leader had resigned and Mizzi contested the vacant post and was elected. He was destined to be raised to number two or three in the cabinet. Or so it seemed.

But Daphne's stories could no longer be ignored once the ICIJ published the Panama Papers in April 2016. The consortium presented a series of orange-and-black cartoons depicting prominent politicians who were revealed by the Panama leaks to have been clients of Mossack Fonseca. The colourful cartoons quickly became recognisable icons of corruption, money laundering, and tax evasion.

They were called 'the power players': 140 politicians from 50 countries in a tax dodging hall of infamy that included the presidents of Argentina and Ukraine, the prime ministers of Iceland and Australia, and former heads of government from Georgia, Iraq, Sudan, Mongolia, and other countries.

There were only two figures from within the European Union, one of them the industry minister in Spain and the other Malta's energy minister Konrad Mizzi.

Daphne's story had been confirmed.

The Panama Papers, a Pulitzer Prize-winning ICIJ story, had a transformative effect worldwide. The first impact would be on the fingered politicians in office.

Within days of publication on 5 April 2016, Iceland's prime minister Sigmundur Davíð Gunnlaugsson was forced to resign. Five days later Ukraine's prime minister quit. Five days after that, the Spanish industry minister was forced out. Resignations flowed at Transparency International in Chile, in the FIFA ethics committee, at ABN AMRO.

Pakistan's prime minister Nawaz Sharif was also named and shamed in the Panama Papers. Eventually he would be tried and convicted for corruption on the back of the leaks. The revelations proved politically harmless to Vladimir Putin and to senior Chinese government officials. But not to Ukraine's President Petro Poroshenko who eventually lost elections to the comedian who lampooned him on TV.

In this context, Daphne expected her story to lead to Mizzi and Schembri's resignations or, failing that, their dismissal.

That did not happen.

Muscat squarely defended Schembri's right to set up offshore companies where he pleased. Schembri had been in business before he accepted to serve as his chief of staff. He had considerable commercial interests which required 'international banking structures' and it was frankly nobody's business where he banked.

Mizzi, the prime minister conceded, was a different matter. The setting up of an offshore company was not necessarily illegal but perhaps ever so slightly inappropriate for someone in politics. For this reason, he asked Mizzi to relinquish the deputy leadership of the PL which he had secured just a month previously.

He would keep Mizzi in cabinet, however. He would officially no longer be minister for energy but would still retain ministerial rank within the office of the prime minister, allowing him to retain his portfolio.

Muscat told the press that Mizzi had listed the ownership of the Panama company in an early draft of his annual declaration of assets. While the draft had not been published, Muscat said he had seen it and was therefore satisfied that Mizzi had had no intention of keeping his Panama company secret.

But there was a flaw in that argument. The Panama documents leaked from the Mossack Fonseca servers documented the exchange of emails between Brian Tonna's junior partner at Nexia BT, Karl Cini, and his counterparts at Mossack Fonseca in Panama City.

These emails detailed the setting up of Mizzi and Schembri's companies in Panama and were dated March and April 2013, almost three years previously. The first company Hearnville, would be owned by a New Zealand trust called Roturoa but its real owner would be Mizzi. The second company, Tillgate, would be held by New Zealand trust Haast but its real owner would be Schembri. A third company would be called Egrant but Cini would not say on the email exchange with Mossack Fonseca who the company would belong to. He instead said he would hand over the name orally over a Skype call later.

The significance of the Skype-only communication is that it would leave no trace of the instruction. Why would anyone want to do that? And why would this higher level of security be necessary for the owner of Egrant when it had not been so for Schembri and Mizzi?

When news broke that three companies had been set-up at the same time, some people wondered if Muscat was connected to Egrant. This explanation could fit his rather odd behaviour. Joseph Muscat had previously fired ministers when their conduct threatened his public image. Why did he feel the need to defend Konrad Mizzi and Keith Schembri? Why did he symbolically admonish Mizzi but ensure that in effect he would suffer little punishment?

That year's political satire, an annual panto-style affair called *Comedy Knights*, included a knowing call: 'Prime minister, who owns the third company?'

Adding fuel to the fire, Muscat repeatedly insisted he did not consider it particularly problematic for a government politician to own an offshore company. It would have been a problem, he argued, if Mizzi kept it a secret from his boss, but Mizzi had not.

Mizzi had not been altogether transparent about the existence of the Panama company. Under Maltese law, tax-payers who own companies abroad are obliged to make this known to the tax office. Mizzi had not done that and he had been outed by the Panama Papers. He had to pay a fine to close the issue and did so.

But, for Muscat, that was not a resigning offence.

Investigators at Malta's anti-money laundering intelligence agency, the FIAU, looked into Schembri's and Mizzi's activities. Though under-resourced, under-trained, and stepping on some very important toes, their investigations led to the conclusion that Konrad Mizzi and Keith Schembri may have broken the law. The technical term they use is 'reasonable suspicion of money laundering' because the FIAU is not a police force or prosecutor. As an intelligence agency, its job is to compile the evidence and pass it to the police for action. From then on, its staff act as advisors and witnesses.

The FIAU was then headed by a respected professional called Manfred Galdes. He recruited investigators from a shallow pool of suitably-qualified people. One such was a police inspector named Jonathan Ferris who was, at the time, half of the 'economic crimes unit' of the police.

In April 2016 Manfred Galdes handed the police a report that concluded the FIAU had 'reasonable suspicion' that Konrad Mizzi had laundered money.

The FIAU's report was handed over to the police chief, then career policeman Michael Cassar. Cassar sat sweating behind his desk. On it lay a case against a government minister, and facing him across his desk was the financial intelligence chief. Cassar did not feel he could ignore the evidence. He was not going to use it either. Instead he went on sick leave while he negotiated an exit from the police corps. He resigned within the week.

His replacement was Lawrence Cutajar, the fifth police chief in Muscat's first three years in power. Cutajar describes himself a fan of two things in life: Inter Milan FC and Joseph Muscat, whom he once described as a 'prime minister with brass balls'.

The FIAU report into Konrad Mizzi's Panama affair went in the drawer. As did another investigation that accused Mizzi of collecting kickbacks for purchasing an offshore gas storage ship to supply the new power station. And another investigation that accused Keith Schembri of collecting kickbacks from the sale of passports to Russian oligarchs.

Manfred Galdes resigned in disgust. His replacement shelved the reports and fired investigators recruited by Galdes, including Jonathan Ferris who turned from police inspector to specialist corruption investigator to unemployed whistleblower in the space of less than six months.

From April 2016 when the Panama Papers scandal broke to a year later, the question on everybody's lips was: who owns Egrant?

There was one person who knew for sure, Karl Cini of Nexia BT. But he was not talking. And yet no one could know more than the person who gave the instruction to Mossack Fonseca.

At the Nexia BT offices in the northern suburb of San Ġwann, seven kilometres from Valletta, one would have expected to find documents confirming whether Nexia BT had clients that were laundering proceeds from corruption. Although in April 2016 it was probably already too late.

On 11 March 2016, the day after Daphne broke the news that Cini had set up three shell companies in Panama, she reported that a large number of black bags of shredded paper had been left in a pile for collection right outside the Mossack Fonseca (Malta)/ Nexia BT offices in San Ġwann. Later that day Daphne reported that the pile of shredded paper had been collected from outside the Nexia BT offices and not by city waste collectors, but by a van belonging to Keith Schembri's KASCO Group, a privately-owned paper manufacturer and processor in Malta.

Remember Neville Gafà? He is the government official who took the last photographs of Daphne Caruana Galizia the day before she was killed.

Four months earlier, a Maltese court heard evidence from a Libyan national, Khalen Ben Nasan, who had been charged with blackmailing Gafà.

Ben Nasan had told the police that Gafà had asked him for more money than he expected to pay for visas for Libyans escaping war. He told the police that friends of his in Libya had video evidence of Gafà asking them for money.

The police 'raided' an old office Gafà had not used for months. They found 'nothing'. They did not raid the office he was using at the time or his house. Instead the police ended up arresting not Gafà but Ben Nasan.

Before March 2013, Neville Gafà was an optician's assistant in a local shop. He has no academic training to speak of. However, he was employed as a 'person of trust' along with hundreds of other PL campaigners after that election. His only apparent qualification was that he is a personal friend of Keith Schembri and Konrad Mizzi.

For entirely inexplicable reasons he was assigned the job of handling applications for Libyan civilians wounded in the civil war there to be granted medical visas for treatment in Malta. A visa to Malta is a Schengen visa and is therefore of considerable value to people escaping a war, wounded or unscathed.

Ben Nasan, and other witnesses who never made it to the stand in Malta, testify that Neville Gafà 'sold' medical visas to tens of thousands of Libyans for what the Italians would call *tangenti*, loosely translated as 'backhanders'.

Ben Nasan presented text messages from Gafà urging him to 'resume their business'. But the police did not ask Gafà what 'business' he was seeking to resume.

In November 2018 Libyan sources informed the Maltese press that they saw Neville Gafà in Tripoli, Libya. When challenged he said he was there on holiday which, given the civil war there, is, to be kind, unlikely.

Days later official photographs appeared on the official Facebook page of Libya's government of Neville Gafà having what appeared to be talks with the Libyan home minister. Gafà is accompanied by Kenneth Camilleri, the prime minister's personal bodyguard.

Libyan sources would tell the Maltese press that, on his Tripoli 'holiday', Gafà used the Maltese embassy's official car and other resources of the embassy that was technically closed because of security concerns.

The Maltese foreign ministry said Gafà doesn't work for them and he wasn't there on their business. The health ministry, which is shown on Gafà's business card as his employer, said they had thrown him out. The prime minister said Gafà was doing 'important work' but could not say who Gafà really worked for.

Then sources produced another piece of information. While on 'holiday', Neville Gafà was seen having a chinwag with Haytham al Tajouri, one of the most powerful warlords of Tripoli. Gafà said in his defence he 'stumbled' on Mr al Tajouri and he was just being polite, as one does when on holiday.

In 2016 the United Nations Panel of Experts on Libya reported to the UN Security Council on the situation in that country and accused Tripoli militia leader Haytham al Tajouri of financial fraud and human rights infringements.

The UN report says:

Haytham al Tajouri created a private detention centre in Tajura's ostrich farm, where he detained former regime officials and sympathisers. He extorted large sums of money from visitors. During Operation Fajr operations in July 2014, 12 former regime officials disappeared from his facility. His claim that he had handed them over to their families was denied by government sources.

Another possibility is that Gafà was not on holiday in Libya at all but trading in medical visas with a brutal warlord. The warlord denies any wrongdoing. The former optician's assistant denies any wrongdoing as well.

When Muscat succeeded Alfred Sant as leader of the Labour Party, there was no tradition of the Labour leader's spouse playing a prominent role in politics. Dom Mintoff's wife was English, timid, private, and lived most of her life avoiding the limelight and her abusive, philandering husband. Karmenu Mifsud Bonnici was a lifelong bachelor. Alfred Sant and his wife were separated before he was elected.

In contrast, the PN politicians were models of Catholic probity. Eddie Fenech Adami and Lawrence Gonzi were married, monogamous, heterosexual heads of picture-perfect nuclear families.

Joseph Muscat bucked his party's trend. When he became leader of the PL, he was married to Michelle, who was in Daphne's sights as vain, shallow, and greedy.

This March 2017 post on Daphne's blog should give you a taste:

Why are we paying to keep Mrs Muscat's father in private healthcare when they spend €15,000 on a six-day holiday?

No, really, it's just so bloody insulting and offensive. And this is a point that has been completely overlooked. The taxpayer has to foot the bill to keep Mrs Muscat's father in a private care home, and until late 2015 paid €40,000 a year to keep both her parents at Villa Messina, where they abusively occupied two government-sponsored places to the detriment of people who genuinely can't afford to pay.

While taxpayers pay for her father to stay at a private care home, probably while their own parents are at St Vincent de Paul Hospital or paying their own way, Mrs Muscat thinks nothing of blowing around €15,000 on a six-day holiday in Dubai – just one of several holidays she takes every year with her children and occasionally with her husband.

This is disgraceful. If she can afford those holidays, she shouldn't expect the rest of us to pay her father's bills at a private care home. And we should demand an explanation.

Michelle Muscat may have not been Daphne's favourite person, but she was a blessing to PL spin doctors, who were not unaware of the advantages of pitching Muscat as a family man to a broadly Catholic electoral base.

Michelle, then Tanti, graduated with a bachelor's degree in communications from the University of Malta. Professionally, she only really put her skills to productive work as personal secretary to Sant when he was leader of opposition.

Muscat courted Michelle at a time when their engagement would prove useful to him. There is no suggestion their love was not genuine. His direct access to the party leader's office would have come in handy.

During Muscat's first term as MEP in 2007, the couple had had twin daughters and Michelle's fulltime job was being photographed beaming for her husband's political flyers.

A year earlier, Michelle had set up an online accessories business called Buttardi with her friend Michelle Buttigieg. She used the nom de guerre Michelle Muscat-Tanti and was listed on the Buttardi website as 'European Sales and Promotion Manager'.

In 2012 Daphne wrote how she had found herself picking out a Buttardi necklace at an accessories shop when looking for a gift. In her inimitable style, she wrote:

Hang on, I said to myself when I saw the Buttardi label. That's Michelle Muscat's pin-money thing. No way am I going to buy one of her frigging giżirani *(necklaces), no way am I going to give it to a friend (she'll think I'm spoofing her – 'Here's one that the* Mexxej tal-Partit Laburista *(Labour Leader)'s wife made earlier') and no way would she ever wear it, on principle.*

'I've changed my mind,' I told the girl behind the counter. 'I'm taking this handbag instead.'

Years later Buttardi would be back in the news.

When Muscat became prime minister in 2013, Michelle was determined to be quite unlike all the previous spouses, who had dabbled in charity work and tagged along to events, but whose life generally remained private.

Michelle, however, took on a greater role. She patronised local fashion designers and wore their creations on public occasions. She polished her edges with cosmetic surgery. And she set up an office of her own with staff and a public calendar.

Daphne in November 2013:

The Sunday Circle *is running an interview with the prime minister's wife, who has been photoshopped to the point where she looks like a cyborg. It's not as though we don't get to see her in real life, so this extreme photoshopping business is a really bad idea as it makes her look terribly insecure about her appearance.*

The entire interview is carried in the link below, so you needn't bother getting the magazine unless you wish to cut out Mrs Muscat's photographs and frame them with a red candle lit beneath.

The Hello *magazine style of questioning is all about how Mrs Muscat is a mother first and foremost (because nobody has ever had children before) and how she is determined to give them a normal life – you know, by flying them to Manhattan during school days, taking them to receptions at Dar Malta in Brussels in the evening, and hauling them off to meet the Pope ('he's just like a village priest' says Mrs Ignorant, missing all the signs of somebody gracious who is scaling his conversation down to her level).*

How many more of these Evita Peronesque interviews are we going to have before the situation is completely milked dry? At least Evita Peron had no children. Mrs Muscat is hell-bent on shoving hers down everyone's throat while her political sidekicks become hysterical at any criticism of the situation, describing it in terms of a Herodian massacre of innocents.

Perhaps inspired by the comparison to Peron, Michelle set up her own charity, the Marigold Foundation, a catch-all NGO 'that addresses social behaviour, health issues, special needs and education'.

For her efforts, in March 2017 she was awarded the title 'Volunteer of the Year' by the government-controlled Council for the Voluntary Sector. It later emerged she had signed her own nomination for the award.

In 2015 Michelle started an annual solo swim to raise funds for her charity. That first year she crossed the Malta-Gozo channel which is 5km wide. Daphne wrote:

I don't know about you, but I didn't have her down as a long-distance swimmer – more as one of those women who get into the water and then swim on the spot while nattering to each other.

Since then the event has grown into an annual carnival. Michelle is escorted by army boats and helicopters and stretches of her swim are broadcast live on national TV.

In 2019, her husband congratulated her for swimming 15 kilometres in choppy open seas in just over four hours, a swimming pace comparable to Olympic open sea events.

When out at sea, she is prevented from speaking which helps manage the risk of political embarrassment. Her public utterances are kept to a minimum, mostly because they often prove awkward and counter-productive. When the Muscats first moved into Castille, the prime minister's wife told an interviewer the family had every intention of 'making the most' of their time in high office.

They would live up to that promise. The couple's children travelled first-class to every imaginable destination on their father's official business trips, frequently missing school to be wheeled out on official events where the presence of children was, many felt, inappropriate.

This behaviour would not escape Daphne's criticism. Nor would the fact that Michelle would open up the prime minister's official residence to her friends to use as a setting for commercial fashion shows, ostensibly promoting local talent.

In 2014, a minor scandal erupted when one of Michelle's designer friends, Mary Grace Pisani, used the prime minister's wife's good offices to 'encourage' female prison inmates to work for her curtain manufacturing business. The project was introduced under the auspices of Michelle's charity but the curtains produced by the prison inmates were sold commercially. The inmates were paid a pittance to produce the curtains and were paid late, had no recourse to complaint, and had no one looking out for their interests.

Michelle defended her charity and her friend, but her public quotes to the press were replete with contradictions and failed even the most basic fact checks.

That same year Michelle, whose husband had been prime minister for less than a year, was commissioned to do a little informal international diplomacy. An uninteresting photo exhibition was being held at the presidential palace in Valletta with the rather grand title of 'Children's Eyes on the Earth'.

Malta's presidents are figureheads and hold no political power. Apart from constitutional symbolism, their main efforts go towards raising money for charity by, for example, organising an exhibition.

But this particular exhibition was brought to Malta by Leyla Aliyeva, daughter of Ilham Aliyev, president of the fabulously corrupt Azerbaijan. Aliyeva has no official or state role in Azerbaijan. Ostensibly for that reason, she was hosted in Malta by the prime minister's wife who also holds no public office. During her sojourn in Malta, Aliyeva stayed with the Muscats at the prime minister's official summer residence in Girgenti in the west of Malta.

Daphne 's antennae went up:

Why in heaven's name are we sucking up to Leyla Aliyeva, the Azerbaijan dictator's daughter, a woman who makes the international news for all the wrong reasons? Azerbaijan does not have a royal dynasty. This woman is not a hereditary princess, but the daughter of a man who rigs elections to stay in power, controlling his country through a corrupt and oppressive regime.

Yet here she is, hosted like royalty by Malta's head of state and by the wife of the Maltese prime minister, feted, and toasted. 'Oh but it's an exhibition for children! A photography exhibition!' Wrong, and wrong. You have to ask yourself WHY the exhibition was held in Malta and why, more pertinently, it was held at the presidential palace, hosted by the head of state, and why Mrs Muscat entertained this corrupt dictator's daughter at her husband's official summer residence, Girgenti Palace, which she has somehow made her own personal territory.

There's something very wrong going on here.

There wasn't much more than intuition in those remarks. And, of course, knowing enough about Azerbaijan to connect some dots. Leyla Aliyeva owned three banks in Azerbaijan. In 2010, the *Washington Post* had reported that, along with the rest of her family, she owned real estate in Dubai worth some $75 million.

Azerbaijani journalist Khadija Ismayilova, who is a target of regular acts of oppression by her country's government and who collaborated with Daphne, had been documenting the Aliyevs' corrupt conduct for several years.

In 2018, *The Guardian* reported that, a few months after her visit to Malta, Aliyeva and one of her sisters Arzu agreed to buy a £60 million property in London using secret offshore companies.

There was more to raise Daphne's suspicions in those glamorous photo-ops of Michelle Muscat and Aliyeva.

As an MEP starting in 2004, Joseph Muscat spent some time serving on the European Parliament's joint commission with the Azerbaijani Parliament. The Azerbaijani Parliament, such as it is, is a satellite of the political and personal interests of Aliyev. The president's own party holds a considerable majority in the assembly, facing a minority made of government-leaning parties, so-called independents and a 'soft opposition'.

This effectively means that engagement with Azerbaijani parliamentarians amounts to engagement with Aliyev.

When Muscat became PL leader and prime minister he was in a position to help those friends he had made while MEP, such as the Azerbaijan regime. In October 2013 Aliyev's party won the parliamentary elections by a staggering 85% of the vote in a ballot which the OSCE described as being beset by 'widespread irregularities, including ballot-box stuffing and what appeared to be fraudulent counting'.

Muscat's appointee, Speaker Anġlu Farrugia, he of the dodgy teen arrests, was present in Azerbaijan and he judged the elections as 'fair, democratic and transparent'. But he would, wouldn't he?

It is hard to imagine a fair, democratic, and transparent election electing any party, let alone one that belongs to an autocrat, with 85% of the vote.

By 2013, the Azerbaijani government had already become notorious for its ways of persuading Western politicians to take rather surprising positions sympathetic to the regime. A year previously, a report by the European Stability Initiative rocked the parliamentary assembly of the Council of Europe when its members accepted absurdly generous gifts from the Azerbaijani government including black caviar worth hundreds of euro.

Azerbaijan's form of trading in influence was swiftly branded 'caviar diplomacy'.

The final piece of information hanging on the washing line was the apparently innocuous opening of a photo exhibition almost no one would go to see. And as always, Daphne was on it.

In September 2013, five months before Aliyeva's visit, Malta's state-owned energy company sealed a deal for a new power station and the energy it would produce for the next 18 years with a consortium named Electrogas. A third of the consortium was owned by Azerbaijan's state-owned energy company, Socar.

There's something very wrong going on here.

Daphne wrote about the setting up of shell companies for Mizzi and Schembri in 2016. But there were many loose ends and many unanswered questions and she would be busy looking into them for the next several months.

In February 2017, when the question 'who owns Egrant, the third Panama company?' had been on everyone's lips for a year, Daphne got in touch with a source who had written to her a few months previously, complaining about the unfair employment practices of a small, obscure bank where she worked.

The source was not altogether *au fait* with the intricacies of Maltese politics or even the character of Michelle Muscat. She was a Russian woman and had only lived in Malta for just over a year.

Her name was Maria Efimova and Daphne would help her become Malta's most famous whistleblower.

THE PASSPORT KING

Daphne's scorn was a flight of red tracer bullets arching through the night sky. Sometimes her writing had beauty and power but it was always deadly.

Take Henley & Partners. The name of the company sounds like it could be the manufacturer of posh biscuits. Instead, Henley & Partners describe themselves as 'the world's leading expert in private client residence and citizenship planning, and specifically in providing advice on comparative citizenship law and the acquisition of alternative citizenship.'

Daphne didn't quite see it the same way. 'These scamming crooks,' she called them. She went on to say that:

> the scamming crooks… are treating us Maltese in the same way they might have treated a tribe of jungle natives 200 years ago: profiteering off us because they think we Maltese are all as stupid, greedy, backward and corrupt as our tribal leaders. I'd like to see them putting up travelling sideshows selling British or Canadian passports – but it's not going to happen, is it, because we're the remote island natives who've been gulled into selling our land for beads and a couple of bolts of cloth.

The chairman of Henley & Partners is Christian Kälin, a Swiss entrepreneur who is widely known as 'The Passport King' and likes to declare that 'citizenship is inherently unjust'.

His solution to this injustice is to find microstates in the Caribbean or Europe and get them to enact new laws which allow the sale of passports to people with a lot of money. Funnily enough, people with a lot of money who wish to obtain a new passport often turn out to be crooks.

In January 2014, prime minister Muscat, his cronies, and the Passport King flew to Brussels to pitch to the European Commission their new passport-selling wheeze. The European Commission hated it, concluding the sales of citizenship 'called into question the very concept of European citizenship.'

The European Parliament voted on a motion knocking down the passport sales scheme: 560 in favour, 22 against. The then Commissioner for Justice, Viviane Reding, snapped: 'It is legitimate to question whether EU citizenship rights should merely depend on the size of someone's wallet or bank account.'

But in the EU, nation states determine immigration, citizenship, and passport laws, not Brussels. Malta gave the Passport King the green light and he started flogging his wares in the bazaars where rich people who want a new identity hang out.

Henley & Partners sell Maltese passports. It works like this. The passports belong to the government of Malta. The marketing, the checks, the fine details, that's all done by Henley & Partners. What the company sells, in a technical, narrow sense, is the know-how so that you end up with a passport. They're the middlemen and they take a cut. They then 'add value' with products and services. In the case of Malta, for example, they act as real-estate agents, making extra cash from passport-buyers who need to fulfil their residency obligation to get their new Maltese passport.

Right at the top of the list of questionable partners of Henley & Partners was Cambridge Analytica, the entity now infamous for scraping data off Facebook and using it to target swing voters and thus, the story goes, helped facilitate Brexit in Britain and Donald Trump's election in the United States. The world owes a lot to the pioneering British journalist Carole Cadwalladr for spelling this out in the pages of *The Observer* and *The Guardian*. But, long before Cambridge Analytica and its parent company SCL became infamous, they were in bed, so to speak, with Henley & Partners in the Caribbean.

The nation of Saint Kitts and Nevis is the smallest state in the western world, both physically and by population. The country has around 53,000 people. It is a democracy, true, but it is more like a small town than a nation state. The potential for corruption is huge. Saint Kitts is a crack in the pavement in the international rule of law, into which all manner of creatures of the night scurry and slide and slither.

To sell passports, you need a country willing to do it. Quite a lot of states around the world now sell passports, including Britain. The catch is, the wealthier the country, the more the government and/ or its journalists check up on the source of the individual's wealth. So if you're a dodgy crook with a stash of ill-gotten gains, then you might think twice about knocking on Britain's door because they might not let you in or, if they do, it could get embarrassing quite quickly. But Saint Kitts is a different matter. Henley & Partners took over the government's passport-selling operation in 2006 and made it much, much bigger.

The problem for Henley & Partners is that governments in countries big or small often change. To ensure that their passport-selling wheeze was not reversed by an incoming new government they and their friends went to work on the general election in 2010. That year Henley & Partners and SCL rocked up on Saint Kitts. The prime minister of Saint Kitts was behind in the polls and the leader of the opposition was being critical of the passport sales. Watch this space.

Alexander Nix of SCL/Cambridge Analytica was caught with his metaphorical pants down in 2018 by the UK's Channel Four News boasting of dirty tricks or 'counter-ops' in a classic sting. Nix told Channel Four News' undercover cameras that his company deployed honey traps, bribery stings, and prostitutes, among other tricks, to swing more than 200 elections around the world for his clients.

Old Etonian Nix wasn't all fur coat and no knickers. SCL really did sting the leader of the opposition on Saint Kitts in 2010, Lindsay Grant. They offered him a sweetheart deal, a $1m bribe in return for support in a land deal. Grant bit on the worm and suggested some nice offshore accounts the crooked money could be paid into. SCL's people filmed the sting and then stuck it up on the internet. The result was that Grant tanked at the polls and the government, and Henley & Partners' passport scheme, were safe, at least for a while.

Henley & Partners and their pals also got involved in an election on the islands just up the road, as it were, in Saint Vincent. Officially, Henley & Partners boasts it 'does not get involved in political campaigns' but both Freddie Gray in *The Spectator* and Juliette Garside and Hilary Osborne in *The Guardian* got hold of a chunk of emails showing the Passport King, Christian Kälin, getting very closely involved in the election. His candidate lost, by the way.

In 2019, the UK House of Commons select committee on the media reported on big tech's abuse of data. Their report was called 'Disinformation and Fake News'. In a section of their report, the MPs looked at Henley & Partners. The Passport King would not have enjoyed the write-up.

The select committee report is worth quoting at length:

As we said in our Interim Report, SCL Elections and its associated companies, including Cambridge Analytica, worked on campaigns that were not financed in a transparent way, overstepping legal and ethical boundaries. Our Interim Report described the relationship between SCL Elections' campaigning work and Christian Kälin, Chairman of Henley & Partners. We were told that, behind much of SCL Elections' campaigning work was the hidden hand of Christian Kälin, Chairman of Henley & Partners, who arranged for investors to supply the funding to pay for campaigns, and then organised SCL to write their manifesto and oversee the whole campaign process. In exchange, Alexander Nix told us, Henley & Partners would gain exclusive passport rights for that country, under a citizenship-by-investment (CBI) programme. Alexander Nix and Christian Kälin have been described as having a 'Faustian pact'. With the exclusive passport rights came a government that would be conducive to Mr Kälin and his clients.

All concerned deny any wrongdoing.

The MPs in their report noted that, in 2014, the UK issued a warning that 'illicit actors' – crooks in layperson's English – were buying passports 'for the purposes of evading US or international sanctions or engaging in other financial crime'. One reason for this warning was the fact that Saint Kitts (SKN) had removed 'Place of Birth' on its passport.

The MPs noted the following people had acquired Saint Kitts and Nevis (SKN) passports:

- *Ali Sadr Hashemi Nejad: Iranian, acquired SKN passport via application managed by Henley & Partners in 2009; arrested by the US in March 2017 for money laundering sanctions violations and was bailed in May; currently subject to electronic monitoring and curfew; his Maltese bank, Pilatus, had its licence withdrawn in October 2018, for money laundering;*

- *Houshang Hosseinpour, Houshang Farsoudeh, and Pourya Nayebi: Iranian, acquired SKN passports in November 2011, December 2011, and November 2012 respectively; they used their SKN passports to acquire a bank in Georgia; all three men were sanctioned in 2014 by the US;*

- *Ren Biao: a Chinese national, who obtained his SKN passport in September 2013; he moved to SKN with his family in 2014, after China issued an Interpol red notice. He was wanted for allegedly acquiring $100m by defrauding state institutions;*

- *John Babikian, fled Canada in 2012 in the wake of tax evasion charges, holder of an SKN passport, prosecuted by the US Securities and Exchange Commission (SEC) in 2014 for stock fraud, and fined $3m.*

Of the four cases cited by the MPs, Ali Sadr Hashemi Nejad was the one who got his Saint Kitts passport via Henley & Partners.

For the record, the MPs noted Henley & Partners' rejection of any allegation of wrongdoing:

Henley & Partners denies directly funding any election campaigns in the Caribbean on citizenship-by-investment at the same time that SCL was active in the region. A letter from Global Citizens, on behalf of Henley & Partners, was sent to the Committee in December 2018, stating: 'It is natural that there would have been a certain amount of interaction among the numerous advisors and consultants. It is entirely incorrect, however, to suggest that Henley & Partners was a formal partner to SCL in any way.'

Sven Hughes used to be a reservist in the British Army and served for a time in Afghanistan. He was also a copywriter for an advertising agency. One day in 2009 Alexander Nix popped into his office and made him an offer he couldn't refuse. Work for SCL, go to the Caribbean, help out with an election in Saint Kitts and we will double your pay. Hughes said yes. Early on, he tripped over Christian Kälin's operation. In 2018, when he was interviewed by Freddy Gray of *The Spectator*, Gray asked: 'Did you meet Christian Kälin?' Hughes said:

> It's an interesting name. I didn't meet him. The way we were asked to engage with him was through the use of Skype or invisible emails accounts, which you would neither send or receive emails but rather save your correspondence into the drafts folder.

This unusual method of communication is also used by members of Islamic State to exchange messages with each other. It works when both parties know the password to the email account. The beauty of this method is you can delete the correspondence easily and then there is no proof it ever existed.

Islamic State denies any wrongdoing.

Did Hughes think that at this stage he should have smelt a rat, asked Gray?

> Within two weeks I had a conversation with Alexander Nix which was: 'I'm worried to be here ethically, morally, and in some of the things I am seeing.' Nix said: 'If I'd told you the truth, you would never have joined us.'

On the podcast Sven Hughes and Freddy Gray are both heard laughing.

Hughes set out to try and reshape the election team in a proper way, as he saw it. He was employed by SCL and spoke to Nix every day but also found that he was communicating with Kälin every day or very often. Gray put it to him that Nix admitted (while being secretly filmed by Channel Four News) to dirty tricks, sting operations and so on. Hughes referenced the Saint Kitts campaign:

> It was not something I chose to do or actioned. I was winning the election … by running a clean campaign … In each campaign, there was an occasion where, between Alexander Nix and Chris Kälin in some capacity and I don't know to what extent whose idea it was each time, but some sort of doubling-down, sting was introduced to make sure the campaign won. So in Saint Kitts

and Nevis, the very thing he spoke about on Channel Four News, with paying bribes, yes, that was a technique that they utilised in Saint Kitts and Nevis. I'm equally frustrated by this. We didn't need to do this. We were winning. It wasn't necessary. However, I wasn't the boss.

Hughes was privy to the Lindsay Grant sting but unhappy about it. There was a second operation in Saint Vincent, the amplification of sexual abuse charges against one politician. Hughes did not like this either but found it happened. Gray put it to Hughes, that Nix won the election, then Kälin sold the passports. That was how Hughes saw it too. In one of his campaigns, Hughes and his team insisted on a live-in armed guard in the villa where his team was based. He feared that his bosses were not paying enough attention to their duty of care: "I explicitly stated, 'You are going to get someone killed.'"

Hughes was so worried about safety on one Caribbean island that he worked out a fast exit route, a fast boat or a plane, in case of trouble. After a year, he left SCL in 2010 and created his own company which, he says, is more ethical.

In 2012 Hughes's former deputy at SCL, Daniel Muresan, was found dead in a hotel room. He had been working for SCL on the tightly fought elections in Kenya. Daniel was the only child of a former Romanian agriculture minister, Iona Avram Muresan, who had been sentenced to seven years in prison for embezzlement. The Romanian newspaper *Adevarul* reported his father saying:

They found him in his hotel room. He had his laptop on his lap, the telly was still on and there was a glass of wine next to him. He enjoyed drinking a glass of wine before going to sleep.

Muresan, who was thought to be in his early 30s, died of a heart attack. That was listed as the cause of death on the certificate sent by fax to the Gherla prison in Romania where his father was serving his sentence, *Adevarul* reported. His father reportedly feared his son had been poisoned in relation to his own embezzlement case.

'Dan,' said Hughes reflecting on the time they had both worked for SCL, 'was my deputy on the election side of the business. A wonderful man, we were living together under armed guard in Saint Vincent.'

In 2012, Hughes, now working for his own company, got a call from Alexander Nix: 'he wanted me to work for him in the US.' Hughes said no. 'And then Nix said at the very end of the call: "oh and by the way Dan's dead." He said he'd got so drunk he drowned in his own vomit on the Kenyatta campaign.' Hughes said he didn't know what had happened but on the podcast repeated his concerns that SCL in his experience did not do enough to ensure the safety of their team.

Cambridge Analytica whistleblower Chris Wylie – he of the dyed pink hair – told the British MPs on the media select committee in 2018 that he had been worried that Muresan, his predecessor as head of elections, might have been murdered. Wylie said Muresan was poisoned after 'a deal went sour. People suspected he was poisoned in his bedroom,' Wylie said, adding that the Kenyan police had been 'bribed not to enter his hotel room for 24 hours'.

Wylie added that the claims were merely 'speculation' he had heard from others inside the company and that he had no proof of the allegations. 'What I heard was that he was working on some kind of deal of some sort,' he said. 'I'm not sure what kind of deal it is. But when you work for senior politicians in a lot of these countries you don't actually make money in the electoral work – you make money in the influence brokering after the fact – and that a deal went sour.' He added: 'Again, this is what I've been told, so I'm not saying this as a matter of fact, but people suspected that he was poisoned in his hotel room.'

The authors asked Alexander Nix to comment about the death of Dan Muresan. Nix pointed out that the tragic death of 'my very good friend and colleague, Dan Muresan, in Kenya was thoroughly investigated at the time by the local police and the Romanian Embassy and there was no suggestion that his death was anything other than a terrible accident'. Nix also quoted an independent report by Julian Malins QC saying it concluded that:

(Dan Muresan's) death was certainly unexpected, but I have found nothing in the circumstances to suggest that he was murdered. None of those closely involved at the time (the police and family and embassy staff) thought that he was

murdered. The autopsy findings did not suggest murder. His death was, in fact, the kind of very sad event that can happen to a young man on a Saturday night, who has been drinking. To suggest to the world's press that he was murdered was an irresponsible act, no doubt causing pain to his loved ones.

Wylie painted a picture of SCL/Cambridge Analytica as a lawless organization that had dealt with hacked material, illegal data, and the use of intimidation techniques to win elections.

Sven Hughes was more measured in the podcast but his message was similar to Wylie's. Was Hughes aware of accusations that Cambridge Analytica was doing fake news, asked Gray? Hughes recalled that 'at the time, because I was asking inconvenient questions through my year there, I became cut off from my dealing with Christian Kälin pretty much completely and was set aside from those techniques … So I left. I voted with my feet.'

Hughes's answer is striking. When asked about fake news, Hughes refers to Kälin of Henley & Partners, not to Nix of Cambridge Analytica.

After establishing their business model in the Caribbean, Henley & Partners made a move on Malta. The beauty of Malta is that it is a European Union state and allows free movement of people and capital inside the world's biggest market, passport-free travel inside the Schengen Area, comprising 26 states and 400 million people, and visa-free travel to almost anywhere in the world, including the United States.

But a passport that good costs money. Whereas a Saint Kitts passport could cost $250,000 at most, a Maltese one costs around €650,000 for the passport alone but there are also the trimmings. Family members cost €25,000 each. You have to buy €150,000 worth of government stock, an outlay you can get back in five years' time. To buy a passport you need to own property in Malta or rent for five years. So if you have a spouse and two kids, purchase the government stock and buy or rent, the whole shebang could set you back something close to €1 million. The numbers of golden passports sold via Henley & Partners's know-how with the sanction of Malta's government amounted to, by December 2018 (the time of the last available data), around 2,500. That's a revenue stream worth, roughly, €2.5 billion. The exact amount of money coming in is not known. The lion's share of that money goes to the government of Malta. But Henley & Partners' cut – 5% or more, again the exact numbers are not known – adds up to a tidy sum.

Henley & Partners are making a killing.

In a nutshell the governments of little states in the Caribbean, and Malta too, were offered a deal: we – SCL/Cambridge Analytica – will help you win your election and in return, once elected, you pass laws enabling a different crew – Henley & Partners – to sell passports.

The evidence suggests that the Mr Big of the whole operation may not be the obvious figure, Alexander Nix of Cambridge Analytica, but in fact could be the clever Swiss, Christian Kälin, because selling passports is where the big money is. One should note three things: first, that according to Companies House in London, both SCL and Cambridge Analytica are in liquidation; second, that Henley & Partners issued a statement in 2018: 'Dr Kälin has not interacted with Alexander Nix for many years and does not consider him a "friend"'; and third, that Henley & Partners is thriving.

The pattern set up in the Caribbean repeated itself in Malta long before the 2013 elections. The visitors from outer space, sorry, Cambridge Analytica/SCL and Henley & Partners, arrive, offer their deal, 'we will help you win your election, then you will rewrite your passport laws'. The election is won, the passport laws are rewritten, then the crooks, sorry high value clients, come in.

One of the authors of this book, Manuel Delia blogged in early April 2018 that correspondence showed that Kälin asked SCL to introduce him to Joseph Muscat in June 2011 – two years before the election that the PL won big. Muscat's success in 2013 is partly due to the electoral cycle; voters thought it was time for a change and local businesses were happy to donate to the likely winner. But the PL had been virtually bankrupt in 2008 and five years later its campaign was awash with money. The scale of their wealth is very hard to explain purely from local resources alone. At the time political parties were under no legal obligation to declare the source of their wealth. However, under Maltese law any party funding from outside the country is illegal.

Kälin also visited the PN in Malta in 2011 and made his passport-selling 'consultancy' pitch. The then governing party was not interested and they heard nothing more from him. But his other half, as it were, Alexander Nix, rocked up on the island in November 2012.

Co-author Manuel Delia blogged that the information in the correspondence between Henley & Partners and SCL, originally unearthed by Freddy Gray in *The Spectator*, confirmed that the two organisations have consistently worked hand-in-hand in several jurisdictions and there were indications that they had also done so in Malta since 2011, before PL announced its new policy to sell passports.

The MPs on the UK House of Commons media select committee read Manuel Delia's blog and cited it as a source in their interim report. As soon as it was published in 2018, the government of Malta and a dodgy PR outfit called Chelgate fired back. Both Malta's High Commissioner to the UK and the Chelgate PR company wrote to the committee, denying statements in the Interim Report that Malta's Labour Party had had dealings with the SCL Group 'for several years before the 2013 elections'.

The final report by the British MPs retorted that:

We understand, however, that SCL certainly had meetings in Malta, that Christian Kälin of Henley & Partners was introduced by SCL to Joseph Muscat in 2011, and that Christian Kälin met with both political parties before 2013.

So the MPs told the government of Malta and Chelgate to stick it up their jumper. That halo of smugness you see is from co-author Manuel Delia. Joking aside, he was spot on.

It is something of a mystery why Chelgate PR should jump to the defence of Malta's government and its dealings with the Passport King and, perhaps his one-time pal, Mr Nix. Chelgate's boss is a character called Terence Fane-Saunders. Its website boasts that TFS is 'widely regarded as one of the leaders of the international public relations profession'. He once worked for Burson-Marsteller, a PR company that lied about the Dirty War in Argentina while its client the Fascist junta there was torturing and murdering people. In 2017 Chelgate hit the headlines in *The Sun*: 'Company behind Grenfell Tower "death trap" cladding hired a PR firm "before fire had been put out".' *The Sun* reported: "Harley Facades, who were paid £2.6 million for cladding, reportedly appointed Chelgate to manage the fallout as the death toll rapidly rose.'

There has been no admission by the government of Malta that it hired Chelgate to wash its dirty linen. But that is what Chelgate did.

There is one other point worth weighing up in relation to the assertion made by the Maltese government that it had had no dealings with the SCL group or Cambridge Analytica.

In 2015, before the Cambridge Analytica scandal hit the news, Malta placed one of the shareholders of SCL, Jonathan Peter Marland, on its annual Republic Day honours list. He was made honorary officer of the national order of merit and President Marie Louise Coleiro Preca stuck a medal on his chest.

Jonathan Marland owned shares directly in SCL Group Limited and, through JP Marland & Sons Limited which he fully owns, he controlled further shares in the SCL Group.

Marland is also a member of the House of Lords as Lord Marland of Odstock since 2006.

In the months leading to his decoration by Malta he was closely active with Adrian Hillman – a character that will feature again later in this story – with whom he coordinated the Commonwealth Business Forum on the fringes of the Commonwealth heads of government meeting held in Malta in 2015.

He also operated in close association with Phyllis Muscat, close personal friend and travelling companion of prime minister Joseph Muscat. In 2015 Jonathan Marland employed Phyllis Muscat's daughter in the Commonwealth unit he ran.

Daphne Caruana Galizia reported at the time how Phyllis Muscat used her relationship with Jonathan Marland to secure lucrative employment for her daughter while studying in the UK.

The Times (of London) identified Jonathan Marland, formerly a trade envoy for David Cameron's government, as one of the high-profile connections that SCL exploited for its business. *The Times* said about Jonathan Marland and others that 'the men who run Cambridge Analytica are no strangers to scandal and intrigue and have social and business links to the heart of the Conservative Party, royalty, and the British military'.

The Guardian reported in 2015 that Jonathan Marland denied he interfered in SCL's business. Marland said he had not been involved in running the company and had refused a request to introduce it to Conservative Party HQ.

> *I have had very little engagement with the company and in fact am fairly sure I have only met (Cambridge Analytica former CEO Alexander) Nix once,* he said. *I also know very little of their operations as my initial investment was over 10 years ago. As such I had no idea of their Facebook data and am naturally concerned about current events.*

As well as Jonathan Marland, all concerned deny any wrongdoing.

Who, exactly, are the beneficiaries of the Passport King's cunning wheeze? Daphne chased up a number of Christian Kälin's clients.

Step forward, for example, Vietnamese MP Nguyen Thi Nguyet Huong. In July 2016, she was found to have violated Vietnamese law by holding dual citizenship, which the country does not permit. She had secretly acquired Maltese citizenship and was kicked out of parliament for breaking the law. Daphne blogged:

> *Sources in Malta have informed me that she paid for her Maltese citizenship under the Maltese government's 'sale of citizenship' scheme, euphemistically known officially as the International Investor Programme (IIP). The Muscat government, which introduced the scheme three years ago, touted it as being a way to 'attract talent to Malta', and said that those who 'invested' in Maltese citizenship would have to live in Malta for part of the year. It is unclear how a Vietnamese member of parliament fits these requirements. Malta's sale of*

citizenship to individuals from countries which do not allow their citizens to hold dual nationality also raises questions about Malta's diplomatic negligence – to say nothing about all the questions this particular case raises about the careful due diligence scrutiny to which candidates for the purchase of Maltese citizenship are supposed to be subjected (as we were told).

There are several other newly minted Maltese citizens thanks to Henley & Partners who made the world headlines and these are a few examples:

- Pavel Menlikov: Russian-born and owner of a Maltese passport since 2015. Menlikov lives in Finland. He chaired the Airiston Helmi real estate firm which was raided by Finnish financial police in September 2018 on suspicion that it was a front for a giant money laundering operation;

- Mustafa Abdel Wadood: Egyptian-born and owner of a Maltese passport listed on Malta's government gazette in 2018. Four months later he was charged with fraud and conspiracy by the US government. He awaits trial and his citizenship is being withdrawn;

- Liu Zhongtian: Chinese-born and owner of a Maltese passport since 2016. He is the owner of a huge Chinese aluminium conglomerate and indicted in 2019 by a US grand jury for smuggling aluminium into the US and dodging $1.8 billion in taxes. Daphne had reported Liu's acquisition of a Maltese passport in May 2016;

- Arkady Volozh (founder of Russian search engine Yandex), Boris Mints (owner of the major investment company O1), and Alexander Nesis (founder of equity group ICT): The three are Russian-born holders of Maltese passports and shortlisted by the United States treasury in a 'Kremlin Report' targeting oligarchs close to Vladimir Putin for potential sanctions.

All concerned deny any wrongdoing.

The Malta passport scheme is particularly popular with Russian applicants. It is estimated that the largest contingent of 'new' Maltese citizens is originally from Russia. That's more than 600 which, given that this is a roll call of billionaires, is a large number indeed.

You cannot be a billionaire in Russia or anything like it without getting along with Vladimir Putin. Conversely, it is not viable to be or to remain a billionaire in Russia without some form of toehold in the West.

Henley & Passports' scheme in Malta, though by no means exclusively of interest to Russians, provides for the Russian oligarchy a way of bridging the apparently contradictory aspirations of being both close to the Kremlin and far away from Russia at the same time.

Consider, for example, the case of Grigory Anikiyev, a Russian parliamentarian whose son, Artem, acquired a Maltese passport on his 17th birthday. In a video blog, Artem bragged about his 24 hours in Malta, flying in and out on a private jet to collect his passport and enjoy a spot of shopping while his father exhorts young Russians to be good patriots and love their country.

The access given by passports sales schemes in Malta and elsewhere raise security concerns in the West, not least because of the back door that is opened to the Russian oligarchy and to Chinese nationals who break the laws of their own country seeking citizenship of another.

US-based financial crime consultant Kenneth Rijock blogged in April 2018 that his sources in contact with government officials in the US, Canada, and the EU 'engaged in joint preparations to create regulations that will effectively combat the threats posed by criminal elements who have obtained citizenship by investment passports from five East Caribbean countries'. Most of those countries used Henley & Partners to promote their passports, including Saint Kitts where Pilatus Bank owner Ali Sadr Hashemi Nejad obtained his.

Rijock reported that these countries 'have intentionally engaged in activities designed to conceal the actual true identity of their dodgy clients' such as minimal but real changes to the legal name of the client or altering their place or date of birth. So, by way of example, co-author Manuel Delia could get a new passport as Emmanuel Delie with a slightly different date of birth — and that way the US and other law enforcement authorities would not pick up the real identity of the holder of the freshly minted passport.

In the meantime, Henley & Partners have expanded and are now selling the passports of Kazakhstan and Moldova. The 'Passport Index' which ranks passports according to how 'powerful' they are because of the number of countries in the world that permit their holders to enter them without needing a visa, ranks Kazakhstan's passport the 53rd most powerful in the world. Moldova ranks 42nd.

Those rankings are unlikely to be attractive to buyers from the nationalities that typically purchase passports from other countries. Russia's passport ranks 40th and South Africa's 44th, to name two. A passport from Kazakhstan and Moldova is hardly an upgrade.

Analysts have suggested that Moldovan and Kazakhstani citizenship could help their buyers acquire citizenship from countries with much more powerful passports who would not accept them if they did a background check on them.

So if you are a Russian crook and your name is Ivan Killalotov, even the due diligence process of Malta, such as it is, might refuse you a passport given your history. However, if Mr Killalotov buys a passport from an interim country under a slightly different name, say Ivor Kyllotov, then he would become a different person altogether and his history would be wiped clean. This process could even fox the FBI, at least for a time.

'Interim' passports from Kazakhstan or Moldova open the door for dodgy customers that could have a problem securing a Saint Vincent passport (23rd most powerful in the world) or a Saint Kitts passport (22nd). Or a Maltese passport, 5th most powerful in the world. By the way, all of these ratings are supplied by Henley & Partners who, of course, are paid by these countries to flog their citizenships.

Although the 2014 agreement between Malta and the European Commission allowing the passports scheme obliged the government to regularly publish the names of 'citizens by investment', the Maltese authorities have found a crafty way of dodging that bullet.

Maltese law already required the government to publish in the gazette the list of people who are naturalised as Maltese citizens, that is people who are not born Maltese but become so by proving Maltese ancestry, say, or by showing they have become eligible having lived in Malta for a long time or having been married to a Maltese citizen for a number of years.

Since 2014, the government has added citizens who have acquired citizenship through the Henley & Partners scheme to this list. There is no distinction between, say, people who marry Maltese citizens and people who buy passports. When someone marries a Maltese, that's an individual. But Ivan Killalotov is likely to buy a passport for Mrs Sveta Killalotova and their children, Nasty and Nastya and Nastieryet as a package. That could be five Killalotovs popping up on the new citizens list and they would immediately look like they paid for the privilege.

The government has therefore changed the A-Z rules on the published list, listing, exceptionally for a Maltese official record, the names of the new citizens in alphabetical order by their first given name, instead of by their surname so that billionaires and Maltese-Australian third generation migrants are shuffled together like an enormous deck of cards. So, in our example, Mr Killalotov and Mrs Killalotova will feature on different pages of the very long list under the letter I for Ivan and S for Sveta, rather than K. You can work out their connection but it has been made deliberately difficult because in Malta opacity rules.

Transparency International Russia has been documenting the identity of Russians acquiring Maltese citizenship for the past five years. But it is no easy task.

To add to this obscurity, the addresses indicated by the applicants for Maltese citizenship (where they are required to have lived for a year before applying, according to Malta's commitments with the European Commission) are kept secret.

A few addresses have, however, leaked, most of them by administrative error, when around 80 'new' citizens were listed by mistake on the electoral register which necessarily contains the voters' addresses to identify them with a constituency. Before they were removed from the list, reporters went out knocking on doors to look for billionaires.

Co-author Manuel Delia found new passport owners 'living in' boarded up basements, uninhabitable garages, or modest homes clearly inhabited by other people. None of the addresses were places you would expect 'high net worth' individuals or families to choose to live.

Although there is no way for journalists to verify all the addresses since these are kept secret, it is safe to say that people who purchase a passport under the Henley & Partners scheme and choose to live in Malta are rare.

Consider, for example, the case of 62 Saudi nationals belonging to two of the richest families of that country who were named on the 2018 citizenship list as Maltese citizens. There's no other way of saying it: if 62 oil rich Saudis lived in a small place like Malta for an entire year, someone would notice them.

Of course, just because they were not in Malta does not mean that someone somewhere on the island was not delighted to cash monthly cheques from oil sheiks they have never met.

Maybe that is one reason why not many people wanted to hear of Daphne Caruana Galizia's concerns about the scheme.

Writing in November 2016 she observed that:

a report published by the regulator for the sale of Maltese citizenship has found that selling EU passports and the property/rental spin-offs therefrom now account for almost 3% of GDP. Because it is unsustainable, it follows that this is insane. The government is now caught in a trap where it has to keep selling EU passports – good luck with the consequences of that – to keep up the GDP figure, or stop selling them and watch GDP shrink by 3%. The alternative – finding a sustainable and properly productive way to grow the economy – is apparently beyond the people whose main concern now is entering into deals which will grow their assets and 'populate' their companies in Panama and the British Virgin Islands (and those are just the ones we know about).

Inevitably that sort of dependence breeds corruption.

Daphne also closely followed revelations by Malta's then leader of the opposition, Simon Busuttil, in April 2017 that someone close to Prime Minister Muscat got nice bungs from three Russians in return for passports. A leaked report by Malta's Financial Intelligence Analysis Unit on the passport wheeze details three Russians who became Maltese citizens in 2016: Irina Orlova, Evgeny Filobokov, and Viktor Vashkevich. Investigators believe that the three ultimately paid bribes totalling €166,832 ($206,725) to Willerby Trade Inc., an offshore company directed by Muscat's associate Brian Tonna. Around €100,000 of that money was moved to a Pilatus Bank account controlled by Keith Schembri, the prime minister's chief of staff.

All concerned deny any wrongdoing.

Keith Schembri has admitted receiving the funds paid by Willerby into a Pilatus Bank account but he claimed Brian Tonna was settling a personal loan Keith Schembri had advanced him when Tonna was going through an expensive divorce. A private agreement between Tonna and Schembri was presented to 'prove' this was the case.

Loan agreements are classic money laundering tools used to cover illicit payments which Tonna and Schembri deny this was.

Brian Tonna served as the auditor for Keith Schembri's personal business interests. The code of ethics for auditors prevents them from borrowing from or lending money to their clients.

Brian Tonna and his junior partner Karl Cini resigned from the voluntary professional Institute of Accountants to preempt any disciplinary proceedings against them.

The Accountancy Board, which is a statutory regulator with the power to withdraw an accountant's license, has said that it will only consider Brian Tonna and Karl Cini's cases if and when they are convicted by a criminal court of law.

The Passport King's funny business enraged Daphne. Henley & Partners hired a fancy London law firm Mishcon de Reya, to try and shut her up. Fat chance of that.

This was one salvo from her blog on 12 May 2017:

The damage caused to Malta by the sale of citizenship is unquantifiable. Malta is not Saint Kitts & Nevis. It is interlocked with the rest of the European Union and has a European economy. Keith Schembri and his sidekick Joseph Muscat think that selling Maltese/EU citizenship is free money, because you're selling a small piece of paper document, that costs you nothing, for €650,000. They and a legion of other bell-ends who are so busy selling passports that they can't see straight because they're blinded by $£€$£€ look only at the revenue and don't see the massive cost in terms of reputational damage to Malta, and the fall-out from that which we are seeing now.

I and thousands of others are glad that Busuttil – then leader of the opposition Nationalist Party – *has committed himself to ending it. No wonder Henley & Partners has broken out into a cold sweat. Regardless of their claims to the contrary, Malta is their only EU-passports-like-pastizzi money-tap. And the Maltese government is the only EU member state government with which they have a contract – and not just a contract but crooks at the wheel, including the Prime Minister's chief of staff. Note to Henley & Partners: if you send me another cease-and-desist letter with a warning not to publish it, I'm going to publish it, then print it and use it when I next take the dog for a walk. If I'm angry enough, I might then even post it back to you.*

She finished off her blog with the following hashtag: #nomorecrooks.

Christian Kälin replied, sounding more hurt than angry. Daphne, being Daphne, posted Kälin's reply on her blog:

Hi Daphne. I just was made aware of this post. Did you receive another letter that upset you or what is the issue? I understood from our interactions, and from Mishcon's last communication (which was, however, quite some time ago) that you had agreed to remove the defamatory and incorrect posts on your blog. Kindly advise. Basically we will need you to remove not everything of course, but those statements that are clearly defamatory and incorrect. If that is not done we have no other choice than following the advice of our lawyers and start proceedings in London as this is where all of this internet blogs has most impact on our business. Hopefully we can avoid that and continue a reasonable dialogue, which I always find is better than any alternative. We simply want to stay out of the political issues Malta faces and do our business – in Malta or elsewhere. Hope you understand …

Best Chris

Dr. Christian H. Kälin TEP IMCM Group
Chairman & CEO Henley & Partners Holdings Ltd.

Daphne fired back on 12 May:

Christian, I am extremely annoyed at your lawyers' high-handed attitude and more than annoyed at the fact that a company feels itself empowered to sell a country's citizenship against the will of the citizens of that country and by underhand agreement with a government that does not have an electoral mandate for it and then has the sheer brass neck to begin going after journalists and real citizens of that country who object to it.

If this government is voted out, you will have no trade in Maltese passports at all, and the vast majority of citizens of this country hope it happens.

As I had occasion to tell you when we met, Malta is not Saint Kitts & Nevis. You can behave like a colonial power, throwing your weight about against the press and legitimate criticism, in Saint Kitts & Nevis, but you can't do it here.

I do not appreciate your threat to sue me in London. The reason you are doing it is not because 'most of your business is there'. Most of your business comes from shady people in Russia and the Middle East, with the occasional Vietnamese MP thrown in.

The reason you are threatening to sue me in London is because you imagine that I am somebody from the sticks who is frightened of the words 'London', 'UK courts', and 'high costs'.

I would be fascinated to see the adverse publicity surrounding any court case in which your shady outfit goes after a blogger in the EU member state where you are abusively selling Maltese citizenship – the fact that you have an agreement with a corrupt government does not make it non-abusive – against the will of the people who hold a Maltese passport by birthright.

Henley & Partners must be the most unpopular outfit in Malta right now after Pilatus Bank – an outfit owned by somebody who bought a Saint Kitts & Nevis passport from you – and that other outfit run by Joseph Muscat and Keith Schembri, with whom you signed an agreement decided upon before they came to power.

I trust you have some understanding of the low regard in which Henley & Partners is held by the real citizens of Malta, and I await your reassurance that you are not bankrolling Muscat's outfit in this electoral campaign so as to ensure that he is returned to power and you can carry on selling the passports of my country. Daphne Caruana Galizia.

On the last day of May 2017 Daphne got hold of – incredibly – an email exchange between prime minister Joseph Muscat, his chief of staff Keith Schembri, and Christian Kälin who, for once, was not sending 'invisible emails'.

Guns blazing, she emailed PM Muscat, Schembri, and Kälin. They will not have liked what she wrote:

Sirs,

I have in my possession evidence, in the form of email exchanges between the addressees of this message, that Henley & Partners' threat/decision to sue me in the UK courts was taken on instruction from, and in collusion with you, the Prime Minister, Joseph Muscat, his chief of staff, Keith Schembri, and the Justice Minister, Owen Bonnici.

Following a meeting on the subject with the Justice Minister, Christian Kälin, who is group chairman of Henley & Partners, outlined a plan under which letters designed to intimidate with the threat of a financially ruinous and extremely cumbersome law suit in the 'UK courts' were to be sent to me, to the Opposition MP Jason Azzopardi, and to 'three media houses' in an attempt at dissuading us from further scrutiny of Henley & Partners and its opaque and damaging activities in Malta.

This plan was then put past you, the Justice Minister, and you, Jonathan Cardona, CEO of Malta's Sale of Citizenship Scheme, for your approval. It was also forwarded to you, the Prime Minister and to you, Keith Schembri, in tandem, and Henley & Partners' group chairman addresses you by your first names: 'Keith, Joseph', in that order.

You, the Prime Minister, reply: 'i don't object' (sic) and you, Keith Schembri, reply: 'Thanks, Chris. This looks good. Very kind regards'.

At some point, you dropped the decision to threaten and intimidate the 'three media houses' and Opposition MP Jason Azzopardi, with a view to focusing solely on me with a barrage of letters and emails from Mishcon de Reya, a respectable law firm with a reputation to protect, who may be unaware that they are being used as a tool to affect the corrupt plans of the Prime Minister of a European Union member state against a journalist who he has marked out as his own personal enemy, and who he wishes to ruin financially because he cannot do so in other ways ...

At the most basic level, it is beyond belief that the Prime Minister of a European Union member state – as distinct from Henley & Partners' favourite stomping-ground, Saint Kitts & Nevis – would allow himself to be addressed in this overly familiar fashion by the chairman of a corporation that has come to Malta to sell European Union Schengen Zone passports through a convenient arrangement with yourselves, to the detriment of other EU member states and with damaging consequences for Malta itself, or that he would allow himself to be addressed by that chairman in the same bracket as his own supposed underling and chief of staff, with his chief of staff even taking precedence: 'Keith, Joseph'.

It is just as disgusting that you, the Prime Minister of my country, stoops so low as to enter into collusion with a corporation chairman, showing him that you deliberately and maliciously use an @josephmuscat.com address for 'official' business rather than your @gov.mt address, and that you have drawn your Justice Minister and the CEO of Malta's Sale of Citizenship Scheme (your former 'Sherpa') into collusion to do likewise, along with your chief of staff Schembri who you clearly treat as a business equal if not actually a superior to whom you concede.

In other words, you, the Prime Minister of Malta, have no problem at all showing a corporation chairman that you are deliberately and maliciously choosing ways and means to cheat the public you have been elected to serve, and to hide information from the civil service, and that you so lack the dignity of the office you hold, that you draw the corporation chairman with multiple passports into this plot to hoodwink your own government and people.

I know that this email will be ignored by you, the Prime Minister, by you, his chief of staff (you have already barred my telephone number), by you, the Justice Minister and also by you, the CEO of Malta's Sale of Citizenship Scheme (who brazenly and disgracefully uses the email address jonathan@josephmuscat. com). But I shall still ask the question as to why you are colluding with Henley & Partners using @josephmuscat.com addresses hosted on a private server in the United States, rather than your official @gov.mt addresses hosted on the Malta government's servers.

This particular question is addressed to Christian Kälin, group chairman of Henley & Partners: Why, despite the fact that you are here operating in a European Union member state and not in the Caribbean islands of Saint Kitts & Nevis, you have agreed to collude with the Prime Minister, his chief of staff, another senior cabinet minister and the head of Malta's Sale of Citizenship Scheme using @josephmuscat.com addresses, when you know — because you operate extensively in corrupt and undemocratic jurisdictions — that the sole purpose of this is to keep the exchanges from being part of official government records as they should be.

As I myself said to you, Mr Kälin, during our sole meeting some weeks ago: 'The fact that you deal with shady members of the Malta government and may have been exposed to corrupt dealings at an official level here in Malta does not change the fact that Malta is nonetheless a European Union member state and not a dirt-poor and desperate Caribbean island without the rule of law or institutions to safeguard it.'

I should add here that, this morning at the Courts of Justice, I informed the inquiring magistrate in the Egrant Inc/Pilatus Bank inquiry that the Prime Minister, his chief of staff, the Justice Minister, the chief of Malta's Sale of Citizenship Scheme and other key henchmen are all using firstname@ josephmuscat.com addresses for their illicit exchanges concerning Henley & Partners, which would indicate that they are doing the same in their other (nefarious) plots.

I also suggested that he should act immediately to gain investigatory access to the josephmuscat.com email server as he will probably find many of the answers he is looking for there.

Meanwhile, a word of advice to the addressees of this email message: if you are going to take the trouble to creep around using @josephmuscat.com addresses to hide your dealings from the public and the civil service, it's a good idea to make sure that you don't automatically pick up your correspondent's @gov.mt address by default when you type in his name, as that will send the entire chain of emails to the Malta government server. Daphne Caruana Galizia

Daphne was killed six months later on 16 October.

One consequence of her murder is that it put the good work of Anthony Julius, a trustee on the board of English PEN, which campaigns to defend writers and freedom of speech, into the shade. Julius is a libel specialist at Mishcon de Reya, the fancy law firm hired by Henley & Partners to shield the force of Daphne's attacks on them. Daphne's family asked English PEN to remove Julius. English PEN decided to retain Julius.

The Caruana Galizia family said they were hurt by that decision. They went as far as asking English PEN to stop participating in campaigns supporting the cause for truth and justice in Daphne's case. Matthew Caruana Galizia said 'the shock and disgust with which journalists and writers all over the world reacted to English PEN's decision is something that's surprised even me. We all feel as though the organisation has abandoned the defence of free expression to serve as a platform for Mischon de Reya.'

National chapters of PEN are self-governing and separate. PEN International continues to campaign for truth and justice for Daphne Caruana Galizia.

A second consequence was that Henley & Partners went the extra mile to improve its public image. To that end, in April 2018, they booked Maltese tenor Joseph Calleja to sing at a Henley & Partners event in the City of London. Christian Kälin was at one point on the platform too. During the day, when *The Spectator*'s Freddy Gray popped up and started asking inconvenient questions, Gray was asked to leave the event.

Later that evening prime minister Joseph Muscat arrived to hear not the fat lady but the not thin man sing. On the street was a small, noisy but very peaceful group of protesters, among them Paul Caruana Galizia, Daphne's youngest lad. Co-author John Sweeney, then working for BBC Newsnight, tried to doorstep Muscat. He asked: "Prime minister, do you stand by your economy minister, Chris Cardona?"

A security guard thumped Sweeney for his impertinence.

There is, of course, no suggestion that Christian Kälin or his associates in Henley & Partners had any hand in Daphne's killing.

BANKING FOR BAKU

In December 2014 Joseph Muscat led a funny peculiar delegation to Baku in Azerbaijan. Official trips overseas by Malta's prime minister are traditionally well covered by the local media. The government pays for the journalists' travel costs to make sure they're on the front line taking good photos of 'Joseph Muscat with …'

But not on this trip.

Nor did the government's Department of Information provide any information.

Daphne would find some details on the Azerbaijani government website.

Joseph Muscat's delegation was composed of himself and three other people: Keith Schembri, Konrad Mizzi, and his press secretary Kurt Farrugia. No ambassadors, no civil servants, no note-takers, no press.

In the photos they sit facing the fabulously corrupt President Ilham Aliyev flanked by his entourage of a dozen big shots and hangers-on.

In April 2015 it was time for a second funny peculiar trip to Azerbaijan. Joseph Muscat had heeded the press's bewilderment that they had been left out of the visit last time. So his office paid for a small press pool to cover his second trip to Baku in four months. The editor of the national broadcaster TVM was invited with a camera crew and a photographer from the Department of Information.

Two years later, in 2017, Daphne Caruana Galizia learned what happened that day:

In April two years ago, the Prime Minister travelled to Azerbaijan for a meeting with Ilham Aliyev, accompanied by Kurt Farrugia and Konrad Mizzi.

Reno Bugeja, head of news at the public service broadcaster, TVM, was supposed to accompany them, along with a cameraman and a photographer from the government's Department of Information. The DOI was supposed to obtain visas for Azerbaijan for the three men, but told them it hadn't managed to do so and that they should leave Malta on their (transit) flight to Paris all the same and wait there for the visas.

The two men from TVM and the DOI photographer ended up stranded in Paris for 24 hours. Reno Bugeja was furious. During those 24 hours, the Department of Information did not take their calls and Kurt Farrugia, the head of government communications, didn't answer his phone either.

When they were finally told that the visas had come through, they left Paris for Ukraine, en route to Baku. They landed in Baku late at night and immediately tried to contact the Department of Information in Malta, or Kurt Farrugia in Azerbaijan, for directions on what to do and where to go.

The three men from TVM and the DOI, who were there at the government of Malta's behest, spent three hours at Baku airport ringing Kurt Farrugia and getting no reply, and eventually left and went to a hotel.

When they finally got through to Farrugia, he told them that it didn't matter that they had missed Joseph Muscat's meeting with Ilham Aliyev, which is what they thought they were supposed to be there for. They were astonished. Shouldn't the head of government communications have been freaking out that they missed photographing and filming such a high-level meeting?

They realised that they hadn't been wanted at the meeting and that the visas fiasco and failure to answer phones was just a ruse to hold them off while at the same time pretending – after the accusations the previous December that Muscat, Mizzi, Farrugia, and Schembri had gone to Baku without the media – that this time, the media had been invited, albeit only TVM.

Instead, TVM and the photographer from the DOI found that they had gone to all that trouble and travelled all that way just for a meeting of old ex-leaders of dodgy countries, who Ilham Aliyev had invited to Baku to show how democratic he is. This was a far cry from the meeting about oil and gas which they had been led to expect.

Joseph Muscat liked having his chats with Ilham Aliyev away from prying eyes.

In 2016, Maria Efimova's husband, a Cypriot, attended a job interview at a bank in Malta called Pilatus. The couple had moved to Malta from Ireland with their two infant children and were trying their luck settling down on the island. The interview was arranged by a recruitment agency next door to the bank.

When he visited the 'bank', it was not quite what he expected. There were no cashiers, no customer waiting area, not even a sign on the door saying 'bank'. It was an office with a handful of people in a posh building that housed several embassies of European countries including the UK, Germany, Ireland, the Netherlands, and Portugal.

The interviewer seemed more interested in learning about his family, questions he had thought were just the warm-up phase. He said his wife was still looking for work. She spoke English fluently and had had some training in banking and anti-money laundering procedures.

The interviewer, Hamidreza Ghanbari, an Iranian national sporting a Dominican passport and CEO of Pilatus Bank, did not appear too keen on the gentleman in front of him. But he told him the chairman was looking for a personal assistant. The bank, he explained, was only just being set up and since it was a very small operation, onboarding new clients was often handled by the main man himself. These were special clients, ultra-wealthy, ultra-demanding. Their banker's personal assistant could be no ordinary secretary.

Maria Efimova's husband left the interview thinking he did not stand much chance of getting a job. His wife, however, who hadn't even been trying, looked set to be earning their keep quicker. He went home to tell her that a banker working in Ta' Xbiex wanted to interview her for the job of his assistant.

His name was Ali Sadr Hashemi Nejad.

At the time, Ali Sadr was 33 years old. He was originally a native of Iran but by then held a portfolio of passports which allowed him to dodge international sanctions against his country of origin and its citizens.

He had no training as a banker. He graduated in civil engineering from Cornell University and had been living in the US for 10 years with his mother and sister. In a 2003 court filing he claimed that, if he were ever to return to Iran, his life would be in danger, because his father, who still lived in Iran, was in trouble with the regime. Or so Ali Sadr claimed.

That claim does not check out. Ali Sadr's father, Mohammad Sadr Hashemi, was at the time one of the wealthiest men in Iran and was decorated by the presidency of Mohammad Khatami as a national hero for being one of the 'great exporters' of the Islamic Republic.

Ali Sadr obtained a US green card in 2004 based on his application for asylum in the United States.

In short order, the asylum seeker ostensibly escaping from the country in which his father was an enormously successful businessman established himself rather well. He registered multiple companies in Malta, Switzerland, Hong Kong, Cyprus, the UK, and the US. He procured properties in Maryland, Washington DC, and Malibu. He even acquired a pistachio farm in California, as you do.

His official US residency opened doors to acquisitions in that country. But his Iranian citizenship would still have proven a barrier to conducting business in several countries. That barrier was removed by Henley & Partners who supplied Ali Sadr with at least one fresh Caribbean passport. Or two.

Writing in *The Malta Independent* on the eve of the June 2017 election Daphne Caruana Galizia reported that she had confirmed with Christian Kälin that Ali Sadr was a Henley & Partners client.

In the UK registry, Companies House, Ali Sadr appears as a director of two companies. In both cases he is listed as a citizen of Saint Kitts but has two different dates of birth. There is a remote possibility that there exist two Ali Sadr Hashemi Nejads from Saint Kitts and Nevis who both registered companies in the UK but given that the population of that country is less than 60,000 this is not likely.

The existence of the relationship between Ali Sadr and Christian Kälin has been confirmed by Kälin himself. In response to questions from *The Shift News*, Kälin part-confirmed a Daphne story that Ali Sadr had been invited to be a guest at a wedding anniversary party hosted by Mr and Mrs Kälin.

> *As a matter of courtesy ... [Ali] Sadr was indeed invited to Kälin's wedding anniversary event, which was one of many social events that Kälin regularly hosts, and to which a large number of people are invited, including current and former clients ... [Ali] Sadr did not attend this event,* Henley & Partners told *The Shift News.*

The existence of a relationship between Ali Sadr, Joseph Muscat, and Keith Schembri was revealed through Ali Sadr's wedding guest list. Photographs taken at his 2015 wedding in Florence show the Muscats and Keith Schembri with the owner of Pilatus Bank in the kind of chummy snaps you would take with old friends.

Since Malta is a member of the EU and the eurozone, a banking license granted by the Maltese authorities is in effect a European banking license. That made Ali Sadr's acquisition all the more valuable.

Ali Sadr started exploring Malta as base for his bank before the 2013 elections, when the Nationalists were still in power. He met the then finance minister who encouraged him to explore Malta as a business location. But his application would need to be assessed by the regulatory authorities.

Ali Sadr applied for a banking licence after the 2013 election. He instructed his staff not to mention his Iranian nationality in any communication. This was revealed in emails exhibited as evidence before the US courts.

'No one should mention any ties from me to Iran. This is only to own Pilatus and the bank in Malta.' He wrote that email as he worked to set up the bank accounts needed to show Maltese authorities he had the necessary funds to run a bank. The US authorities would later describe those funds as 'proceeds of crime'.

By January 2014, the license to set up Pilatus Bank was granted.

Unlike her husband, Maria Efimova was not an EU national. Though she was entitled to work in Malta as the spouse of an EU national, as a Russian citizen she needed to get a work permit before she could secure employment. Local work permit rules do not allow a job-seeker to apply independently for a permit. An application can only be filed by an employer.

Maria Efimova was offered the job of personal assistant to Ali Sadr Hashemi Nejad and was asked to start the next day. But the engagement would have to be informal while the bank's application for her work permit was processed. Since the outcome of the process was a foregone conclusion in view of her eligibility, it was safe for her to start working.

But it would not be right for her to be paid before she had been formally registered.

Apart from a work permit, Maria Efimova was also waiting for her residence permit to be approved. While her application was being considered, she could not leave the country and leave her husband behind as travelling alone she would likely not have been allowed back into Malta on her return. An issue arose when Ali Sadr needed Maria Efimova to travel for work. She told him she could only travel with her husband while her residence permit application was pending. And the children would have to travel with them as there was no one they could leave them with.

Maria Efimova says Ali Sadr Hashemi Nejad agreed. She made the booking and went on the trip.

Three months working at Pilatus Bank gave Maria Efimova a clear idea of what was going on. It did not seem quite right.

The bank was barely interested in the infinitesimal Maltese market. But there were two Maltese names she did recognise.

One was that of John Dalli. The notorious former EU commissioner held an account with a few hundred euro, but as far as she could see it was inactive.

The other Maltese name was Keith Schembri. The name did not mean anything to her. She would later learn that the name and the account belonged to the most senior adviser of Malta's prime minister.

But her attention was drawn to more significant customers with names she would recognise with her moderate familiarity with the Russian news media.

Pilatus Bank held no more than 180 accounts. It was not too hard to remember the ones which provided the highest contribution to the multi-billion value of the bank's deposits.

The bank was primarily a clearing house for the scions of Azerbaijan's ruling elite.

The children of the fabulously corrupt Azerbaijani president Ilham Aliyev and minister for emergencies Kamaladdin Heydarov funnelled hundreds of millions of euro through Pilatus Bank using it to launder funds and purchase properties outside their country.

The game here is hiding the true source of the money. If a president's daughter openly buys a house in, say, London then the world will know about it very quickly. But if the president's daughter uses private banks, shell companies, and other vehicles in offshore jurisdictions to hide her identity, it is much harder to know the true source of the cash. The files in Pilatus Bank documented the payments processed for these secret acquisitions.

Being inside Pilatus Bank meant being one of a handful of trusted people who knew what the Aliyevs and the Heydarovs were hiding: the fact that they were the mystery buyers of fabulous wealth. They needed to hide their identity because being the heir to a minister, or even a president, could not easily explain the hundreds of millions of euro they held. The money was likely the product of corruption or misappropriated from the people of Azerbaijan.

The 'heirs' of this monarchy in all but name owned massive conglomerates in their own country, hotels and luxury properties in Dubai, porcelain and linen factories in France, villas in Spain, and developments in Georgia.

Though the Azerbaijanis were not the only customers of Pilatus Bank, they were the ones with the most money. From the inside, it looked as if Ali Sadr Hashemi Nejad was developing a boutique business as a banker for elite dictators and their families.

One other name was José Eduardo Paulino dos Santos, the 32-year-old son of the dictator of Angola. Old Man Santos was also staggeringly corrupt and had ruled oil-rich Angola with an iron fist longer than his son had been alive.

Perhaps the first abbreviation you learn on an anti-money laundering course is PEP: politically exposed person.

When a banker is faced by a customer who is a politician or a holder of some other public office such as a judge, they need to watch out. Someone trusted with public office who goes rotten and takes bribes or embezzles money by virtue of their office will need a bank to take their money. A banker who takes the proceeds of crime is party to money-laundering.

It is not enough to watch out for the politician. You need to keep an eye on their spouses, children, and trusted others.

Therefore, in theory, it is harder for a politician to open a bank account. They are asked to provide more information about how they obtained their money. And if they cannot explain every cent, most banks would turn the PEP down, declining their business.

Keith Schembri and Konrad Mizzi knew something of that problem. The Panama Papers show that their dodgy companies Hearnville and Tillgate went around the world tryng to find a bank which would take their money. As far as is known, the effort was unsuccessful.

Pilatus Bank was very accommodating to those who knew of its existence.

Maria Efimova could think of half-a-dozen laws and banking rules being broken every time an eminent PEP became a client of the bank. For the PEPs, it was as easy as buying a piggy bank from a toy shop.

She made her thoughts known, particularly to the bank's compliance manager Claude-Anne Sant Fournier with whom she had become friendly. In an office of 10 people, courtesy and familiarity would naturally bring the staff together. Sant Fournier trusted Efimova enough to ask her to babysit her child.

Efimova told Sant Fournier she was not comfortable with the bank accepting millions from clients no bank should accept.

Sant Fournier knew her stuff. Before working at Pilatus Bank, she was a specialist consultant on compliance and anti-money laundering at one of the big four consultancy firms: KPMG.

Her last client at KPMG was Ali Sadr Hashemi Nejad. She helped handle his application for a banking licence and, when he got it, she switched sides and became her former client's head of legal and compliance.

Three months into her job, Maria Efimova saw investigators for Malta's financial intelligence agency, the FIAU, barge into Pilatus bank for a 'routine inspection'. There was no way in hell that some of the files handled by the bank where she worked would pass even the most accommodating and cursory inspection. Files of politically exposed persons lacked the most basic checks and there were documented transactions that would have raised the suspicion of an infant. But they had been processed by the bank without the slightest question.

Claude-Anne Sant Fournier was not looking forward to answering uncomfortable questions from the FIAU. In her position, the law enforcers would expect her to bear the responsibility. She understood she needed to dodge the heat.

While the investigators waited in the lobby, Ali Sadr Hashemi Nejad and Claude-Anne Sant Fournier hid in his office and tried to send Maria Efimova to deal with the investigators.

Maria Efimova refused. She had warned them their processes were not compliant and she didn't think it was fair to be made to carry the can.

Ali Sadr told Maria Efimova to leave and never come back. She had been his assistant for three months and had not yet been paid.

Maria Efimova was an angry woman. She felt she had been used. The least the bank could do, if Ali Sadr wanted to fire her, was pay her for her work. Instead she found herself broke, unemployed, and without an explanation she could give any subsequent employer as to why her job at the bank had not ended well.

After making enquiries, she filed a complaint at the Department of Industrial and Employment Relations, the government office generally known as the 'labour office'. They heard her case and wrote to Pilatus Bank telling them that, unless they paid Maria Efimova for the time she worked there, they would proceed to take legal action.

The bank did not pay and the government office took the bank to court.

Ali Sadr retaliated by going to the police and accusing Maria Efimova of defrauding his bank. He claimed she had bought flights for her family on the company credit card without authorisation. The flights cost less than €2,000. Maria Efimova had no paperwork to show she had booked the tickets on the express instructions of her boss. Instead she looked like she had taken her kids on a joy ride at the company's expense.

The police arrested Maria Efimova, handcuffed her, and held her in a cell for 12 hours. The next day they charged her with fraud. In a later complaint, she said the police had treated her roughly. The police questioned her in front of Ghanbari and Sant Fournier, humiliating her and calling her a thief in front of her alleged victims. Maria Efimova says the police also ignored her pleas for water. She said in her complaint she was pregnant at the time but hadn't told the police. Soon after she miscarried.

Once she was charged, she was released on bail until her case could be heard. Her passport was retained by the authorities to stop her from absconding.

The officer charging her was Jonathan Ferris, a police inspector in the economic crimes unit. He would later have to answer questions in an internal inquiry looking into Maria Efimova's claim that she had been mistreated. He denied her accusations.

The evidence Pilatus Bank had given Ferris clearly showed that Maria Efimova purchased tickets in her name and the names of her children and charged them to the bank's account. The case against her seemed solid and it did not surprise him that she might try to get out of trouble by lashing out at the police.

Out on bail, charged with fraud, her passport withheld, Maria Efimova was unemployed, unemployable, and trapped in Malta. While she desperately tried to find a way out, her mother in Russia died. When she asked for permission to go to her mother's funeral, it was refused.

She had heard of Daphne Caruana Galizia and her blog *Running Commentary*. In October 2016, she wrote Daphne a letter telling her about Pilatus Bank, what the bank had been up to, and what had happened to her at the bank and at the hands of the Maltese police.

Daphne did not reply immediately.

Four months later she did. In February 2017, Daphne got in touch with Maria Efimova and told her she wanted to meet her. The journalist visited the whistleblower at her modest apartment. Speaking to co-author Manuel Delia after Daphne Caruana Galizia was killed, Maria Efimova said that it was clear to her that there was not much she had told Daphne about what was going on at Pilatus Bank that Daphne did not already know.

Daphne must have had another source either from within Pilatus Bank or someone who was aware of the findings of the preliminary investigations into the bank conducted by the FIAU, the same investigations that had led to Maria Efimova being fired.

In February 2017 Daphne published a series of articles about Pilatus Bank, how its Iranian owner had somehow obtained a licence to run a European bank without so much as a day's banking experience and how Keith Schembri and John Dalli both banked at Pilatus, although Dalli's assets at the bank appeared to be negligible.

Daphne reported how fabulously wealthy PEPs who could not deposit money at an ordinary high-street bank without having to answer questions funnelled their cash through Pilatus Bank. And she reported how documents held at the bank showed what was happening with that money, what it was being spent on, how it was being laundered.

Maria Efimova says Daphne then showed her copies of a set of documents and asked if she had ever seen them. Efimova said yes. The documents had been stored in a lockable filing cabinet or safe in the bank's office kitchenette. The location was significant because privacy laws do not allow office managers to set up CCTV cameras in staff recreational areas. Whatever was stored in the office kitchenette was meant to be kept away from the bank's CCTV cameras.

When Maria Efimova confirmed the authenticity of the documents, *Running Commentary* ran the most important and most read story in its nine-year history.

The owner of Egrant, the third Panama shell company everyone had been asking about, had been found, the story went. It was Michelle Muscat, wife of Malta's prime minister Joseph Muscat.

From Daphne's blog, published on 20 April 2017:

In the kitchen at the offices of Pilatus Bank in Ta' Xbiex, there is a safe in which certain files are kept, and also particular documents marked for extreme secrecy. The safe used to be in the bank CEO's office, but for some reason was moved to the kitchen.

In this safe, documents are held pertaining to Russian clients of the bank, and to Maltese PEPs, including John Dalli, consultant to Prime Minister Muscat, and Keith Schembri, the Prime Minister's chief of staff, both of whom have accounts with the bank in their own personal names.

Dalli's account is not used much, but the Prime Minister's chief of staff uses his regularly and his statements show highly suspicious transactions involving people in Azerbaijan. This bank account is separate to the one held in the name of his once-secret Panama company, Tillgate Inc.

The safe in the kitchen at Pilatus Bank also contains the documents that answer the question which the whole of Malta has been asking this past year: who owns Egrant Inc, the third company Brian Tonna set up in Panama, for somebody so important that the name had to be given over Skype, rather than in an email as it was for Konrad Mizzi and Keith Schembri.

Those documents in the Pilatus Bank kitchen-safe are declarations of trust which show that shares in Egrant Inc are held by Mossack Fonseca nominees for 'Mrs Michelle Muscat'.

The declarations of trust were provided to the bank by Brian Tonna, as a prerequisite for opening an account for Egrant Inc, for which the identity of the ultimate beneficial owner is required. Mrs Muscat's name is also given on another document held in the bank's safe: the account opening form for Egrant Inc.

These documents have been scanned and uploaded to the cloud, for security purposes, by third parties so that they cannot be destroyed by the bank.

The scanned and uploaded documents were never published.

Daphne did reveal transcripts of the documents but said that publishing scans of the documents themselves could reveal the identity of her sources which she was duty bound to protect.

When Daphne published this post, the country had already been waiting with bated breath. She had a knack for building up anticipation by putting up curtain raisers on the days leading up to her biggest revelations.

The day before, she had published the following:

A company owned by Leyla Aliyeva, one of the two daughters of Ilham Aliyev, ruler of Azerbaijan, transferred very large sums of money, described as 'loan payments', to Hearnville Inc, Tillgate Inc, and Egrant Inc last year.

The company, which is incorporated in Dubai's free zone, is called Al Sahra FZCO, and Ms Aliyeva is the ultimate beneficial owner.

The payments were made through Al Sahra FZCO's account at Pilatus Bank.

More about this tomorrow.

Eventually Daphne would report that Leyla Aliyeva's company paid over €1 million into the Panama company belonging to the prime minister's wife.

On Friday 21 April 2017, another bombshell:

Ali Sadr Hasheminejad has a sister, Negarin Sadr Hasheminejad – known by the shorter form of Negarin Sadr – who has a fashion business called Negarin London. Both siblings live between London and the US.

In March last year, Pilatus Bank received urgent instructions to open an account for Negarin Sadr, the chairman's sister. It was late in the evening, but bank officials were told that it couldn't wait until the next day.

The account had to be opened immediately and a loan of US$1 million granted there and then to Negarin Sadr for her fashion business.

Then another instruction came in: as soon as the loan was processed, a significant proportion of it – approximately US$400,000 – was to be paid out *from Negarin Sadr's loan account to a bank account held by 'a Maltese woman who lives in New York and has a jewellery business called Buttardi'.*

The Maltese woman was Michelle Buttigieg – no relation to Pete Buttigieg the US Democratic contender for the presidency who has Maltese ancestry. Buttigieg is a common name in Malta. Michelle Buttigieg was in New York because the government had appointed her as 'tourism representative' ostensibly to promote Malta as a holiday destination to American tourists. Buttigieg was also Michelle Muscat's business partner; they had started a jewellery business called Buttardi in 2002.

On 8 April 2015 Michelle Buttigieg and her husband William bought Unit 1E, a single residential unit in 402 East 74th Street, New York, for $790,000. The purchase was registered in September 2015 and was secured by a mortgage granted to Michelle Buttigieg and her husband by JP Morgan Chase Bank.

In April 2017 Daphne reported that Michelle Buttigieg had a year earlier, in March 2016, received a considerable sum of money from the sister of the owner of Pilatus Bank.

On 13 April 2016 JP Morgan Chase Bank informed the New York public registry it no longer held security on the property as it was no longer owed any money on the mortgage it had granted to Michelle Buttigieg just the previous March (2015).

The sudden settlement of such a large mortgage was never explained.

19 to 21 April 2017 were very dramatic days in Malta. As Daphne posted her series of exclusives about Egrant and Pilatus Bank, the entire political edifice of the country was under incredible strain.

The Panama Papers had already led to the removal of two prime ministers in Iceland and Pakistan. One of them was on trial and facing many years in prison. Joseph Muscat seemed immune to the revelations about his underlings but it was reasonable to expect that if a company owned by his wife had taken bribes from the

Azerbaijani regime and the family of an Iranian banker, he would not be able to get away with it.

But Joseph Muscat had other plans.

Speaking to the press, he said:

This is the biggest political lie ever told in this country, he told a press conference. *In front of the Maltese public, I swear, I categorically deny I had, or have, any type of undeclared account or company in Malta or overseas. We never signed any type of document which transfers shares of a company. I have never signed, never been offered to sign …*

That was around 7pm on Wednesday 19 April.

Malta's news reporters were in a frenzy. They ran around, microphones and cameras in hand, looking for quotes. A camera crew tracked down Michelle Muscat coming out of the official town residence of the prime minister in the central village of Ħal Lija with her children and a band of guards and hangers-on.

She gave a short comment to the press which, considering her record on previous occasions, was remarkably well put:

This is a vicious lie against my husband and me. We'll continue working serenely for the good of the country.

Another camera crew found the police chief Lawrence Cutajar on a boys' night out, eating the traditional meal of fried rabbit and chips. Was he going to do anything about Daphne's claims that the prime minister's wife took bribes and laundered them through an off-shore company, he was asked. He batted them away and said he saw no reason for any urgent action. The lot of a chief of police, not even allowed to eat his rabbit in peace.

But the evening was not over. Reporters at Net TV, the station owned by the PN, were tipped off that the lights were on at Pilatus Bank. It was after 9pm and a lot could be happening inside those offices bearing in mind the day's revelations.

At around 9.30pm, the lights inside the bank went out and a man and a woman came out of a rear exit carrying two suitcases. A Net TV reporter and camera operator chased the couple down the 300 metres from the bank to their car, asking them repeatedly in Maltese who they were and what they were taking out of Pilatus Bank so late at night.

All this was captured on camera. The man and the woman marched steadily, ignoring the reporter's questions. It was only when they got to the car that the man spoke, claiming he did not understand Maltese. The reporter, stunned, apologised and repeated the simple question in English. 'Who are you and what are you doing here?' But by then they had driven off.

Net TV aired the footage that evening without a clue who the two were. Daphne Caruana Galizia enlightened them. The woman was a manager at Pilatus Bank and the man was Ali Sadr Hashemi Nejad.

The night would have more surprises in store.

After footage aired of Ali Sadr taking two bags out of the bank, the government issued a statement through the official Department of Information in the middle of the night.

The significance of this was that the prime minister had already addressed the allegations in a hurriedly-called press conference at 7pm. He had denied the allegations and said there was no call for any investigation, let alone resignation. Minutes later, the police chief echoed his view.

But in the middle of the night, the prime minister changed tack. By 6am, online portals were reporting that the prime minister had instructed his personal lawyers to request a magisterial inquiry to determine whether he or his wife really did own Egrant and really did use it to launder proceeds from bribes.

Meanwhile, plane watchers reported seeing a private jet taking off from Malta on Thursday 20 April at 4am without any passengers on board. It landed in Baku in Azerbaijan, then flew on to Dubai.

The private jet was operated by the leasing company Vistajet, a plane-chartering business that operates a taxi service for the ultra-wealthy. The company is based in Malta but operates no scheduled flights and, given its stratospheric fees, does not carry holiday-makers. Nine days later, Vistajet would be paid €1 million, a sizeable chunk of Malta's entire tourism marketing budget, to carry adverts on its inflight magazine.

At about 8am, the police led by Inquiring Magistrate Aaron Bugeja fell upon the offices of Pilatus Bank in Ta' Xbiex, sealing it and collecting evidence. Justice would be served. Or would it? What if the evidence had somehow been spirited away in the 15 hours which had passed since Daphne's report had been published? What if it had been placed in suitcases and flown to Baku in a private jet?

Over the next 10 days, a political crisis ensued. 'Crisis' suggests that the government was unstable or the prime minister's fate uncertain. That would be misleading. Absolutely no one in Joseph Muscat's parliamentary party was of a mind to express even the slightest doubt about his side of the story.

But there clearly was a feeling in the country that this could prove complicated for a prime minister who had overcome many other obstacles previously. None had been quite like this.

Daphne's stories were invariably flatly denied by the government. But time and time again, her journalism stood up to scrutiny. No police action followed any of her reports before Egrant. More libel suits were fired at Daphne, giving PL supporters all the proof they needed to believe their political heroes had been wronged.

The demonisation of Daphne Caruana Galizia was in full swing. Regimented armies of trolls went online, harnessing the vocabulary used to describe her over decades: she was a witch, a traitor, a hater, a liar. And, of course, she was serving the interests of the PN.

No one was going to take into account Daphne's work on the case of John Dalli, a veteran PN politician, for example. In a dual system of politics, Daphne belonged to the 'enemy', the Nationalists, those who would invent any sort of lie to secure power.

In the frenzy, there were other twisters going about. One of them was the witch-hunt for Daphne's source at Pilatus Bank. Ironically, even as they sought to discredit Daphne's reporting, an online lynch-mob was looking for her source. Of course, if the source was somehow lying about Joseph Muscat, then Daphne might have been the innocent victim of a hoax. But logic is rarely the strong point of the online troll.

The term 'magisterial inquiry', as we have seen, can be a little misleading to anyone unfamiliar with criminal proceedings in Malta. It functions more like an inquest than any form of proper investigation. A magistrate's job is not to determine whether a crime has occurred, or to find the perpetrator. It is to collect the evidence and present it with a recommendation to the attorney general, who then takes a decision whether to instruct the police to prosecute.

Although the limitations of a magistrate's powers in this case are clearly known to people working in criminal law, an ongoing magisterial inquiry is often a useful political tool to enable the false claim that a proper investigation is underway. If an inquiry draws a blank, politicians are quick to use that fact alone as an acquittal, which it is not.

The prime minister's supporters may have hoped Magistrate Aaron Bugeja would wrap up his inquiry in a matter of days. He summoned Daphne Caruana Galizia to answer questions in his courtroom and – the assumption was – since there would be nothing to back up her claims, the matter would end fairly quickly.

Maria Efimova was reading the newspapers, perhaps not entirely comprehending the enormous political storm her conversations with Daphne had unleashed. She had grown to admire the journalist. She liked her determination to get to the bottom of things but also her indomitable courage in the face of a regime Maria knew could be corrupt and could turn rough. She had learnt that from her dealings at Pilatus Bank and her experience with the local police.

In an interview with co-author Carlo Bonini after Daphne's death, Maria Efimova says she brought up with Daphne the possibility of physical danger. She had been on a bus in Msida one sunny morning when she found herself stuck in a traffic jam, by no means a rare occurrence on the island, and later learnt it had been caused by a fatal car bomb up the road.

Maria Efimova asked Daphne if she should not be more careful, but Daphne dismissed her fears and replied: 'What are they going to do to me, blow me up in a bomb?'

It wasn't such an unrealistic prospect. Daphne had seen one of her dogs poisoned, another's throat slit. The door of her house had been set on fire, its glass panes shattering and the flames licking sleeping quarters, while she and her family slept, only waking up and escaping death in the nick of time.

As Maria read what was being said about Daphne, she felt responsible. Blowing the whistle on Pilatus Bank was grounded in how badly that bank had treated her, firing her without pay. But the reason the bank had fired her in the first place was that she had repeatedly spoken up against her employer's bad practices. That had been a principled stand. It felt far less principled for the whistleblower to hide behind the journalist.

On 28 April 2017 Maria Efimova showed up at the law courts and asked to speak to Magistrate Aaron Bugeja. She was unceremoniously turned away. As magistrates who conduct inquiries also act as judges in other cases, they do not hold office hours for the public. On the contrary, it is considered unacceptable for a magistrate or a judge to be seen speaking to interested parties outside the formal confines of the courtroom.

Moreover, magisterial inquiries are conducted behind closed doors. Witnesses are warned not to repeat what is said inside, and not even confirm they have testified.

Frustrated, Maria Efimova called Daphne and said she wanted to give evidence. Daphne called the court registry and, after hushed exchanges, Maria Efimova was brought in front of Magistrate Aaron Bugeja to speak of what she knew.

She outed herself to the magistrate of her own free will.

Consequently and unwittingly, she outed herself to the entire population of Malta and the world. Despite all the theoretical secrecy of inquiries, her identity was leaked to *Malta Today*, one of the local newspapers, who published the identity of the whistleblower everyone had wanted to know.

The lifetime experience of Daphne Caruana Galizia testifies to the pathological collective misogyny in Maltese culture. Although it can be argued that the mockery, the vicious attacks and the threats she suffered were in proportion to the seriousness of her revelations, incomparable with the work of any other journalist working in Malta, the fact that she was a woman amplified the attacks many times over.

Because she was a woman, it was easier for people who did not want to believe her to dismiss her work.

Maria Efimova's experience became another example of the pervasive misogyny present in Maltese society. Young, blonde Eastern European women are branded 'strippers' or 'prostitutes' in the Maltese context. And, for some, it was more convenient to view Maria Efimova as a honey-trapping troublemaker, than to accept that she was a public-spirited whistleblower keen to stand up to wrongdoing.

Joseph Muscat exploited that prejudice.

Days after the name Maria Efimova became publicly known, a report on specialist website *Intelligence Online* claimed 'the MI6 and the CIA are highly concerned by what the Russian couple has been up to in Malta. Some officials perceive it as a move to destabilise Malta's pro-western Prime Minister coming from the Kremlin, especially because it occurred at a time when Muscat was openly opposed to Moscow.' The article itself goes on to claim that MI6 and the CIA were concerned about possible Russian interference in the next Maltese election.

The term 'Russian couple' was an error as Maria Efimova's husband is Cypriot. The MI6 and the CIA, if this reporting was accurate, were being unusually sloppy on the details.

Asked to comment on the online report, the prime minister said he was informed by two allied security services that the Egrant story was invented to pay him back for not allowing a Russian ship to enter Malta for refuelling on its way to the Syria conflict. However, he did not have evidence that the people inventing the Egrant story were connected to the Russian secret services.

The prime minister made another claim. At the time Malta held the EU Presidency. One policy pushed by Malta was to speed up the waiving of EU visas for Ukrainians after the 2014 Russian invasion of eastern Ukraine. That policy had, the prime minister claimed, irritated 'certain people' and there was going to be 'some form of retaliation'.

Maria Efimova was, of course, Russian. So Muscat's supporters could have been tempted to think that if the government was being got at by the Russian state, then Efimova could well be a Russian intelligence agent.

The Russian authorities denied any intelligence connection with Maria Efimova. In subsequent interviews, Maria said the Russian embassy had asked her to keep a low profile and avoid public appearances or engagements with the press. She had given one interview to *The Malta Independent*, for whom Daphne wrote a regular column, basically restating what Daphne had already reported, and confirming herself as the source.

After the warning from the government of her native country, Maria Efimova clammed up.

By then, however, Joseph Muscat had created the impression that he was the innocent victim of an international conspiracy in which Daphne was a central player, though not necessarily the mastermind.

On 1 May 2017, at a massive PL gathering right outside his office, Joseph Muscat said Daphne, her allies in the PN, and anyone else whose nefarious interests were served by the instability of his government, had brought the country to a crisis it did not need.

He would therefore be calling a general election a year ahead of schedule, and it would be held on 3 June 2017.

The general assumption was that Muscat had called an election in reaction to Daphne's stories. This is contradicted by evidence Daphne Caruana Galizia would later publish showing that the campaign slogans and website URLs for the 2017 campaign (in theory, the next general election was due in 2018) had been decided and registered weeks before she was in possession of the information she used to publish the Egrant scandal.

Joseph Muscat went to the polls in effect a suspect in a criminal inquiry for bribery and money laundering. His chief of staff Keith Schembri was the subject of a separate inquiry on the back of a leaked FIAU report that concluded there was a reasonable suspicion he had taken kick-backs from the sales of passports. Muscat, Schembri, and the former Energy Minister Konrad Mizzi, were appealing another court order calling for an inquiry into the findings of the Panama Papers.

Under normal circumstances, this would not have been the best setting for an electoral campaign.

High-profile people who had endorsed the Labour Party in 2013 were openly saying they were switching sides in disgust at the corruption of the 'Panama Gang'.

At the climax of that electoral campaign, Joseph Muscat wheeled out some very famous friends who stepped up to endorse him. Italian centre-left PD leader Matteo Renzi spoke about his 'friend' Joseph Muscat and said 'beyond politics there is loyalty and friendship. Joseph Muscat is a friend and I believe he will be the one to lead Malta into the future' and former British prime minister Tony Blair recorded a video describing Muscat as 'a great example of what a progressive politician could do in power'.

I know elections are always tough and sometimes they don't always focus on the issues that matter, Tony Blair's video informed the cheering crowd, *but they're a moment of great decision. And so, as Malta approaches election day, I congratulate him and wish him every luck.*

What was Tony Blair doing, ten years out of power, toasting a political leader of a very small country in the middle of an election called ostensibly because of corruption allegations? To try and answer that question, we have to look at Blair's cosy relationship with the fabulously corrupt regime of Azerbaijan's President Ilham Aliyev.

Since stepping down from office, the former UK prime minister has set up what cruel wags call the BlairRich project. He works as a consultant for a number of big money contractors, one of the richest being a pipe-dream, literally, of President Aliyev. The president of Azerbaijan is planning the Trans Adriatic Pipeline (TAP) running gas from oil-rich Azerbaijan through Turkey, Greece, Albania, then along the seabed of the Adriatic to Italy. The pipeline is a competitor to Nord Stream 2, running from Russia to Germany. The logic behind the pipeline is simple, that it diversifies Europe's energy sources, lessens its dependence on Russia, and helps energy poor southern Europe. Along the way, a lot of people could make a ton of money. They might include President Aliyev and Tony Blair.

The fly in the ointment is that Aliyev is a brutal dictator who fakes elections and locks up satirists. In Azerbaijan, an ex-Soviet Muslim country on the Caspian Sea, north of Iran and east of Georgia, President Aliyev's nickname is 'The Donkey'. When two satirists released a video with donkeys in suits, they were beaten up by thugs, then arrested and jailed for 'hooliganism'. While they were still rotting inside, Blair rocked up in Baku in 2009 and gave a speech for a reported minimum of £90,000.

Peter Kilfoyle, then a Labour MP, said:

The very least he can do is donate his fee to a charity that works in the area of human rights. He should not be profiting from a country that flagrantly ignores human rights. There have long been questions about the Azeris and their approach to human rights.

Norman Baker, a then Liberal Democrat MP, said:

This is dirty money. It is demeaning for the former British prime minister to hawk himself around the world getting what cash he can. If he had an ounce of decency and self-respect he should now give this to an appropriate outside charity.

The father of Eynulla Fatullayev, a prominent journalist who was being held in solitary confinement at the time, said:

Why did Tony Blair come here? It was another blow to us – pure propaganda by the regime. The government was showing him off and saying: 'Look who is with us.' He was not here to support the Azeri people, or our democracy movement. He was here to support an authoritarian government, a dictatorship.

Blair's spokesman said at the time:

This was a one-off speaking engagement, organised by the Washington Speakers Bureau in the usual way. It was not organised by the Government. Neither Tony Blair or Tony Blair Associates has any commercial or pro bono relationship with the president or the government of Azerbaijan.

But the bigger mystery is why did Blair bother to boost Muscat in the 2017 election? If Daphne's journalism was right, the Aliyev 'royal family' were using Malta's Pilatus Bank as a laundromat to clean up millions, maybe even billions, of dollars. For that to work, the Aliyevs needed the Muscat government to turn a blind eye.

The 2017 election posed a (slight) risk to that strategy, so, one possibility is, that to keep in with his fabulously rich friend, President Aliyev, Blair spent a little of his political capital on Joseph Muscat when most democratic leaders were supping with him using a long spoon.

A second possibility is that Blair liked Muscat because he grinned a lot.

Come 3 June 2017, Joseph Muscat would be re-elected prime minister with a consolidated majority.

Along the bumpy road of Panama scandals and Egrant troubles, Joseph Muscat lost the support of some high-profile switchers who had voted PL for the first time in 2013 because they had seen in him a great white hope. Corruption lost the PL some votes. But it also won the PL some others. The willingness to bend the rules is an attractive proposition for voters who want the rules bent for them. Corruption is, theoretically, a vote loser. But June 2017 proved it can be a vote winner as well.

Joseph Muscat's charisma had not yet worn off. The PL core vote was still infatuated with its leader. A wider circle, a majority, thought it should give the prime minister the benefit of the doubt. In any case, the political cycle still favoured him.

On top of that, the economy was pumping. The low points of the international crisis of 2008 and the oil crisis that followed were in the past. Fair winds favoured Joseph Muscat. Add to that a construction boom caused by the relaxation of planning rules and a bullish demand for properties by a growing foreign population and you have 'an economic miracle'. Hardly the atmosphere for the electorate to try something new.

After the election, the criminal case against Maria Efimova for allegedly defrauding Pilatus Bank was due for a fresh hearing. She did not show up in court. The court ordered her arrest for the next hearing.

At that hearing, the police informed the court they were unable to find Maria Efimova. Three months previously, before the Egrant scandal had erupted, the court had returned Maria Efimova's passport on condition that she only travelled to Spain, Germany, or the Czech Republic, the three countries where her new employer had offices.

In the EU's Schengen area, where people travel freely across borders without any passport checks, such a 'condition' is practically unenforceable.

After Joseph Muscat's election victory, Maria Efimova used her passport to leave Malta. She was not planning on coming back.

The police said they would not allow her to escape justice and had issued an international arrest warrant against Maria Efimova to be dragged back to Malta to face fraud charges and fresh charges of lying about being mistreated by the police.

An international arrest warrant over a complaint of less than €2,000 is extraordinary. The costs of such a process far exceed any possible recovery from the crime, assuming it is proven, and is very seldom used for such relatively minor crimes.

The harder the Maltese authorities looked for her, the more scared Maria Efimova became. When she learnt of Daphne's assassination in October, she knew she had made the right choice to leave the country. There was no reason for her not to assume Daphne's killing was not connected to 'the biggest lie in Maltese political history' as prime minister Muscat described Daphne's Egrant story. She believed she, too, was in danger.

Needless to say, her former boss Ali Sadr Hashemi Nejad, owner of Pilatus Bank, had been vehement in his denial that any wrongdoing had ever occurred at his bank. His denials were categorical. He denied banking for the Aliyevs and just about everything else Daphne Caruana Galizia had written.

The week Daphne Caruana Galizia was killed, Ali Sadr took his efforts to clear his name a notch further.

Through his attorneys he wrote to every English language news organisation in Malta with a '.com' website, demanding that any story ever published about Pilatus Bank in the aftermath of Daphne's revelations be deleted and expunged from the online record.

The legal letters from Lawrence Law Group of Wisconsin Avenue, Washington DC, were accompanied by the threat, unusual for Maltese news organisations, that if they failed to comply, the bank would open multi-million dollar lawsuits against them in the US where their .com websites were registered. Attempting to respond to such lawsuits in an US court would financially cripple the cash-strapped Maltese organisations, let alone contesting them.

Ali Sadr liked firing off letters from fancy law firms to pesky journalists. In January 2018, co-author John Sweeney, then working for BBC Newsnight, got a letter from Schillings, a very expensive London law firm specialising in libel. Its client was Pilatus Bank and the letter complained that points 'Mr Sweeney now raises are demonstrably false, which the most cursory of online searches would have revealed …' It goes on to refer to a previous letter which gave notice of the 'true position' and repeated 'the obvious and demonstrable falsity of Mr Sweeney's new points'.

Oh dear.

The Maltese press community had also just been introduced to SLAPP lawsuits. SLAPP is an Americanism and stands for Strategic Lawsuits Against Public Participation, in other words libel tourism where wealthy corporations look for aggressive jurisdictions where they can file ruinous defamation suits. The threat of such a lawsuit is often a sufficient deterrent to prevent a story from being published, or have it retracted.

Although several jurisdictions have legislation to protect their journalists from this corporate vindictiveness, the Maltese government refused to back a private members' bill filed in Malta's parliament by Nationalist MP Jason Azzopardi. The government argued that the bill would be contrary to Malta's international obligations.

When that failed, Nationalist MEP David Casa lobbied the European Parliament to introduce legislation against SLAPP. That process continues.

But, in October 2017, Maltese newspapers faced the choice between certain bankruptcy or doing Ali Sadr's bidding. Reluctantly, reports about Pilatus Bank were pulled, including the detailed interview Maria Efimova had placed on record, testifying to what she had witnessed at Pilatus Bank.

The sense of danger for a whistleblower increases when, after having spoken out, her message is silenced.

As it happened, Ali Sadr never threatened Daphne with legal action in the US if she did not remove her stories. Instead, without warning, he started proceedings in Arizona where the URL of her website daphnecaruanagalizia.com was registered. He demanded $40 million in damages from Daphne and the removal of her stories about him from the record.

Weirdly, Ali Sadr and Pilatus Bank did not alert Daphne to their Arizona case. She was unaware of it at the time she was murdered.

But Daphne's execution did not stop the effort to smoke Maria Efimova out of hiding.

In a January 2018 interview with co-author Manuel Delia, Maria Efimova said her father in Russia had received visits from people enquiring whether it was true his wife had died, a claim Maria Efimova had made in her request to have her passport returned. Maria suspected that the visits were from private detectives but she did not know who they were working for. The pressure on her and on her father in Russia was all too real.

Maria Efimova's father received a second visit, this time from Russian police claiming they were looking for his daughter at the request of the authorities in Cyprus, where Maria Efimova had been living four years earlier, before she moved to Ireland and then to Malta. She had worked for a Russian jewellery company in Cyprus and this company was now making allegations that she had defrauded the business.

On 18 January 2018 the *Cyprus Business Mail* reported that Cyprus had issued an international arrest warrant for Maria Efimova on a complaint that was unrelated to Malta's original warrant.

The next day, Cyprus news websites *SigmaLive.com, Offsite. com.cy, Kathimerini.com.cy,* and *24sports.com.cy* reported that Maria Efimova was wanted as a suspect in the killing of Daphne Caruana Galizia. That may have been the result of a chain of ghastly misunderstandings but Cypriot journalist Stelios Orphanides, then working for the *Cyprus Business Mail* told co-author Manuel Delia 'some Cypriot media are owned by people with agendas, some of whom are corrupt, who are not interested in necessarily employing adequately qualified journalists'.

Stelios Orphanides filed a complaint before the media complaints commission in Cyprus. It found that claiming Maria Efimova was wanted for murder was not just a horrible mistake. The story was false and intended to discredit her as a whistleblower and reduce the significance of the evidence she had given against Malta's prime minister.

Someone had provided fake news to the Cyprus media. And some of them had gobbled it up.

Cyprus's arrest warrant issued in January 2018 was on the back of a complaint filed by her former Russian employer who found out, some four years after the fact, that Maria Efimova had cheated him of about €40,000. She denies this, and questions why the complaint took four years to surface. At the time of writing, the issue is still unresolved.

The fake news stories alleging that Maria was in some way responsible for Daphne's murder suggests there was an effort to bring her out of hiding. People who had checked she was not with her father in Russia may have assumed she had returned to Cyprus, her husband's native country.

In March 2018, it became known that Maria Efimova was in Crete.

On 21 March 2018, Maria Efimova travelled from Crete to Athens and handed herself in to the police. She was booked and eventually transferred to an Athens prison where she spent 15 days behind bars, waiting for an extradition hearing.

But, on that same day, half way around the world in Washington DC, the sound of rolling metal bars shutting rudely would ring in someone else's ears.

Ali Sadr Hashemi Nejad was arrested at Dulles airport in DC, on his way out of the US. The attorney for the Southern District of New York charged Ali Sadr with six counts of bank fraud and busting sanctions against Iran. If convicted, Ali Sadr faces 125 years in prison.

Ali Sadr Hashemi Nejad denies any wrongdoing.

The charges themselves do not relate to Pilatus Bank but to alleged actions before he opened his Maltese-European bank.

The US public prosecutor has remarked in pre-trial proceedings that Pilatus Bank is effectively a money-laundering exercise, as it has been funded from the proceeds of other crimes.

The European Central Bank eventually shut down Pilatus Bank and withdrew its licence to operate.

But before that happened, while under administration, Pilatus Bank was found guilty by a Maltese court of employing Maria Efimova without paying her. The government-appointed administrator issued a cheque in her name to compensate her for the complaint that had started all the trouble.

Even though Pilatus Bank no longer exists, the Maltese police have kept open their request for the arrest of Maria Efimova so she can face charges that she cheated the bank of less than €2,000.

After 15 days in an Athens prison, a Greek court heard arguments for Malta's request for Maria Efimova's extradition. European Union countries are treaty-bound to facilitate mutual extradition requests. It is a rare event indeed for an EU court to refuse the request for extradition from another EU country's police force.

This would be one such rare event. The Greek court denied Malta's request, fearing for the safety of Maria Efimova's life should she be forced to return to Malta. The Maltese authorities insisted on an appeal, which was also turned down.

Maria Efimova, the whistleblower, and Daphne Caruana Galizia, the journalist, had brought down Pilatus Bank, the bank that cashed the dirty cheques of the Azerbaijani regime.

Joseph Muscat survived the Egrant scandal. But journalism alone had achieved what no Maltese enforcement agency would even attempt to do: challenge the viscous flow of dirty money from Baku to Malta and onwards to the rest of the world.

GAMBLING ON PANAMA

Down these mean streets a man must go who is a member of the Institute of Chartered Accountants. Our apologies to Raymond Chandler, but the image is irresistible.

Brian Tonna was the accountant who sat one office down from the prime minister in Malta. His Nexia BT firm was a minor operation before the March 2013 election. This was all set to change. His junior partner, Karl Cini, flew to Panama City in February 2013 in the thick of the electoral campaign as a guest of Mossack Fonseca. He struck up a relationship with the law firm that would help his clients organise themselves financially once they attained power.

A key issue in the electoral campaign was the cost of energy for domestic consumers. The PL sent out two messages before the election. The first and more important message was that the government-in-waiting knew just what it had to do to rejig Malta's energy supply and therefore cut the cost of energy for consumers. The second message was that the PL was clean. It certainly did not sign back-room deals.

Malta is a small country and, although under EU rules there can be no monopoly in the generation of electricity, the inescapable reality is that in Malta there's only space for one supplier.

In 2013, the government owned the energy provider Enemalta, a behemoth in a perpetual state of quasi-bankruptcy because its owner was keen to keep consumer rates as low as possible. Obviously, a state-owned company never quite goes under because its owner has access to taxpayers' pockets and would always see to it that it did not.

The new PL government wanted to 'restructure' Enemalta's finances. It renamed the corporation 'Enemed' and sold a third of its stock to the Chinese state-owned Shanghai Electric Power.

Brian Tonna was at the heart of the deal. He sat right in between the negotiator for the Maltese side, Energy Minister Konrad Mizzi, for whom he had secretly set up a New Zealand trust and a Panama shell company, and the negotiator for the Chinese side, an Accenture Strategy employee called Cheng Chen.

Scouring through the Mossack Fonseca leaks, Daphne Caruana Galizia learnt that Brian Tonna had helped with the setting up of a British Virgin Islands (BVI) company for Cheng Chen through Mossack Fonseca. She also found emails from Brian Tonna's office to Mossack Fonseca showing that they were setting up a bank account for Cheng Chen as well.

Cheng Chen's hidden nest in the BVI was set up at the same time that Brian Tonna was setting up a spare one for himself. Tonna set up 'Willerby', a company that an FIAU investigation would later find was used to pay thousands of euro into a Pilatus Bank account held by Keith Schembri, the prime minister's chief of staff.

Predictably, Cheng Chen and Brian Tonna's companies also held accounts at Pilatus Bank, the clearing house for the corrupt.

All concerned deny any wrongdoing.

Brian Tonna went deeper into the energy restructuring programme.

Upon his election in March 2013, Joseph Muscat made Brian Tonna and Nexia BT his advisers in the prime minister's office. One of their first overt operations, in parallel with the covert operation of setting up three Panama companies, was to draw up a feasibility report for a new power station.

The issue was simple. How to fix Malta's steep energy bills? The answers could be, first, to use the undersea electricity cable from Sicily to import more electricity. Second, to build an undersea pipeline to bring oil or gas to Malta. Third, to build a brand new Liquid Natural Gas plant fed by ships.

In a matter of a few weeks, Nexia BT published a report that confirmed the assumptions the PL had made before the March elections. It concluded that the third option was the way to go: a new LNG power station was indeed desirable.

Nexia BT and Brian Tonna personally were the lead evaluators of the contractors commissioned to sell energy to the government. Having blessed the decision to go with LNG, they would also get to choose the company which would get the fattest contract in Maltese public procurement history.

The choice would fall on a group called the Electrogas Consortium. The ownership of the consortium is fiendishly complicated but the single biggest Maltese player is a man called Yorgen Fenech, one of the island's richest men, an entrepreneur, casino owner, and man about town.

The consortium included some highly reputable names and some less so. It was led by London Stock Exchange listed Gasol PLC, an international group focused on the supply of natural gas in contracts mostly in Africa and central Asia. Gasol was the lead partner in the bid holding 30% of the consortium. Another 30% was held by a grouping of Maltese businesses called GEM Holdings. 20% each were held by the 'technical' components of the consortium, Siemens, the German manufacturer, and Socar, Azerbaijan's state-owned energy company.

GEM Holdings Limited in turn is owned by four entities: three companies and an individual. The three companies represent three of the largest family conglomerates in Malta. Tumas Energy Limited and Gasan Enterprises Limited hold a third each of GEM Holdings Limited. The other third is split again into thirds. Two-thirds — that's 23.9% of GEM Holdings – is held by CP Holdings Limited for Malta's Apap Bologna family.

Then there's a 9.1% share in GEM Holdings Limited held by a company owned solely by Yorgen Fenech. Yorgen Fenech is CEO of the Tumas Group that owns Tumas Energy Limited. He is the scion of the Fenech family that owns the Group and he is also CEO of GEM Holdings Limited. So Fenech's company owns a bite of of a bite of the Electrogas Consortium and by virtue of this 9.1% share he is also personally an indirect owner of the consortium.

Yorgen Fenech is also close to Brian Tonna, the man responsible for evaluating the consortium's bid for the energy contract.

It would later emerge that Brian Tonna's Nexia BT did not just evaluate Electrogas's bid on behalf of government. Nexia BT was also the auditor of GEM Holdings Limited, part-owned by Yorgen Fenech.

A national audit office investigation found this potential conflict of interest disturbing. When asked to explain, Nexia BT produced a copy of an engagement letter dated April 2014. This meant that Nexia BT was appointed auditor of GEM Holdings after – not during – its evaluation of the Electrogas Consortium. The law requires companies to record the appointment of auditors in the public registry. GEM Holdings had not done so, so the national auditor remarked that the proof that Nexia BT had produced in its defence was not conclusive.

The National Auditor reported:

An engagement letter to this effect was provided by GEM Holdings Ltd to this Office; however, verification with the Malta Financial Services Authority was not possible.

This potential conflict is especially significant when one considers that the evaluation of this bid proved to be more of a negotiation of the terms of the contract to accommodate the shifting needs of Electrogas than a thorough examination of what was best for the Maltese consumer.

The consortium outlived many setbacks that might well have finished off other contenders.

The first setback was the collapse of its lead partner. Gasol PLC, the owner of the company that held 30% of Electrogas ran up debts approaching €100 million and at one point had to borrow €1 million from one of its subsidiaries merely to pay urgent bills. Eventually, in 2018, the company went into administration.

Gasol's shares in Electrogas were sold to the other three partners who upscaled their holdings so that Electrogas was now divided equally three ways. The sum paid for those shares was never disclosed. Gasol's own financial statements left a blank space where their accounts were supposed to report the value of the sale.

The transfer of shares from Gasol to its partners was concluded on 22 July 2015.

The Panama Papers would reveal that on that very same day Konrad Mizzi's Panama company Hearnville was transferred from its administrators – the front working for Mossack Fonseca in Panama – to the New Zealand trust set up for him by Nexia BT.

Konrad Mizzi dismissed this as an irrelevant coincidence. Which it very well could have been. Except that a detail places it in context. Mossack Fonseca did not only secretly handle the financial affairs of Konrad Mizzi. Its customer profile also included Gasol's parent company African Gas Development Corporation Ltd. The shared connection with Mossack Fonseca may also be another coincidence.

All concerned deny any wrongdoing.

With the exit of Gasol, the rest of the consortium lost the promised source of the capital funds needed to build a new LNG power station. They would have to come up with the money themselves but at €450 million any bank would have needed considerable collateral to take such an enormous risk.

If only the government would remove that risk.

It did.

Firstly, the government leaned on a bank that would advance a cool €450 million.

Although Malta's government is the biggest shareholder of Bank of Valletta it only owns a fifth of its shares. But the bank used to be state-owned and the government still has legacy controls. It chooses the bank's chairman who holds a lot of influence on the big banking decisions of the group. The bank was asked to lend €450 million with a government guarantee of €360 million. To give an idea of just how considerable this loan was, Bank of Valletta's total revenue in 2018 was just over €230 million. The loan Electrogas needed was almost double the Bank's net annual revenue.

Such exposure could have broken the Bank of Valletta. So the government provided Electrogas with its guarantee for €360 million of the €450 million it needed to borrow. If Electrogas went bust the government would step in, which meant the consortium's (and the bank's) risk was now to be carried by taxpayers.

The guarantee was supposed to be temporary and capped for 22 months, but on the eve of the June 2017 elections the guarantee was extended again. The press would only find out about this in November 2017.

But that was not all. While the government was facilitating a private consortium to build a new power station, the framework of the deal was such that the power station itself would remain the property of its builders. They would then sell the energy they generated to the grid owned by the state-owned energy distribution company Enemed.

After the sale to Shanghai Electric of 30% of Enemed, the term 'state-owned' became a slight misnomer. 'States-owned' became closer to the mark as the governments of Malta and China now owned the corporation. Enemed had its own relatively new fuel-oil power station already. It had come on line in 2012. And in 2015 a new undersea interconnector between Malta and Sicily was commissioned.

Enemed had plenty of sources from where to buy electricity. Electrogas's risk was that it could end up generating excess capacity. Their financial model could go south.

The government again shifted the goal-posts to accommodate Electrogas and undertook to purchase enough energy from Electrogas to help the business stay in the black no matter the demand and no matter if other sources of energy could provide Maltese consumers with lower-cost electricity.

In April 2018, Juliette Garside of *The Guardian* reported on an analysis by experts in fuel markets about how the Electrogas deal was impacting Maltese consumers' expenditure.

Benchmarking indicated Malta was paying a significantly higher rate than similar purchases from the wider market negotiated at that time by Greece, Italy, and Turkey. Estimates by The Guardian *suggest Socar paid $40m less for the gas than the sum it charged Malta.*

That's because Socar, the Azerbaijani state-owned company, which owned a third of the Electrogas consortium did not actually sell its own gas to the Maltese company.

Instead it purchased gas from the market (from Shell, as it happens), set its own hefty mark-up cushioned by the government's purchasing guarantee, and then proceeded to make extra bucks from its share of Electrogas's own profits. Those profits were generated without much start-up risk as the financing of the operation was guaranteed by the government.

From Socar's point of view this was as win-win-win as they come. But, as *The Guardian*'s analysts put it, Malta was 'losing hand over fist'. And the government had locked itself into the deal for 18 years.

The Guardian's April 2018 analysis was subsequently confirmed by Malta's national auditor who reported in November 2018 that, if the government simply switched off Electrogas's power-station and replaced its electricity by buying it through the under-sea connector from Sicily, it would have saved millions in the period under review. The generous contracting arrangements with Electrogas – and particularly with the Azerbaijan oil company Socar, which is the fuel supply component of the outfit – prevents it from looking for the best deal.

Local consumers pay the difference.

This was not the first time Socar walked away with a handsome deal courtesy of Konrad Mizzi. In 2015, the national auditor reported the energy minister likely overstepped his authority and interfered to ensure Enemed entered into a fuel price hedging agreement with Socar. Konrad Mizzi denies this.

The auditor found considerable chunks of the paperwork it expected on the fuel price hedging deal missing. This was probably why it could not absolutely confirm its suspicion that Mizzi had interfered in a purely commercial matter that gave Socar an advantage.

After the 2017 election, Mizzi was transferred to the tourism ministry, at face value a demotion. It subsequently turned out that Mizzi was still leading the negotiations with Electrogas (despite the appointment of another energy minister) and his signature is on the final contracts.

On 22 February 2017 Daphne Caruana Galizia posted one of her cryptic curtain raisers. The headline for that post was '17 Black – the name of a company incorporated in Dubai'.

There was no text. Only a collage of unflattering pictures of Keith Schembri, Konrad Mizzi, John Dalli, and Joseph Muscat.

If you play blackjack or take a roll at a casino roulette table, 17 Black would mean something to you.

Daphne was two months away from publishing her story on the Egrant scandal when she played the card of telling the 'Panama Gang' that she knew about the Dubai company. She was still working on what 17 Black meant, when she was killed eight months later.

At some point before she was killed, a source within Electrogas leaked to her a dump of emails and internal communications from the consortium's servers. The information, combined with the Panama Papers, contained the elements of an entirely new and massive corruption scandal. Daphne understood the scandal was there waiting to be unearthed. The general election in June, the bullying and the isolation, the apparent futility of it all, were not going to stop her. But a car bomb did.

After her death, a group of journalists from around the world coordinated by the French-based Forbidden Stories group kept her work going. That is how the Daphne Project came about. *La Repubblica*, the Italian newspaper where co-author Carlo Bonini works, is a member. Journalists from *The New York Times*, *The Guardian*, and *Süddeutsche Zeitung* that had led the Panama Papers story in the first place, *France 2*, *The Times of Malta*, Reuters, and several others shared the effort of looking through the notes, the files and the leaks that Daphne was working on when she died to see if they could complete her work.

The Daphne Project published findings on fuel smuggling in Maltese waters, on Mafia infiltration of Malta's gaming sector, the sale of Maltese passports to crooks, off-shore nests hidden by Maltese ministers, the Malta branch of the Azerbaijani laundromat, even stories about the alleged assassins who killed Daphne and their connections with powerful people in Malta.

There's no doubt, however, that the biggest finding of the Daphne Project was the link that finally connected the Panama scandal that exposed Keith Schembri and Konrad Mizzi with the Electrogas scandal.

In February 2016 Daphne had reported that Brian Tonna's Nexia BT set up Panama companies Tillgate for Keith Schembri and Hearnville for Konrad Mizzi.

In March 2016 the Panama Papers were published by the ICIJ, confirming this information.

The Panama leaks would also include emails between Nexia BT and Mossack Fonseca discussing the worldwide hunt for bank accounts for Tillgate and Hearnville. The leaked communication stops at December 2015, the date of the last data dump from John Doe, the ICIJ's source in Panama.

Up to December 2015, Mossack Fonseca had not succeeded in securing bank accounts for its two Maltese clients. Banks repeatedly turned them down because of their political exposure.

The email exchanges leaked with the Panama Papers show that Keith Schembri and Konrad Mizzi claimed their Panama shell companies would be conducting international business in recycling, remote gaming, infrastructure projects, maritime projects, fisheries, and tourism. They were going to conduct this business while serving as full-time government minister and senior official.

While briefing Mossack Fonseca, Brian Tonna's Nexia BT said its clients Konrad Mizzi and Keith Schembri were expecting their companies to earn $2 million in their first year of existence alone.

In the same correspondence, Nexia BT identified two Dubai companies as 'target clients' for Tillgate and Hearnville. The two Dubai companies were named 17 Black and Macbridge. That email is, serendipitously, from December 2015. If it had been sent any later, we might never have known.

It is unclear whether Daphne had become aware of the correspondence that had identified 17 Black and Macbridge as 'target clients'. The matter became public knowledge in April 2018, published by the Daphne Project six months after her murder.

But Daphne did know this: that 17 Black was at the centre of the Electrogas scandal.

FIAU investigators working before its diligent former director Manfred Galdes resigned had looked into 17 Black and found that the Dubai shell company had received money from the Maltese agent that handled the purchase of an off-shore gas tanker, *Armada LNG Mediterrana*, that would be berthed alongside the new Electrogas LNG power station to supply it with fuel.

The investigation was suppressed but the information was eventually leaked to *The Malta Independent* in May 2017.

The FIAU investigation found that 17 Black received a deposit of $200,000 in July 2015 from Orion Engineering Group, a company owned by Maltese businessman Mario Pullicino, agent for the company that supplied the *Armada*. Mario Pullicino denied the payment was intended as a bribe.

There was a second payment into 17 Black the FIAU had found, and that was considerably larger. $1.5 million was deposited into 17 Black's account in November 2015 by a Seychelles company called Mayor Trans Limited. Mayor Trans Limited is owned by Rufat Baratzada, an Azerbaijani businessman.

Rufat Baratzada holds several business interests, some of which are in the United States. To make this fat payment to 17 Black he passed his funds through Latvia's third largest bank at the time, ABLV. When the money went through, the Latvian bank flagged the payment as 'suspicious'.

ABLV's standards of suspicion were notoriously low. In February 2018 the European Central Bank shut it down after a run on the bank caused by a US financial intelligence unit (FinCEN) notice that blacklisted the bank as a money-laundering engine.

Within three months a Latvian bankruptcy lawyer, Mārtiņš Bunkus, 38, was shot point blank in the streets of Latvia's capital Riga. Many in Latvia suspected that the murder was connected to the bank going bust.

Latvia's financial intelligence unit looked at the transactions in and out of ABLV. Documents published by MEP Ana Gomes showed Malta's FIAU asked for information from their Latvian counterparts about this transaction between ABLV and 17 Black. The Latvians provided the Malta police with information in response. The content of that information remains unknown.

The sequel to the question 'Who owns Egrant?' was 'Who owns 17 Black?'

The answer to the question would explain why an Azerbaijani national was using a money-laundering engine in Latvia to deposit so much money in a Dubai shell company that, as far as could be determined, did nothing at all, although it also accepted fat payments from a company acting as an intermediary for the purchase of a gas tanker.

In November 2018, the question would be answered. Stephen Grey and Tom Arnold for Reuters and the Daphne Project published a story that named the owner of 17 Black as Yorgen Fenech.

To recap, Yorgen Fenech is one of Malta's richest men. He is one of the owners of the Electrogas Consortium. He is CEO of GEM Holdings that owns a third of the Electrogas Consortium. He also owns 9.1% of GEM Holdings. He is CEO of the Tumas Group that owns a third of GEM Holdings that owns a third of Electrogas.

Yorgen Fenech is the third boss of the Tumas Fenech family business founded by his grandfather. The business has investments in casinos, property, hotels, entertainment. In Malta, they have fingers in lots of pies. Yorgen Fenech's rise to power was, people say, at the expense of his cousins who felt they could no longer work with him. The word on the island is that he had something of a Napoleon complex about him. No one is quite sure how much Yorgen Fenech is worth. He's certainly a multi-millionaire and may indeed be a billionaire. After the cousins left the business, they carved out their share of their grandfather's legacy and are now competing with Yorgen Fenech and the Fenech brand.

The Electrogas deal was sealed by Konrad Mizzi and Keith Schembri. Secret paperwork for Mizzi's Panama shell company, Hearnville, and Schembri's Tillgate, identified 17 Black as the 'target client' that would pay millions into their accounts.

The estimated figure that 17 Black and Macbridge – whose true owner is still unknown – would pay Keith Schembri and Konrad Mizzi's companies was $2 million.

The circle was complete.

Yorgen Fenech personally retained approximately a tenth of the local holding in Electrogas. Why so? Could this tenth actually be destined for someone else, person or persons unknown, outside the consortium? Could it possibly be a continuing bribe? No one knows for sure, but the circumstances are such that the questions hang in the air.

Yorgen Fenech has not denied owning 17 Black. He has not explained why he owns it or what the company does.

The rest of the Tumas Fenech directors and all the other Maltese families holding shares in Electrogas distanced themselves from 17 Black. All shareholders of Electrogas insist they have been contracted to provide energy to Malta on the merits of their bid and not because of corruption. They deny any wrongdoing.

Electrogas denies any wrongdoing.

Yorgen Fenech denies any wrongdoing.

Keith Schembri and Konrad Mizzi deny any wrongdoing.

A magisterial inquiry continues.

THE MYSTERY PROFESSOR

There is a photograph of British Prime Minister Boris Johnson and Joseph Mifsud together. One is a fraud, a cheat, a conman and almost certainly a Russian stooge. The other is a mystery professor from Malta.

All good jokes – and the above is obviously a joke – bite into the apple of truth. Joseph Mifsud was a dodgy academic, originally from Malta, and an associate of Prime Minister Joseph Muscat.

That does not make Joseph Mifsud a suspect in the assassination of Daphne Caruana Galizia. No one in this chapter seems directly connected to the murder itself.

But Joseph Mifsud sat shoulder-to-shoulder with Joseph Muscat on the eve of the 2013 election, at a time when Muscat's governing plan for the following years was clearly set out. But behind the scenes other planning was also being carried out. That work likely included Pilatus Bank. It almost certainly included Henley & Partners. It would include the money laundering services for the Azerbaijani 'royal family'. It would include EU citizenship for dozens of Russian oligarchs in Vladimir Putin's sphere.

Joseph Mifsud came to the world's attention because he was allegedly used as a Russian asset serving Vladimir Putin's interests in the west. Then he disappeared.

Why him?

Mifsud conned five universities something rotten and then ended up at a tiny university in Rome with extraordinarily close links to Moscow's biggest spy factory. In Rome in March 2016, he met a bit-player on Team Trump, George Papadopoulos. The next month they met again in London where Mifsud introduced Papadopoulos to a young Russian woman he called 'Putin's niece'. At the meeting he offered the man from Team Trump 'the dirt' – thousands of emails belonging to Team Hillary Clinton. The emails had been hacked by the Russians. The Democrats only became aware that they had been hacked in June 2016, so Mifsud was touting the stolen goods two months before the victims realised they had been robbed.

Funnily enough in that very same month, April 2016, Mifsud had been in Moscow. He appeared on a guest panel with a big Kremlin player and a German millionaire based in Switzerland who once bought a British nuclear company and then suggested that the British nuclear engineer at its heart go to Moscow on an all-expenses paid trip for a conference.

Before his disappearance Mifsud was the networker *par excellence*. He had been snapped with everyone who is anyone: Boris Johnson, Joseph Muscat, the Russian ambassador to London, Alexander Yakovenko, and even the Russian foreign minister, Sergey Lavrov.

Somehow, Mifsud managed to leverage his career from being a dodgy academic into becoming a figure in an extraordinary story of espionage. He boasted to his Ukrainian girlfriend Anna that 'I have dinner with Lavrov tonight. Lavrov is my friend. Lavrov this, Lavrov that,' she told Alberto Nardelli of *BuzzFeed News*.

In November 2017, the investigation by FBI special counsel Robert Mueller set out the evidence against Papadopoulos and Mifsud's name emerged as the go-between for the Russian hackers. When cornered by a reporter from *La Repubblica*, Mifsud denied any contact with the Russian government, saying: 'I am an academic, I do not even speak Russian.' Immediately after that interview, Mifsud disappeared, with the American government and the Italian state hunting him.

The Democratic National Committee sued the professor, their lawsuit stating that he 'is missing and may be deceased'.

Only, Mifsud did not vanish. Where he ended up over the next six months is an extraordinary story and one which is deeply disturbing for anyone who cares about how Europe deals with the threat from the secretive Russian state.

There's an old KGB handbook which details the tricks Russian intelligence got up to in the bad old days of the Cold War. The gossip is that these techniques are still very much in use. Lesson One, roughly translated, goes like this: 'When targeting the enemy, don't use a Russian if you can find someone from a third country who will do your dirty work for you.' That seems to have been what happened with the vanishing professor.

Joseph Mifsud was born in Malta in 1960 and grew up and attended university on the island. He also studied at the University of Padua in Italy before going on to Queen's University Belfast where in 1995 he completed a PhD in comparative education. He returned to Malta where, according to his online biography, he became chief advisor to the ministry of education. He claims to have served as Malta's representative to the Council of Europe in education and at Unesco. He taught at the University of Malta and married another Maltese academic with whom he had a daughter. The couple are now divorced.

Daphne's son, Matthew had sat through a lecture by Mifsud in 2006: 'bluster and bollocks from start to finish' – proof, if proof were needed, that Matthew is a chip off the old block. Mifsud resigned from the University of Malta in 2007 'under something of a cloud' – a phrase that crops up again and again in this story.

In 2008 Mifsud became the head of the private office of Malta's foreign minister but he stayed for only a few months. Throughout his life, he appears to have been rather good at blagging his way into a job but piss-poor when it came to doing it. 'He exaggerates,' according to a former foreign ministry colleague, 'there's a lot of big talk ... but he didn't deliver.'

Many of the academics Mifsud has worked with in recent years are under the false impression that Mifsud was a diplomat. There is even a photograph of him speaking at an event with 'Ambassador

Mifsud' on his nameplate. But one senior figure who worked with Mifsud at the foreign ministry is clear that he was never an ambassador. Maltese journalist Jurgen Balzan told co-author John Sweeney: 'There's absolutely no evidence of Mifsud being an ambassador or deployed in some Maltese foreign ministry office abroad.'

However, by the mid-2000s, Mifsud did have a network of international contacts and he was particularly well-connected in the nascent states of the former Yugoslavia. He became a close friend of Miomir Žužul, Croatia's ambassador to the United States from 1996 to 2000. Žužul is a practising Roman Catholic, a knight of the Order of Malta, and now lives in Georgetown. The relationship between Mifsud and Žužul has endured. The two men go on holiday together in Europe every summer and are so close that it is apparently inconceivable that Mifsud would visit DC without hooking up with Žužul.

In 2008, after leaving the Maltese foreign ministry 'under something of a cloud' Mifsud became the president of a university at Agrigento in Sicily. A decade on, he was tried in absentia for fiddling the books by hiking pay for some of his colleagues and fined €49,500. Having left Agrigento 'under something of a cloud' he was appointed head of a new 'University of the Eastern Mediterranean' or EMUNI in the Slovenian coastal town of Piran. It's around this time that the ambassador who never was started calling himself 'Professor'.

EMUNI was never a proper university but flogged itself as a centre for students from Southern Europe, North Africa, and the Levant to study for short periods, the money coming from the Slovenian government and a small number of feeder universities. In 2008/09 EMUNI had no students and no faculty. That's a bit of a clue, some say. Its sole activity was to host a short summer school for 20 visiting Tunisians.

To make EMUNI look busier than it actually was, Mifsud allegedly cooked the books, regularly preparing false paperwork to conceal the truth about the university's lack of activity. The image of an EU success story was created and some fell for it. Greek MEP Rodi Kratsa visited and was genuinely impressed.

'Mifsud is very clever on one side but very dumb in other ways,' according to someone who saw him in action in Slovenia. A source says that Mifsud tried to get EMUNI to pay for his apartment, dinners, and car hire. But the Slovenian public sector has strict rules which restrict the payment of personal expenses. Mifsud left 'under something of a cloud' in 2013, accused of owing €39,332 in wrongly-claimed expenses and excess mobile phone charges. To this day the full story of EMUNI has never been told. 'Nobody in Slovenia talks about this,' says a source with knowledge of Mifsud's fraud.

That year he popped up in Malta again, holding a joint press conference with Malta's coming man Joseph Muscat, a few days before the election that would make Muscat prime minister. The two men were toasting the success of a new academic initiative which would see thousands of students come to Malta from abroad. Nothing ever came of this initiative. More interestingly, the brand new prime minister also got to meet the Russian foreign minister, Sergey Lavrov, very early on in his tenure: possible fruit of Mifsud's work behind the scenes? It's hard to know.

What is clear is that when Mifsud realised his days at EMUNI were numbered, he called an old friend in London, Nabil Ayad, for a job. Ayad was closely connected to the Palestinian Liberation Organisation (PLO) and director of the London Academy of Diplomacy (LAD) which he had founded in 1978 and was then part of the University of Westminster. Its students were generally low-order dips from the naffer embassies, seeking to touch up their CVs. Ayad appointed Mifsud director of international studies.

In 2009, Ayad took the LAD brand with him to a joint venture by the University of East Anglia and an educational company, INTO, run by a British man called Andrew Colin out of a Brighton office. Five years later, UEA dumped LAD. It moved on to Stirling University in Scotland. The hook-up cost Stirling a small fortune.

In September 2014, 'Professor' Mifsud organised a three-day trip to Stirling, attended by a group of diplomats from African, Caribbean and other non-G20 countries, plus some of LAD's visiting fellows, including lawyer Dr Stephan Roh – an exotic German-born, Swiss-based millionaire, with a Russian wife, of which more anon. There was a series of lectures and seminars, lots of networking, and a gala dinner. There was something funny peculiar about the bunfight according to one academic who attended. Dr Andrew Glencross said: 'I smelt a rat. There was champagne and everything …'

Is there normally champagne at events in Stirling, asked co-author John Sweeney?

'No, not at all,' replied Glencross bleakly.

After the bunfight, the hook-up between the London Academy of Diplomacy and the University of Stirling started to unravel. Mifsud lacked the skills to manage people and the administrative staff were tense around him. LAD failed to attract students from foreign embassies under Mifsud. By the end of 2014, the student body was mostly Chinese, with one source saying that Chinese students numbered as many as 90%. One professor expressed doubt that many of the Chinese students could understand what was said in seminars because their English was so poor. Concerns were raised with both Mifsud and some of the Stirling academics about the quality of students but nobody seemed to be bothered.

Nobody mistook Mifsud for a serious academic. 'He's more of an educational entrepreneur,' said one of the LAD's former academics. 'Mifsud is part of a massive network of academics and semi-academics who all do favours for each other. There's a lot of back-scratching. It's not corrupt, just normal academic networking but on steroids.'

Mifsud's appearance was scruffy, his tone self-important. 'He was one of these people wearing 10-year-old suits but carrying himself like an important person,' according to one academic. He was constantly name-dropping and promising to link people up with others who could help them. But senior academics at Stirling were starting to tire of his big talk and lack of delivery.

LAD became run-down and chaotic. Several visiting lecturers from the Mifsud era complain about not being paid for work done. Academics from Stirling say that nothing much came of the LAD relationship after the initial three-day trip and a couple of big dinners hosted in London with 'C-class ambassadors'. The leadership at Stirling were beginning to suspect that they had been conned. Mifsud's success at pulling the wool over the eyes of academics in Malta, Sicily, Slovenia, East Anglia, and Scotland shows that very clever people can also be bloody fools.

In mid-November 2014, Mifsud visited Washington DC where he delivered a lecture at the American University on the topic of 'Diplomacy and Development in a Global Environment', sponsored by AU's Program on International Organizations, Law, and Diplomacy in collaboration with the Organization of American States. He also gave an interview to journalist Larry Luxner for an article in *The Washington Diplomat*. If the Russians were watching out for someone they might be able to use, Mifsud was popping up in all the right places.

From 2015, Mifsud's operational base moved to Rome. He reportedly bought a stake in what was the old Italian campus of the University of Malta, renamed the Link Campus University and established the Rome Academy of Diplomacy – a chip off the London Academy of Diplomacy. Link Campus University appeared on the surface to be a credible institution, having respectable names on its advisory board including a magistrate well known for prosecuting corruption cases. It had a beautiful building but hardly any students: 300, if that. There were rumours that the institution was dodgy and secretly linked to Russians. Mifsud was part of the senior management at Link Campus University. When money troubles surfaced, Stephan Roh bought a stake in Link via Drake Global Limited, his UK-registered company.

The inner circle at the top of Link Campus University featured Italians with important political and security connections. The biggest security fish was Vincenzo Scotti, the president of the university, and Italy's minister of the interior from 1990-92, then minister of foreign affairs. Link also boasted Pasquale Russo, who is the president of the Consortium for Research on Intelligence and Security Services, and Professor Franco Frattini, a former foreign affairs minister under Silvio Berlusconi who is rumoured to be close to the Kremlin.

Link Campus is where, in 2018, Luigi di Maio, then Italian deputy prime minister presented the foreign policy programme of the Five Star Movement. Italy's former Minister of Defence Elisabetta Trenta and Deputy Foreign Minister Emanuela Del Re were both members of the faculty before they rocketed to power. And it is where, on 14 March 2016, Mifsud and Papadopoulos met for the first time.

Mifsud had been working at Link, schmoozing, building up contacts with Colonel Ghaddafi's people in Libya. On Mifsud's watch there was, according to a former Link academic, an attempt to promote Dr Roh as an academic figure 'which is ridiculous'. At least one academic was under pressure to book him as a speaker at an academic conference. One of Roh's employees – a French guy based in Monte Carlo – was given a platform as an expert. The Roh employee told an academic that Roh's firm specialised in due diligence and anti-money laundering. According to the former Link academic, Roh speaks Russian. While Mifsud was a very open person, Roh was much more guarded. Some of the academics were worried that the university was being turned into a centre for Russian soft power. There is a photograph of Mifsud at the Link Campus surrounded by young Russian women from a Moscow university. In the photo, Mifsud is smiling like a wolf.

The evidence suggests that Mifsud had first gone to Moscow in 2010 or even earlier. In 2012, the London Academy of Diplomacy hooked up with the Lomonosov Moscow State University's Faculty of Global Processes. An advert said that the faculty was a stepping stone for graduates to work 'in the Russian government, the presidential administration, federal ministries and agencies, the special services'. Bit of a clue? Lomonosov University is a spy factory. Mifsud has boasted that he once met Vladimir Putin himself, but with a track record as rickety as Mifsud's, you have to doubt his word. The Kremlin deny it, but they would, wouldn't they?

The website of the Russian embassy in London shows that in April 2014 Mifsud attended the Global University Summit in Moscow and in May 2014 he met the Russian ambassador to London, Alexander Yakovenko to present his views 'on the results of the Global University Summit'.

They also 'discussed different issues of the Russian-British cooperation in the sphere of international relations, diplomacy, science and education'. On 10 July 2014, according to the Russian embassy website, the counsellor of the Russian embassy Ernest Chernukhin visited LAD with a delegation from the Lomonosov Moscow State University. They discussed the collaboration between the faculty of global processes of MSU and the London Academy of Diplomacy.

After Mifsud met Papadopoulos at Link University in Rome in March 2016, they met again in London the following month.

We have some sight of how Mifsud operated around that time from an extraordinary source, Simona Mangiante, an Italian woman who became Papadopoulos' girlfriend. Mangiante accepted a post working for Mifsud in London in the autumn of 2016 at the London Centre of International Law Practice or LCILP. The LCILP had all the hallmarks of a Mifsud operation: very grand-sounding name, no substance, no real business.

Mangiante suggested that Mifsud, in a manner of speaking, played cupid. She says that Papadopoulos, who also worked at the centre, got in touch with her via social media and asked her out.

The centre's office was in a smart Georgian terrace close to Lincoln's Inn Fields in London. But it was tiny. Mangiante and her colleagues perched around a single table. They used their own laptops. The place was 'very messy', Mangiante told *The Guardian*.

It felt like something was weird. I never met any Russians there ... But the centre certainly wasn't what it pretended to be. He is sneaky, someone you can't read. He was vague about everything. He wouldn't answer questions directly. I could never understand what was behind it.

The centre seemed 'fake', 'artificial'. 'I didn't smell a culture of academia', she told *The Guardian*. And she was not being paid – another classic Mifsud tell. When she complained about not getting any money from Mifsud, he replied via his Stirling University email, writing in Italian: 'Dear Simona, I hope you are fine … I was in Moscow … Now I'm in London. Can we meet in person? I'm here until Tuesday night. A hug. J'

The meeting never happened and Mangiante quit her post there after three months, in November 2016.

In November 2017 Papadopoulos pleaded guilty to making false statements about contacts he had had with the Russian government and admitted to the FBI that a mystery Maltese professor was his go-between with the Russians. The go-between was Mifsud. In the Mueller report, the US special investigation found that Mifsud 'maintained various Russian contacts while living in London' including an unnamed person who was a former member of the Internet Research Agency, the Russian troll farm based in Saint Petersburg.

One former visiting professor from LAD who knew Mifsud well says that if he was involved in helping the Russians interfere in the US election, 'then it will not be out of naivety. He is cunning.' Mifsud was, the academic says, part of a 'third-rate diplomatic community where there is an element of braggadocio'. So maybe he exaggerated his closeness to Russia to impress Papadopoulos. 'But it's clear that Mifsud knew something before the world did. And that raises questions.'

John Schindler, former member of the US National Security Agency told co-author Sweeney: 'the Russians will use third-country nationals as access agents, to use the proper term, meaning they're out there spotting and assessing for targets for Russian intelligence, particularly people who might not want to talk to a Russian or would be put off by talking to a Russian for security or personal reasons. Someone who's a third-country national can be a lot better person to be the face of Russian intelligence.'

So why would a minor Maltese academic, working chiefly in British and Italian universities, be of interest to the Russians? Schindler said:

He is a very typical kind of character in this world, on the fringes of academia, think tankery, and governments. He looks non-threatening. He's a hanger-on, he's at all the parties, he's a wannabe, not a real player. In a strange way that could actually help the Russians because the threat perception drops considerably. He's Maltese which is not associated a lot with threats of any kind, frankly. He can get along in a lot of places.

In May 2017 Mifsud chaired a session at a conference in Saudi Arabia to coincide with US President Donald Trump's visit. Trump didn't attend the conference but Ashcroft Carter, former defense secretary was there. Speakers included former MI6 head of counter terrorism Richard Barrett. The conference was organised by an influential Saudi think-tank called the King Faisal Center for Research and Islamic Studies. Based in Riyadh, its president is Prince Turki Al Faisal, a former Saudi ambassador to the UK and a former head of Saudi intelligence.

Mifsud had told the management that he could help them get a high placing in an international league table of think-tanks. Concerns were expressed about Mifsud to the think-tank's management and whether they had considered that he might be a spy trying to get close to Prince Turki. But Mifsud was apparently so influential with the think-tank's management that they arranged for him to have a special visa which allowed him to travel in and out of Saudi Arabia freely. Some of the researchers at the think-tank had doubts about Mifsud's value and credentials – and, without reference to the management, they removed Mifsud from the security conference programme. When the management of the think-tank became aware that Mifsud had been excluded from the programme, they insisted that all the glossy brochures for the event were pulped, that Mifsud should be reinstated, and that a new set of brochures printed.

In May 2017 Stirling University made an honest man of Mifsud by appointing him as 'a full-time Professorial Teaching Fellow in the University's Politics department'. There's no denying the benefits of networking.

Here's another nugget from that old KGB handbook – international conferences and seminars are great for recruiting. Stuffed with clever academics, scientists, and business people, they're the perfect place to 'get information and influence foreigners'.

The very same month that Mifsud tipped off the man from Team Trump about the dirt on Hillary – April 2016 – the professor had been in Moscow for a Kremlin-backed Valdai conference. It's a talkfest for Kremlin trustees and useful idiots from the West who like the idea of rubbing shoulders with Vladimir Putin and chums. In one photograph to Mifsud's left is Ivan Timofeev, who works at a think-tank linked to the Russian ministry of foreign affairs. *The Washington Post* has reported that email correspondence suggests that Mifsud put the Trump team in contact with Timofeev. Also at that same Valdai conference was Dr Stephan Roh, the Swiss-based entrepreneur who had been on the jolly to Stirling University.

With Mifsud and Papadopoulos, Dr Roh is, you could say, the third man. He and his Russian-born wife Olga have homes in Switzerland, Monaco, London, and Hong Kong. And then there's a castle in Scotland. Buying it made Stephan and Olga the Baron and Baroness of Inchdrewer.

In 2014 Stephan Roh had become a visiting lecturer at the London Academy of Diplomacy. A very wealthy man, he invested in Link University in Rome where Mifsud was part of the management. And Mifsud became a consultant at Roh's legal firm. Mifsud and Roh did the Valdai event in April 2016. On 12 May 2017 Mifsud and Roh appeared together in Moscow at the Russian International Affairs Council to launch an energy report they had worked on together. There's a clip of Mifsud talking about the report which can be summed up in Matthew Caruana Galizia's phrase: 'bluster and bollocks from start to finish'.

And Olga Roh was on Fox TV's 'Meet The Russians'. The TV show has Olga relaxing in her posh home, saying: 'The way we always were in my family, very achievements orientated.'

When co-author Sweeney made a BBC Newsnight film about George Papadopoulos, Mifsud, and Roh in 2018, Olga was running an upmarket dress shop in London's Mayfair. Among her customers was Britain's then prime minister, Theresa May. There is a photograph of prime minister May meeting the Queen in an Olga Roh coat. The shop has since closed.

Most intriguingly are Stephan's business interests, which appear extensive. Newsnight revealed the story of one. Sweeney and his team tracked down a British nuclear engineer, Dr John Harbottle who had his own nuclear consultancy firm. He told the *BBC*:

In the autumn of 2005, I received a phone call from a Dr Stephan Roh, showing an interest in the company and explained very briefly that he intended to be involved with some technology transfer from Russia to Europe and he would like to do this through my company.

Dr Harbottle's company, Severnvale Nuclear Services Ltd, specialised in the effects of radiation on fuel materials in reactors in Britain, France, and the United States. So what did Dr Roh want from him?

Harbottle said:

He explained that he would like to acquire my company but he wanted to retain my services on the technical side because he was a lawyer and had no technical background at all.

Dr Roh bought the nuclear consultancy, then invited Dr Harbottle on an all-expenses paid trip to a conference in Moscow. But the nuclear scientist was alert to the danger that visitors to Moscow can be targeted or even honey-trapped into compromising situations. Dr Harbottle told the BBC: 'We smelt a rat. It didn't sound as if it would ring true and I decided that I wasn't going to go to this meeting.'

So Dr Harbottle declined to go. Shortly afterwards, he was fired.

Under Dr Harbottle the company's turnover had been £42,000 a year. Within three years under Dr Roh, Severnvale Nuclear was turning over more than $43 million a year, with just two employees.

Bob Shaw, weapons and intelligence expert, told co-author Sweeney:

On the face of it, it could be a legitimate business, highly successful in a short space of time. However, my concerns are that it has only got two employees, neither of which are experts in the field of consultancy. So it could be money laundering, up from that it could be a way of obtaining nuclear capability for the Russian energy sector within Russia.

Dr Roh co-authored a book, *The Faking of RUSSIA-GATE: The Papadopoulos Case.* The book sets out the case that Mifsud was not a Russian spy but 'deeply embedded in the network of Western Intelligence Services.' Papadopoulos, too, is a 'western intelligence operative', the authors assert, who was 'placed' in the Trump campaign by the FBI. There is no evidence for this Kremlin-friendly claptrap. *The Faking of Russia-Gate* is a bit rubbish, frankly.

The case of Joseph Mifsud and Team Hillary's emails and Stephan Roh and Severnvale Nuclear raises big questions about these types of international characters and their links to Russia.

When the scandal broke, Mifsud denied that he was a spy. When approached by Italian newspaper *La Repubblica* in November 2017 he said: 'Secret agent! I never got a penny from the Russians: my conscience is clean.'

And then the man with the clean conscience vanished, as is his custom, under something of a cloud.

The Italian newspaper *Il Foglio* discovered that, while the whole world was looking for him, including private detectives working for the Democratic National Committee and the Italian courts for the €49,500 he had embezzled from the university in Sicily, he was holed up in a flat paid by Link University. *Il Foglio* reported: 'The house where Mifsud hid is in via Cimarosa 3, behind Villa Borghese.'

The house was within spitting distance of the Russian embassy. Fancy that.

THE OPPOSITION LEADER
WHO WON'T OPPOSE

When Joseph Muscat contested a general election in 2013 for the first time, the Nationalist Party (PN) he opposed had been in government for most of the previous 25 years. The PN had had two party leaders for almost his entire lifetime. Eddie Fenech Adami became PN leader in 1977 and prime minister ten years after that. He ruled until his retirement from politics in 2004, with a 22-month break when Labour's Alfred Sant won the 1996 election but lost the government in a crisis before its mid-term.

In 2004 the PN elected Lawrence Gonzi who defeated Alfred Sant in 2008 but lost to Joseph Muscat in 2013. It was, by any measure, time for change.

The PN's last term in government was unpopular. It was perceived as tired and arrogant and by the end it could do no right.

Lawrence Gonzi tendered his resignation from the leadership of the PN immediately the election result became known. He was, however, sworn in as leader of the opposition and stayed on as party leader until a new leader was appointed.

His replacement was Simon Busuttil, who had spearheaded the EU information office in the run up to the EU referendum campaign and is widely credited with helping the Yes vote to win 54% of the vote.

Simon Busuttil had been a member of the European Parliament for nine years (2004-13) when he was called upon by the prime minister to return to Malta and serve as deputy PN leader in a desperate bid to rejuvenate the party ahead of the 2013 election.

Daphne Caruana Galizia's initial opinion of Simon Busuttil as party leader:

Simon Busuttil was a fabulous MEP, but, so far, he is really not shaping up as a natural-born leader. As an MEP your job is to be factual and dispassionate. As a leader, you need passion and conviction, because without them you can't motivate people.

Put simply, you can't lead with the outlook, attitude, and comportment of an accountant or lawyer. Leadership is about MORAL pronouncements, about reminding people where their priorities should lie, about giving a human dimension to the nuts and bolts of bald issues.

But first, you have to be able to recognise those issues. A political leader must have a nose for issues in the same way that journalists must have a nose for a story.

She was particularly annoyed with Simon Busuttil's initially tepid reaction to Joseph Muscat's decision to 'push back' migrants saved from the sea through forced repatriation:

And now we have Busuttil's latest bit of absolutely hopeless moral and political leadership. 'Ridiculously inadequate' doesn't even begin to describe it. Faced with public outrage at the push-back of immigrants who will be flown out by Air Malta at midnight and 4am tonight, he says, clinically, that 'this is a very worrying situation' and he 'expects the prime minister to honour all international obligations'.

That's just a part of it, Simon – what about his moral obligations towards the people involved?

I quote Times of Malta: 'Asked about an article he had written in 2010 about sending migrants back, Dr Busuttil said he was now opposed to push back because of a ruling by the European Court of Human Rights.'

Again, unbelievable. He opposes push-back not because of the reasons the ECHR ruled against it (inhumane, exposing people to torture, mass deportation, violations), but because the ECHR ruled against it. This is like saying that you are opposed to murder because it is illegal.

What Busuttil should have said is that he was wrong to support push-back, that he regrets that stance, and now understands the full horror of the implications for the individuals involved. And the fact that the ECHR ruled against it only serves to convince him further that it is immoral, only now we also know that it really is a violation of human rights.

Simon Busuttil should be right out there calling a press conference and slamming the government and Muscat to hell for their behaviour. He should be calling them immoral, racist, violators of human rights. Instead, what we have is a cold-fish approach by somebody who doesn't understand the media and mass political communication at all. If he doesn't shape up fast, he has created a vacancy already. Quite frankly, we barely even know he's there.

It is safe to say she was not a fan.

In the four years between 2013 and 2017, however, Simon Busuttil would grow in stature.

As more and more stories of corruption at the highest levels of power surfaced, the PN increased its focus on good governance, or better, the lack of it in Malta's administration, and campaigned for the next election under the banner of *Politika Onesta* (Honest Politics).

As government scandal followed government scandal, so did the outrage from the opposition. Simon Busuttil no longer waited for others to suggest he call a press conference to slam the government for their ethically objectionable failures.

There were campaigns over the electricity deals, street marches protesting the Panama scandals, indignant calls for resignations over the Egrant revelations, and protests in support of Daphne Caruana Galizia when government minister Chris Cardona won a bid to freeze her bank accounts after she ran a series of embarrassing stories about him.

Another sustained PN campaign was over the privatisation of three public hospitals in Malta, including the only hospital on the smaller inhabited island of Gozo.

The PN had mild misgivings about the principle of hiving off a big chunk of the national health service. But it was angry about the fact that the hospitals were being transferred to unknown people with shareholding structures in offshore jurisdictions clearly designed to obscure who was making money from the deal.

Predictably familiar figures were at the centre of the scandal. The initiative was the legacy of John Dalli, the product of the consultancy he had provided to Joseph Muscat as 'advisor on health matters' following his resignation from the European Commission after he had floundered in corruption allegations.

In 2014 Konrad Mizzi met a group of people who called themselves the Vitals Healthcare Group. They had no hospital to their name and did not appear to exist except for a purpose that had not yet materialised.

Economy Minister Chris Cardona would follow up on that discussion and sign a memorandum of understanding with this 'Group' whose shareholding included a 30% stake buried in the secrecy and anonymity of the British Virgin Islands.

Six months later, the government issued a request for proposals for anyone interested in taking on the running of three government hospitals. Vitals, signatories of the memorandum of understanding that came before the public procurement process, were rather predictably awarded the deal. The announcement came in September 2015.

The public still did not know who was in control of the three hospitals the government used to own. Malta was instead introduced to a Canadian citizen by the name of Sri Ram Tumuluri who talked up the deal as a major development for healthcare in Malta.

Ram Tumuluri's background did not provide much bedside comfort. In his previous job he ran a health spa in rural Canada which went bust within two years.

A company Ram Tumuluri owned with his wife in British Columbia was dissolved by the regulator after declaring bankruptcy three years after it was set up.

In November 2016 Daphne showed that his assets were all tied up as collateral for his debts in Canada. He had no way of covering the guarantees he needed to bid for the Malta hospital contract, let alone win it.

And yet, win it is what he and his unknown associates did. The hospitals were granted as a concession for 30 years during which the government would pay the new owners €2 billion to cover operational costs to continue providing free healthcare. That's €67 million a year: a 30% increase on the operational cost budgeted for the same hospitals while the government still owned them. A classic lose-lose arrangement.

The government refused to publish the contract and details about the scandal trickled out as journalists tried to understand what had really happened. All the equipment in the hospitals, some of which was relatively new, was transferred to the new owners for the princely sum of €1. Vitals held an exit clause of an €80 million payment should any future government decide to terminate the concession before it expired.

The supposed plus side was that the Vitals Group undertook to refurbish two and rebuild one of the hospitals. In two years not much has happened, much like Mr O'Reilly's construction project at Fawlty Towers. Thus far, no garden gnome has been inserted à la Basil Fawlty into Mr Ram Tumuluri or his associates.

By the end of 2017, 21 months into their 30-year concession, Vitals said they had run out of money. They took out an emergency loan to pay salaries and, incredibly, put up one of the state hospitals as surety for the loan. They somehow secured the government's permission to sell on their concession to an American for-profit hospital business when the government had every legal right to rescind the concession on the simple grounds that Vitals failed to deliver on several of their commitments.

The project appeared designed to fail. Secret owners stood to gain from the speculative flip of a public concession with their profits stashed in off-shore jurisdictions away from prying eyes.

In 2017 the Maltese investigative news website *The Shift News*, set up by Caroline Muscat in the aftermath of Daphne's killing, cracked the secret identity of the shareholders of the Vitals Group. Ram Tumuluri was in business with Gupta Ambrish, a Virginia cardiologist, Ashok Rattehalli, a Washington DC 'healthcare executive' and Mark Pawley, a Singapore based consultant.

Mark Pawley had already outed himself in an earlier newspaper interview on Malta's *The Sunday Times*. He was only the second known face in the outfit that called itself Vitals Global Healthcare. In a November 2014 post Daphne wrote:

Vitals is neither global nor has it ever carried out any healthcare to speak of. It was incorporated last year and is, to use industry jargon, a start-up. You might give your website development project to a start-up if they gave you a good enough pitch, but the running of three public hospitals on a budget of $55 million a year? I don't think so.

Chris Cardona and Konrad Mizzi, as well as finance minister Edward Scicluna who was responsible for public procurement, deny any wrongdoing.

Simon Busuttil disagreed and made this one of his loudest battle cries.

Another scandal broke over the American University of Malta (AUM). Somewhat like Voltaire's remark that the Holy Roman Empire was neither holy nor Roman nor an empire, the American University of Malta is an optimistic misnomer.

The project was announced in 2015 by the government. The promoter of the project was Hani Hasan Al Salah representing a Jordanian construction company called the Sadeen Group. The group's educational portfolio was limited to for-profit schools for expatriates in Jordan. They had no higher education institution in their portfolio.

The connection to America was the school's provost, John Ryder. His last academic posting before the AUM was a rector of something called the Khazar University in Baku, Azerbaijan.

The government granted the Sadeen Group use of waterfront historical buildings in the Valletta harbour and a whopping 90,000 square metres of pristine land on which to develop their campus. After nationwide uproar, the concession was reduced to 18,000 square metres. Had the proposed concession been 18,000 square metres to begin with, it would still have been a controversial plan. As it turned out, going from 90,000 to 18,000 square metres satisfied most critics that the government's worst excesses had been curbed and the new deal was an improvement on the old.

The AUM promised to attract 4,000 students by 2021. It hasn't reached one hundred yet.

Simon Busuttil, Daphne Caruana Galizia, and many other people in Malta criticised the AUM scheme as a cover for the transfer of valuable open space to a construction magnate.

One further detail would emerge that would do nothing to dispel that suspicion.

One of the revelations of the Panama Papers was that Adrian Hillman, at the time managing director of the company that owns Malta's newspaper of record, *The Times of Malta*, had a British Virgin Islands shell company.

Keith Schembri owned companies that supplied paper to the newspaper as well as the machinery used by its printing press.

Keith Schembri paid over $600,000 into Adrian Hillman's BVI account.

Daphne wrote in May 2017:

Adrian Hillman – Keith Schembri's friend, unofficial business associate and, at the time, managing director of Allied Newspapers Ltd (Times of Malta, The Sunday Times) – laundered more than €600,000 after the Labour Party was elected to government in March 2013, according to his own accounts which were prepared by corrupt accountants Karl Cini and Brian Tonna of Nexia BT.

The money was laundered through Hillman's company in the British Virgin Islands, Lester Holding Corp, which was not declared to the Maltese authorities or to his employers at Allied Newspapers Ltd.

Lester Holding Corp was set up in 2011, but restructured for greater secrecy, using layers of nominees to hide his ownership, by Mossack Fonseca, Brian Tonna, and Karl Cini shortly after the Labour Party came to power in 2013.

At the same time Lester Holding Corp was set up for Adrian Hillman in 2011, another two companies were set up in the same jurisdiction for Keith Schembri and his business partner Malcolm Scerri, both of the Kasco Group, the leading supplier to Allied Newspapers and Progress Press, the companies controlled by Hillman.

These British Virgin Islands companies, Colson Service Corp (Schembri) and Selson Holding Corp (Scerri), were also restructured for greater secrecy after March 2013.

Adrian Hillman, Keith Schembri, and Malcolm Scerri are all the subjects of a report prepared by the Financial Intelligence Analysis Unit because of these and other money-laundering transactions.

Adrian Hillman resigned his position as managing director of Allied Newspapers in disgrace. Both Adrian Hillman and Keith Schembri deny any wrongdoing. A magisterial inquiry continues.

Editors working at the newspaper at the time insisted Adrian Hillman never sought to influence editorial content and, if they had appeared supportive of Joseph Muscat in the years leading up to the 2013 elections, that had been an editorial judgement they reached autonomously.

There is no doubt, however, that the episode caused considerable harm to the otherwise solid reputation of *The Times of Malta*.

Daphne Caruana Galizia, almost by accident, picked up in May 2017 that there was a connection between the disgraced Adrian Hilllman and the Jordanian promoters of the so-called American University of Malta. A source had told her Brian Tonna was meeting people from the Sadeen Group at a hotel. Her source was wrong and lawyers sent her a threatening letter.

That's when she found out who was really meeting the Sadeen visitors.

Henley & Partners, Pilatus Bank, Keith Schembri, Joseph Muscat, Konrad Mizzi, Phyllis Muscat, Chris Cardona – now I've got Hani Hasan Naji Al Salah, the Jordanian to whom Joseph Muscat gave a large tract of public land at Zonqor Point, and who is represented in Malta by Deo Scerri, the Labour Party's accountant and the Labour government's appointee to the chairmanship of the Bank of Valletta, on my case with threatening letters too.

It's a very crooked queue.

A few days ago, I received a letter from a firm of lawyers, who are linked to Chris Cardona, about a blog-post in which I reported that Brian Tonna was at a meeting with the Jordanian Zonqor Point fixers and Prince Jean of Luxembourg at the Hilton hotel. The letter was exactly what you would expect from people with no breeding who use outrage as a form of defence. It was not Brian Tonna ... sue you ... libel ... unfounded ... blah blah blah.

I rang up the friend ... who had told me it was Brian Tonna. 'I'll just check with X who was with me at the time. I don't know Tonna that well so I might have made a mistake.' Two minutes later he was back on the phone: 'It was Adrian Hillman, not Brian Tonna,' my friend said. 'X is 100% certain and can say it on oath. He knows him very well.' How did you confuse them, I said. 'Oh, they're both as bald as an egg, the same height and involved in the same crooked business.'

I must confess that I was delighted. There the Jordanian camel-trader was, ranting and raving through Chris Cardona's favourite firm of lawyers (after Pawlu Lia) that they're going to sue me for libel for saying that they were in a meeting with Brian Tonna, and all the while they were in a meeting with Adrian Hillman, which is just as bad if not worse.

That shows you the value of libel suits, doesn't it? They sue you for saying they were with Brian Tonna, when all along they were with Adrian Hillman and think that you have no way of knowing this.

In October 2017, the month Daphne was killed, the government appointed Adrian Hillman as its representative on the board of trustees of the American University of Malta.

The June 2017 electoral clash took on a Manichean dimension. Joseph Muscat campaigned on the back of the economic success of the country. The campaign mantra was *l-aqwa żmien* (the best of times). The pitch was that prosperity required the flexibility of a government like Muscat's and the rigid moralising of someone like Simon Busuttil would endanger it.

The message was resoundingly received by a majority of the electorate.

A post written by Daphne in March 2013 went some way towards explaining the sway of the electorate:

Amoral familism is the reason people in Malta use their vote as currency and do not think in terms of the common good or choosing the right government, but in terms of spiting/rewarding, getting/preventing others from getting.

It is also the reason why even monied and supposedly educated individuals are not embarrassed – rather, they are proud because they think it is a heroic act and that it is perfectly normal and civilised – to talk openly about not voting for this or that party, or not voting at all, on the basis of personal matters and what they wish to obtain personally (or prevent others from obtaining).

This sort of talk, and the reasoning it betrays, is completely unacceptable and questionable in societies more civilised and democratically developed than ours. It is considered to be irrational, inward-looking thinking that is completely at odds with what more developed European societies, built on the notion of the common good, stand for.

Daphne applied this analysis to the 2013 election results that had just seen the PL returned to government for the first time since 1998:

The Labour Party campaigned in the context of amoral familism, fully understanding it and working with it. The Nationalist Party failed at garnering the support of sufficient numbers of people precisely because it took the more European, civilised approach – the truly progressive and liberal approach.

In public relations terms, the situation was turned on its head and the positions of both parties reversed in the public mind. The Labour Party, campaigning on the basis of really backward amoral familism, became the progressive and liberal one. The Nationalist Party, campaigning on the true European ticket, became the retrograde outfit.

The Labour Party's leaders no longer just hinted at 'flexibility'. They promoted the notion to attract disgruntled PN voters denied some development permit, say, because of a strict and faceless enforcement of rules.

In a small island like Malta, the government is always a major player in people's lives. There are obvious needs like healthcare and schooling, though corruption in those sectors is relatively rare. Slipping a €20 note to a policeman to try to dodge a parking ticket would be as alien in Malta as it would be in Sweden, say.

But on the other hand, politicians have traded votes for public sector jobs for generations, retaining a bloated public sector of grossly under-employed, under-skilled armies of salaried loyalists. Famously, on the eve of the 1987 election, a Labour Party facing electoral defeat employed 8,000 people in the space of three months. The burden of that rush would continue to be paid until the 2010s when the last of that intake retired.

The mass recruitment of 1987 was the biggest offence but the PN was not innocent of this system of patronage.

By 2017 the PL had reinstated jobs-for-votes as a system of government. It started by transferring the PL's payroll cost to public expenditure employing 'as persons of trust' analysts, propagandists and salaried mobilisers of the PL.

On the eve of the 2017 election an estimated 1,000 people were engaged on the island of Gozo alone. The island has a total population of 35,000, making this a staggering intake.

Another currency traded by Maltese politicians for votes is land, the most valuable asset in the country, its price held high by virtue of its mere scarcity.

Foremost on many people's minds when voting in 2017 was the question whether a new PN government would again tighten restrictions on construction and development, whether the green 'outside development zone' would revert to a status of protection, whether building heights in traditional village cores would be enforced.

People who owned a previously unused basement or a holiday apartment that was now the address of an invisible billionaire who called themselves Maltese were nervous their effortless inflow of money would be dried up by PN puritanism.

Estate agents, cashing commissions from selling and reselling the same properties changing hands on the back of enthusiastic speculative trading, did not want the party to stop.

Some outspoken people who voted PL for the first time in 2013 switched back to PN in disgust. But for most people, it did not matter who was right or who was wrong. The PL was resoundingly victorious in June 2017 and Simon Busuttil's brief sojourn as leader of the PN was over.

Writing a few days after the 2017 election, Daphne said:

People, on the whole, tend to do what's best for themselves. This is quite normal. The thing that has gone wrong in Maltese society is that the link between what's best for yourself and what's best for society in the medium to long term was never forged. There are glimmers of hope, though. It seems quite obvious to me that the ABC1 switchers who voted Labour for the first time in 2013 and who now switched back in droves – they were visible everywhere – did so because they fully understand that a society poisoned by top-to-bottom corruption and the undermining of institutions is one in which it becomes increasingly unsafe to live.

She was commenting after one of Konrad Mizzi's supporters posted a selfie with the beaming minister on Facebook, captioned 'Thank you Panama! Thank you Pilatus! Thank you Konrad!'

Supporters of the PL held a celebratory street party outside the offices of Pilatus Bank. Corruption had won. Hallelujah.

After the June 2017 elections, Daphne Caruana Galizia took a break from her blog, her first in a long time. For years she had barely stepped away for longer than a couple of days. Speaking to co-author Manuel Delia after her death, her husband Peter said Daphne had spent the last five years of her life tethered to her blog. When she travelled, she rushed to find time to keep up with her blog. She couldn't socialise, she had to be around to give meaning to what was happening in Malta.

For around three weeks in June and July 2017 she flirted with the idea of calling it a day. Perhaps to begin with, the apparent futility of it all had got to her. But in conversations with friends at the time, Daphne also spoke about how good it felt to focus on what she enjoyed doing best.

Apart from being a powerful investigative journalist, an influential commentator, an abrasive critic, a witty satirist, and a defendant in 42 civil libel suits and five criminal defamation cases, Daphne was also an accomplished editor and producer of a food and home magazine that by far exceeded the expectations of the minute Maltese publishing market.

Her *Taste & Flair* magazine was a professional reflection of her personal side: an aesthete, a lover of colour and unpolished beauty, a collector, and a foodie. Through her monthly magazine, one could catch a glimpse of the very private woman behind the very public journalism.

Her home in the Bidnija countryside is surrounded by a beautiful and deceptively chaotic garden. After her death, her sons Matthew,

Andrew, and Paul spoke of how much their mother loved their garden, refuting conventional notions of pattern and alignment and seeking to regain an untamed wilderness sheltered from the oppressive ordinariness of the agricultural landscape outside her gate.

In a speech to the European Parliament a month after she was killed, Peter Caruana Galizia said of his wife: 'The more frustrated Daphne grew at the state of our country, the more beautiful our garden became.'

Speaking to co-author Manuel Delia, Peter spoke of how he could claim no credit for the attractive, sometimes quirky, decor of their beautiful home. Daphne collected figurines of elephants made of porcelain, wood, or glass; of shapes and colours that shuffled together left one with the idea of the Platonic elephant, an archetype of memory, patience, strength, constancy, courage, and a maternal instinct that is playful and teasing but fierce when needed.

By the time she had finished preparing the July 2017 edition of *Taste & Flair*, the political scene in Malta had spun beyond all recognition. With a heavy heart, she knew she had to get back to her laptop and continue her *Running Commentary*.

As soon as the election result was announced, Simon Busuttil tendered his resignation and kickstarted a process to elect his replacement by Independence Day on 21 September.

There was no obvious successor to Simon Busuttil, unlike previous transfers of power.

In the context of recrimination and desperate disappointment, in the painful soul-searching, and in the absence of any obvious candidate to take on the top job, a man walked in from outside and said he would give the PN a 'new way' to winning days.

His name was Adrian Delia (no relation to the co-author Manuel Delia) and 'the last time he did anything for the Nationalist Party, he was 17', Daphne said in a post published on 29 June 2017. That would have been 30 years earlier.

The new candidate presented himself as a political fighter in contrast with Simon Busuttil who, he said, was not.

On that latter point, Daphne did not disagree. On 30 June she wrote:

Now that all is done and dusted, I can say that the single factor that most contributed to Simon Busuttil's electoral undoing is that he does not have that essential fighting spirit, the sort that says inside you: 'Come and get me, you f**king bastards, and watch me flatten you into the pavement.'

I got the impression that he would never even think words like 'f**king' and 'bastards', or their equivalent in Maltese, and that he would bridle and be genuinely upset if anybody so much as used them in his presence.

In ordinary life, this is a huge advantage, because the way we get along in ordinary life is by cooperating with others and not fighting them, not thinking of them as bastards and not being aggressive towards them. But politics is not ordinary life. It is as far from ordinary as it is possible to get without actually living with the Kardashians.

When the Nationalist Party's television station broadcast footage of Joseph Muscat emerging from a television debate and saying about Dr Busuttil, 'Imur jieħdu f'sormu' (which means literally 'he can take it up the arse', the technical way of saying 'he can bugger off'), it did so thinking people would be scandalised.

I thought that was a mistake. Nationalist supporters of the sort who don't like that kind of language and attitude would have been upset, but they would have been voting Nationalist anyway. Labour supporters wouldn't be changing their vote on that basis alone, but a whole bunch of people would have thought, 'That's the right attitude' and many of them would have been Nationalist supporters.

Adrian Delia quickly earned a reputation for being perfectly willing to use unparliamentary language in conversation, in contrast with his predecessors. But that didn't mean he had the fighting spirit so necessary to a party leader:

We should have noticed already that Adrian Delia, who is being promoted hard and fast as the Nationalist Party's Moses (except that he has no intention of spending 40 years in the desert and has only popped in now because he is prepared to give it five years in Opposition max) has no fighting spirit to speak of. Anybody with any kind of fighting spirit would have been out there fighting the Labour Party long ago, but Dr Delia hasn't so much as written a Facebook comment or newspaper article.

Even in the two interviews he gave he had absolutely nothing to say about the government or the Labour Party, totally oblivious to the fact that he is going to be elected for no purpose other than to fight them.

In that last sentence, Daphne Caruana Galizia showed she had immediately perceived what Adrian Delia's core strategic approach to his leadership of the PN would be. The demons he would confront would be within the party he would lead, not outside it. He would seek to overthrow the party's ethical attitude to governance. He would seek to overturn '*djuq*', best translated as 'holier than thou'. He would seek to remould the PN in the image of the PL.

Adrian Delia spoke fluently and moved confidently on the stage. By training he was a court litigator and was adept at putting on a show. Party activists, who felt the previous leadership was staid, rallied to him. As did people who found all the talk about good governance too cerebral or too far from the minds of ordinary voters.

Party activists are propagandists in the street where they live. For decades they faced the ire of their neighbours, who were wont to claim their support of the PN was not getting them anywhere, if they had been denied a public sector job or a building permit. Life was much easier for their PL counterparts, armed with the currency of favours and gifts from above. Adrian Delia looked like he understood how the Maltese voter's mind worked.

Daphne Caruana Galizia went about profiling this man who had come in from the cold.

She found that for several years Adrian Delia had represented a Soho landlord whose apartments had been raided by the British police for prostitution and people trafficking. She also found that his clients were able to clear daily cash deposits from 'rent' paid by the prostitutes using an account in Adrian Delia's name in Jersey.

She challenged Adrian Delia to declare whether he had bank accounts in offshore jurisdictions, which he categorically denied. She then proceeded to publish a screenshot of a bank statement from HSBC Jersey bearing his name. His reaction was that he was no longer sure if he had a bank account in Jersey and that when he called the Jersey branch they told him their records did not go that far back.

The flimsy responses did not dent his support. On the contrary, pressure from Daphne Caruana Galizia became a political asset for Adrian Delia as he campaigned for the leadership post in the summer of 2017 ahead of the leadership election in September.

When Joseph Muscat called the June 2017 election a year earlier than it was due, he blamed Daphne and claimed her 'lies' had destabilised his government and he wanted voters to decide whether he was guilty or not. It was a kangaroo court presided over by the accused and at the end of the five-week campaigning process the prosecutor, Daphne, was condemned to ignominy.

PN supporters who had hailed her a heroine and had marched in her support, now accused her of being the reason behind the PN's losing streak, damning her as a curse.

The change in attitude had a foundation with a long pedigree. The PL often challenged previous PN leaders 'to condemn Daphne' or somehow disassociate themselves from her.

But PN leaders before Adrian Delia did not think it was a good idea to condemn independent journalists or even 'to disassociate themselves'. For one thing, disassociation implies previous association, which was an absurd notion. Daphne was not beholden to the PN. But more importantly, politicians with some integrity do not thunder against journalists from their seats in parliament. They understand the importance of public scrutiny. At least that was the accepted behaviour in a world of political restraint before populism, before Donald Trump.

In the Maltese context, the Trumpian assault on independent journalism, was now being defined by Adrian Delia and cheered on by an enthusiastic audience grateful for a neat solution to all the problems of the PN: the exorcism of Daphne Caruana Galizia.

Egging on that support was an unlikely ally: the PL media that supported Adrian Delia's nomination. Leading the counter-intelligence operation was Robert Musumeci, he of the #downwithgalizia online campaign and partner of her nemesis, Magistrate Consuelo Scerri Herrera.

Robert Musumeci argued that the PN should vote in a way that would rid it of the devil that had been possessing it, Daphne Caruana Galizia. It later turned out that Adrian Delia and Robert Musumeci were buddies. Friends in high places.

Daphne was not letting up. That summer she published stories about Adrian Delia's abyss of personal debts, about former clients of his who believe he had shafted them in deals where he was supposed to be representing them but turned out he was representing himself, and of his vulnerability to banks and creditors who liked nothing better than having a politician beholden to them.

Adrian Delia's campaign for leadership made Daphne Caruana Galizia its chief antagonist, perhaps sharing pride of place with Simon Busuttil who, in any case, had already resigned the party leadership. The PL narrative – that Daphne Caruana Galizia presided over a coven of puppets in the PN whom she controlled and inevitably drove to destruction at the hands of popular justice – was adopted wholesale by Adrian Delia.

In one dramatic speech at a campaign event, Adrian Delia gave an unhinged performance that has remained imprinted in people's memory as a turning point. This was when lines were drawn within the PN and support for the soon-to-be PN leader and respect for Daphne Caruana Galizia would become entirely irreconcilable.

Delia shrilly described Daphne Caruana Galizia as a '*bicca blogger*' (a two-bit blogger) and the PN needed to be rid of her. The choice of the description was not accidental.

In a previous lawsuit, Pawlu Lia, a lawyer for the PL had argued that a post written by a blogger did not amount to journalism and its author was not entitled to the protections afforded to journalists. The defendant in that case was Daphne Caruana Galizia.

The term 'blogger' was thrown in the same cauldron of deceit and witchcraft that Daphne Caruana Galizia had brewed in the service of the PN and was now using against the promised leader. He would cleanse the party of her, he claimed.

He accompanied his aggressive response with action. Over the next six days, he filed five libel suits against Daphne, exposing her to a liability of €55,000 and presumably hoping that at some point she would give up.

She did not. Daphne Caruana Galizia did not let lawsuits slow her down. At one point, Silvio Debono, a hotelier and PL funder, filed 19 libel suits against Daphne over a single article she had written criticising the government for granting him a prime site of public land on which to build luxury apartments. That was a libel suit for each sentence he found problematic. At the time of writing all 19 cases – a maximum liability of €210,000 (excluding court and legal expenses) which Daphne's husband and children have inherited – are still ongoing and, significantly, under Adrian Delia's leadership, the PN is a habitual user of Silvio Debono's venues for its social events.

That heat and confrontation attracts the wrong sort of people to politics. Adrian Delia surrounded himself with a small vigilante crew of thugs, some of whom were known to police for association with street crime.

Daphne identified some of those people, and connected the support Adrian Delia was enjoying with thugs often seen in the company of the Labour government's Economy Minister Chris Cardona.

That connection proved to be more than a mere coincidence. The Soho brothel business connected Chris Cardona (PL) to Adrian Delia (PN).

The brothel was at 52, Greek Street, London W1. It was registered in the name of a Bahamas company called Healey Properties Limited in order to create a further degree of separation between the prostitution and human trafficking rackets and the landlords who cashed the proceeds from the activity.

Up to December 2003, Cardona and Delia were both practising lawyers and directors of Healey Properties. They resigned their directorships in a letter signed only by Adrian Delia on behalf of both of them.

When that detail became public, the PN old guard felt vindicated in their suspicion that Adrian Delia's election to the PN leadership served the PL's interests better than those of the Nationalist Party that Adrian Delia was seeking to lead.

Consistent polling and election results since September 2017 showed that an element of traditional core support was now withholding its backing from the PN. And no new inroads were being made among people who had voted PL. The PN was further from an electoral victory than it had been since the Second World War.

On the eve of the leadership election, the PN ethics committee reported that Adrian Delia had failed to answer questions about his past dodgy dealings, particularly in connection with the laundering of proceeds from prostitution. Reacting to that report, Simon Busuttil's final act as party leader was to publicly call for Adrian Delia to withdraw his candidature. He did not.

On 17 September 2017, Adrian Delia assumed office as leader of the PN. A loyal MP would resign his seat in Parliament a few days later to allow for the co-option of Adrian Delia so that he could assume office as leader of the opposition.

Writing on the day of his election, Daphne Caruana Galizia said 'overnight, that 36,000-vote gap between the parties has shot to at least 60,000'. The figure was not the product of a poll but her estimation of the portion of the PN that voted for the party not out of tribal loyalty but simply because it had been more decent than the PL.

On 10 October, she headlined a post: 'I wasn't far wrong when I wrote on 17th September that the 36,000-vote gap had shot up to 60,000'.

I had no surveys to work off but only years of experience in writing about Maltese political behaviour and an obvious understanding of how a big chunk of the Nationalist Party's core support thinks. My own views are not at all unusual, as those who would undermine me seek to make out. They are actually pretty typical of a great, big, key category of electors and that's exactly why I have the readership I do: I understand my audience and the fact that I am one of them.

I had spent the past few weeks writing about how the Nationalist Party would be scripting its suicide note by making Delia its leader, not only because he himself is a knave but, crucially, because when the party allows itself to be hijacked by anybody walking in from the outside, it looks weak, vulnerable, and structurally disorganised. And that means people won't feel safe trusting it to run the country.

Two days ago, Malta Today *published a survey that shows how the vote-gap between the two political parties has actually doubled, from 36,000 to 73,000. My instinctive understanding on the day of Delia's election that the gap had shot to 60,000 had been correct – probably because it was not 'instinct' at all but a real understanding of how the people for whom I write actually think, for no other reason than that I am like they are.*

Six days later Daphne Caruana Galizia was assassinated. News of her killing was on the radio around 3.30pm that Monday afternoon. Adrian Delia was being driven home from the office. When the news came out, he told his driver to take him back to PN headquarters and called a friend, a medical doctor, to meet him there.

When he arrived and walked into the lobby of the building, he said he was feeling unwell and swooned on the nearest couch.

He had been party leader for a month and the '*bicċa blogger*' that dominated his electoral campaign had just been killed. He must have realised that the rest of his term would be overshadowed by her murder.

THE MAFIA DENIES
ANY WRONGDOING

One year after Malta's then Nationalist government launched the first online gambling legislation in the European Union in 2004, the Casalesi clan of the 'Gomorra', the organised crime syndicate in the southern Italian region of Campania, decided to invest their capital on the island.

At around that time, the Italian police tapped a call between Nino Rotolo, a Palermo Mafia boss, and Antonino Cinà, a Corleone doctor and 'man of honour' or made man. Cinà had looked after Totò Riina and Bernardo Provenzano, the *Capi di tutti i Capi*, the bosses of all bosses, of the Cosa Nostra, that is the Sicilian Mafia, during their decades on the run from the law.

'Nino,' Rotolo said. 'You see that people are fasting, but they have to play.' That Mafioso circumlocution meant that dirty money needed laundering and a way to do so needed to be found. The fast would be broken by cleaning up dirty money through online betting. Rotolo spoke about where the bets would be laid: Malta, that strip of land close to Italy was the obvious candidate for a Mafia safe haven.

Fifteen years later, Rotolo's prescience proved correct and his vision was fully realised. The island hosts 300 virtual casinos and boasts the highest concentration in Europe of gambling operators domiciled in a single country. Gambling generates revenues of €1.2 billion a year and contributes 12% of Malta's GDP.

Italian criminal organizations – all of them, without exception – hopped aboard that train, making Malta their main money laundering hub in the heart of the Mediterranean. The Italian parliament's Anti-Mafia Investigative Directorate reported every six months since 2015 its estimate that hundreds of millions of euro had been washed of blood and mud in the Malta laundromat.

It works like this. Anyone obtaining a licence in Malta for online gambling can operate throughout the European Union, provided they can show where the money is coming from and how the winnings and losses flow.

Gamblers must register by creating their own profile on the betting site and provide credit card details to pay for bets and collect winnings. If you always know who's playing, the game is clean.

Sicily's Cosa Nostra, the 'Ndrangheta based in Calabria, and the Camorra of Campania set out to find ways of cheating the system.

Dozens of betting shops, often appropriately authorised by the Italian gambling regulator Monopoli to collect bets, opened all over Italy. Authorised by Monopoli, but not necessarily licensed by them, because many used computer terminals with games on websites licensed in Malta. These shops accepted gamblers with cash, dodging the traceability requirement.

Sometimes the criminal organisation itself operates the betting shop. The 'gambler' belongs to the same family. Any winnings come with a receipt from the gaming shop and therefore perfectly clean. Any losses go to the bank operated by the casino, low Maltese taxes are paid, and the now clean money is in possession of the owner of the Malta gaming license. Win or lose, they win.

The Mafia thus become the collectors of an unstoppable flow of money which at that point is anonymous and therefore laundered of its shady or bloody origins.

If something goes wrong, such as when the island's regulatory authorities suspend a license, although this rarely happens, the business changes hands from one family to another; from one nominee to another; in some cases, from one criminal organisation to another: from the Calabrians to the Sicilians, or to the Neapolitans and vice versa.

This is a powerful 'cartel' where the Italian Pax Mafiosa is guaranteed by a common interest in a money laundering system that is unmatched anywhere in the Mediterranean and the entire Schengen area. It is efficient and, above all, it can steady itself quickly whenever it hits a snag.

Between 2014 and 2018, anti-Mafia district prosecutors in Sicily, Calabria, and Campania, investigated illegal online gambling controlled by the three most deeply rooted and powerful Italian Mafia organisations – the Cosa Nostra, the 'Ndrangheta, and the Camorra.

The Mafiosi flew to Valletta and inspected the casinos. There, they mingled with the island's opaque system of relationships that blurs the lines between the incumbents of the palaces of political power on the one hand and the ruthless local entrepreneurs who prefer to ignore or pretend not to know who their Italian customers really are and where their money really comes from.

Some history.

2014: Ciro Smiraglia, believed to be money-launderer-in-chief of the Camorra's Zaza-Mazzarella clan, turned to the Fidanzati clan from Sicily's Cosa Nostra asking for an introduction to a Maltese 'contact'. He wanted to set up a server on the island on which to start a platform for online betting. 'You're on to the golden eggs,' Gaetano Fidanzati reassures him. That's Sicilian slang for 'you're on the money'.

Court documents show Fidanzati gave Smiraglia an important Maltese name: Bastjan Dalli, brother of John Dalli, the notorious 'Johnny Cash'.

'Tell him you're my brother and my friend,' he recommended.

April 2015: Vincenzo 'Enzo' Romeo, nephew of the legendary Catania boss of Cosa Nostra Nitto Santapaola, is on the ferry that connects the port of Pozzallo at the southern tip of Sicily to Malta in 90 minutes. He has €38,000 in cash in his suitcase and a name and address on the island to look for. He will be meeting Massimo Laganà from Messina, a guy who has left Italy to dodge an inquiry into his relations with the Casalesi crime gang of Casal Di Principe.

In Malta he has become the point of reference at the Portomaso casino tables and a business partner in Planetwin365, one of the most well-known online gaming brands in Europe.

Enzo Romeo needs Massimo Laganà to open gambling platforms registered in Malta to bring together the money that the Cosa Nostra clan illegally collects in the betting centres it controls between Catania and Messina.

2016: 'Ndrangheta boss Mario Gennaro, then 42 years old, turns informant and state witness. He informed anti-Mafia prosecutors in Reggio Calabria he had been the manager and investor for the top criminals in that city, laundering money through online gaming in Malta. Gennaro testified he laundered money through a network of about 20 Maltese law firms.

Mario Gennaro was the beneficial owner of a company shielded behind ownership in trust in another Maltese company called GVM Holdings, at the time headed by lawyer David Gonzi, son of former prime minister Lawrence Gonzi, the man who had opened the island to gaming back in 2004. The Reggio judiciary closed the case looking into David Gonzi's conduct, citing lack of evidence. GVM appears to have ceased its activities in 2015.

November 2017: Law enforcement officers in Florence shut down 14 gaming halls in North Italian towns used by organised crime to launder money through Malta-based Media Live Casino. Italian authorities publicly complain of the ineffectual cooperation of their Maltese counterparts.

Between 2018 and February 2019, Sicilian prosecutors unravelled another link between Sicilian organised crime and gambling in Malta. Three Sicilian towns have a heavy Cosa Nostra presence: Partinico, Resuttana, and Mazzara del Vallo.

The crime syndicates support Calogero 'John' Luppino, a bookmaker in Sicily working for Leaderbet, a brand owned by Malta-based gaming company LB Casino. The money he makes for them pays for the cost of hiding Matteo Messina Denaro, the most wanted Mafioso in Italy who took over the Cosa Nostra after the Corleonesi lost control. He has gone to ground but is still running the show.

In February 2018 Sicilian police arrested Benedetto 'Nini' Bacchi, known as the 'King of Slot Machines'. He ran an operation of some 700 outlets generating €1 million a month which were laundered in Malta, again through GVM Holdings. The laundered money would then be recycled in construction projects.

The responsibility to oversee all this belongs to the Malta Gaming Authority (MGA), the regulatory authority for a billion-dollar betting business. Unless suspects are arrested by overseas law enforcement and often even after that, the MGA appears oblivious to what is happening under its nose.

The criminal element harms the rest of the industry and perfectly legitimate gaming giants that operate entirely within the law resent the influx of mafia money that poisons the industry and puts it in mortal reputational danger.

Occasionally, a licence is revoked. It happened with Leaderbet. Media Live Casino was also shut down and in March 2018 at least five Italian gaming companies left Malta of their own accord fearing a clampdown.

But what flows must ebb again and the Mafia finds its way back in.

Consider, for example, the case of Anthony 'Tony' Axisa. He was one of the pioneers of gaming in Malta and helped draw up the initial legal framework. Up until 2006, he worked as a regulator at the MGA.

Then he decided to put his knowledge of regulation to the service of the regulated. He left the MGA and proceeded to register dozens of online gambling companies and brands. Among these, Bet1128, which the anti-Mafia district attorney of Catanzaro said was an instrument used by organised crime to recycle its money.

Prosecutors say the beneficial owner of Bet1128 was Francesco Martiradonna, son of Vitino 'l'Enel', a gentleman from Bari arrested in 2017 and accused of going into business with the feared 'Ndrangheta clan of the Arena from Capo Rizzuto. Martiradonna placed Bet1128 at the service of the Arena. L'Enel had previously been convicted of associating with the Mafia.

Bet1128 was originally registered in the UK. It was transferred from London to Gżira in Malta in 2009 when the Bari authorities asked London police to seize the business and suspend the licence of Bet1128. The brand found haven in Malta. It was bought by Centurionbet, administered by former law enforcer Tony Axisa but held by trust companies in a Caribbean tax haven.

What happened next is just what you would expect. Bet1128 continued to do business in the EU, but the name of Francesco Martiradonna simply vanished into thin air.

Investigators of the Crotone economic crimes police found that his name may have vanished but Martiradonna is no less real and no less busy. In spite of his name appearing nowhere, he never stopped dealing with Bet1128. Martiradonna manages contacts in Malta. He collects cash receipts and travels to close deals with clients who need a fast laundry service for their dirty cash.

Clients such as the Arena clan from the Capo Rizzuto island use Bet1128 to fix bets and control their rate of return from the betting shops. In 2017, investigators in Catanzaro cracked open the scam and put Martiradonna in handcuffs. That's when the Malta Gaming Authority suspended all licences issued to Centurionbet, including the now notorious Bet1128.

The licence is suspended. But what happens to the Mafia's money stashed and laundered through Bet1128? The Maltese authorities did not even respond to the Italians' request for a preliminary seizure of the company's assets. It is not an unfamiliar problem for Italian enforcement authorities. Italy equips its law enforcement agencies and its judges with specific powers governing 'association with the Mafia'. This allows for seizure of assets even before proceedings against suspects start. There is no equivalent under Maltese law, or indeed the laws of just about anywhere else.

The Catanzaro prosecutors already saw Bet1128 slip through their fingers when they tried and failed to catch the perpetrators when it was licensed in London. The brand had bounced to Malta. It looked like it could bounce elsewhere once again.

Nicola Gratteri, the Catanzaro prosecutor, was furious: 'It's easier to work with the police in Colombia or Peru than to work with Malta.' He was complaining to the Italian parliament's anti-mafia commission. 'If Malta decides not to help us out or takes six months to a year to get down to business, all our work would be useless.'

In 2018, Malta's attorney general Peter Grech said he'd carried out what his Catanzaro colleague asked for. A year later the Catanzaro prosecutor's office has still not had any formal notification that this is indeed the case.

While cross-border law enforcement creeps along at a snail's pace, cross-border crime gallops ahead. Centurionbet is no longer at 11, Triq Tas-Sliema, Ġżira, Malta. A physical check in December 2017 showed Centurionbet had disappeared. In its place there is another gaming start-up. A former manager of Bet1128, who had worked with Martiradonna, still works at the same address but he is now working in a 'new' business, Ivy Net Ltd, offering cryptocurrency payments systems.

'Crypto' is Joseph Muscat's new roll of the dice.

Daphne did not miss the murky soup of corruption, collusion, and money-laundering that online gaming had cooked. The industry added a new toxic ingredient to the unhealthy quality of Malta's political and entrepreneurial life. As gaming became a 'fundamental pillar' of Malta's economy, the toxicity only got worse.

From Daphne's blog, writing on 25 June 2015:

While his father was Acting Commissioner of Police, Daniel Zammit – who was then a police inspector with the Economic Crimes Unit and who is in the news right now on other corruption issues – was constantly seen driving about the island in a Ferrari F12 Berlinetta, with foreign registration plates SU128A.

This car belongs to a Sicilian called Francesco Airo, who operates in 'online gaming'. I put the words 'online gaming' in inverted commas because internet gaming is huge in the laundering of Italian Mafia money. When Italy began to clamp down, the laundering operations began moving out and into Malta.

The Malta-based fixer for one Naples Camorra family is Bastjan Dalli, brother of the former European Commissioner John Dalli. Last year I had published an Italian news report which details how Bastjan Dalli's name came up in telephone conversations between two Camorra men. The conversations were tapped and recorded as part of a judicial investigation.

Daniel Zammit's duties in the Economic Crimes Unit included investigations into the gaming industry. And an Italian man operating in the gaming industry in Malta loaned him a €300,000 car for his personal use. But il-papà (daddy) was the Acting Commissioner of Police and il-kuġin (cousin) Manuel was the Police Minister, so let corruption rule.

Daphne again writes on the subject on 29 April 2016, when Joseph Muscat entrusts Manuel Mallia with the ministry responsible for the gaming industry. The Panama Papers had just been published and Konrad Mizzi was forced to resign the deputy leadership of the PL which he had only held for a month:

Using the path cleared for him by default by Muscat's changing of the rules to accommodate his henchman Konrad Mizzi, Chris Cardona is the first to throw his hat in the ring to replace the corrupt non-contender (as Labour Deputy Leader).

It can't be more obvious now why Muscat asked Mizzi to give up the deputy leadership but kept him on in the cabinet (should I be worried that I can read their behaviour?): they struck a deal.

Cardona consented to let go of part of his portfolio – the part that José Herrera (brother of Magistrate Consuelo Scerri Herrera) looked after as his parliamentary secretary for 'competitiveness', which includes remote gaming and casinos – in return for Muscat making him party deputy leader. This has allowed Muscat to give Manuel Mallia what he wanted: the ministry responsible for online and land-based gaming, which has untold possibilities for a sleazebag who is ultra-familiar with the criminal underworld and who thinks nothing of saying that he keeps half-a-million in cash at home.

The Cosa Nostra denies any wrongdoing.

The Camorra denies any wrongdoing.

The 'Ndrangheta denies any wrongdoing.

It is one of the countless lists of coincidences that litter the path to Daphne's killing that a character that features prominently elsewhere in this drama on pages about secret companies and unexplained payments, also moves in the world of online gaming. That would be Yorgen Fenech, the owner of 17 Black.

Planetwin365 is closely embroiled with The Casino at Portomaso, a physical gambling casino owned and operated by the Tumas Group, of which Yorgen Fenech is CEO and one of the owners. That's the online gaming service that Enzo Romeo from the Catania clan of Santapaola with the help of Massimo Laganà had infiltrated to launder money for the east Sicilian crime syndicate.

Massimo Laganà works for both Planetwin365 and The Casino at Portomaso. Planetwin365's 'live casino' is broadcast from within Yorgen Fenech's casino as well.

In her writings, Daphne makes no mention of Yorgen Fenech's gaming business. It is also below the radar of Maltese public awareness. That's until February 2019 when Swedish gaming regulators discover that out of 67 online gaming companies authorised to do business in Sweden, 51 – almost all of them – have registered offices in Malta. They also discover that four of the 51 have been banned from Norway for repeated breaches of the law. In 2017 Norway froze funds being transferred to these four companies in Malta worth more than €51 million.

The Swedish authorities find something else. One of these four companies was L&L Europe Limited. That company is co-owned by Yorgen Fenech.

Online gaming. Mafia money. Yorgen Fenech. There are a lot of steps here and it would be wrong to jump to conclusions, especially in the context of Daphne's killing.

And yet, there's one more link between Yorgen Fenech's casino business and the murder of October 2017.

Alfred Degiorgio is, of course, one of the three men accused of murdering Daphne Caruana Galizia by car bomb. He's also been charged and is being tried for money-laundering, along with his brother George Degiorgio and George's partner, Anca Adelina Pop. In September 2018, a court heard witnesses from a number of Maltese casinos set out how much business they had done with all three. It was clear that neither George Degiorgio nor Pop were heavy gamblers. But Alfred Degiorgio had been a very successful high roller indeed, according to evidence relating to the time period up to 2013.

And that's a little odd because in casinos, more times than not, you lose.

Fools Die was Mario Puzo's favourite novel. In it Alfred Gronevelt, the boss of his fictional casino in Las Vegas, says: 'Percentages never lie. We built all these hotels on percentages. We stay rich on the percentage. You can lose faith in everything, religion and God, women and love, good and evil, war and peace. You name it. But the percentage will always stand fast.'

Mathematically, the made-up casino boss was on the money. Bob Hannum, professor of risk analysis and gaming at the University of Denver where he teaches courses in probability, statistics, risk, and the theory of gambling, has written: 'With a few notable exceptions, the house always wins – in the long run – because of the mathematical advantage the casino enjoys over the player.'

The court heard that Alfred Degiorgio had gambled €570,000 over the years, losing €71,000. Alfred is a very, very, very lucky gambler indeed. The court heard that he had bet €39,000 in three years at the Dragonara Casino, losing €18,000. That's roughly slightly less than half his total stake. At Casino Malta, Alfred had gambled €34,000 and lost around €6,000. So his luck was even better there.

At the Oracle Casino Alfred Degiorgio, had gambled over €40,000 and lost €31,000. That was where his luck was worst. But at the Portomaso casino the court heard that he gambled more than €457,000 and lost €16,000. So he managed to walk away from the casino with €440,000 of certified clean money.

That kind of luck is incredible.

Who owns the Portomaso casino? Yorgen Fenech, the owner of 17 Black, a shell company in Dubai, and one of the parties to the Electrogas Consortium. As Pieter Omtzigt reported for the Council of Europe, 17 Black 'was expected to make large monthly payments to secret Panama companies owned by (Konrad) Mizzi and (Keith) Schembri'.

One should also point that Yorgen Fenech also owns the Oracle casino where Alfred Degiorgio lost money. But the money he lost at Oracle, €31,000, is dwarfed by the sum he walked away with at the Portomaso, €444,000.

The puzzle deepens when you know that Alfred Degiorgio was registered as unemployed and claiming benefits. How could he be on the dole and being able to risk close to a half-a-million euro in a casino, eh?

That is not incredible. That is impossible.

As Sherlock Holmes once said: 'When you have eliminated the impossible, whatever remains, however improbable, must be the truth.'

So one has to search for other, different explanations for the known facts. One would be that the owner of the casino deliberately looked the other way, that a man 'known to the police' who was unemployed was spending close to half-a-million euro on a casino. That would suggest money-laundering on a massive scale. Or, a second possibility, that the gambling was a cloak and that all or much of the money was actually payment for service or services to Alfred Degiorgio. A third possibility marries one and two: that Alfred was both money-laundering and being paid off.

We wrote to Mr Fenech and a lawyer on his behalf replied denying any wrongdoing. The lawyer suggested that the authors may be implying that Mr Fenech and his company, the Tumas Group, had 'some form of association in illicit activity by the Tumas Group with third parties.' Mr Fenech's lawyer continued:

Any statement, suggestions, and/or insinuation to that effect is entirely baseless, gratuitous, and speculative and is herewith rejected in the strongest manner possible as totally unfounded both in fact and at law.

The authors wrote back asking Mr Fenech's lawyer to explain why the casino allowed an unemployed man to walk out with €444,000 from his Portomaso casino, whether the casino tried to investigate the provenance of the money he walked into the casino with, and whether, in fact, the money was in reality a cloak for a payment from Mr Fenech to Mr Degiorgio.

The lawyer replied:

We refer you to the evidence tendered by a representative of the casinos operated by Tumas Group in July 2018 in the ongoing proceedings before the criminal court against Alfred Degiorgio and others relating to money laundering charges, which evidence had clearly established that Alfred Degiorgio's last visit to the said casinos goes back to 2012 in the case of one casino and 2013 in the case of the second casino. Consequently, the inferences and insinuations made in your last paragraph are so spurious, false, and contrived that they do not merit any consideration whatsoever.

The full set of communications from Mr Fenech's lawyers is shown in the annex to this book.

The four- or five-year gap in time between Alfred Degiorgio's last swing at the Portomaso roulette and the assassination of Daphne Caruana Galizia would, on the face of it, discount the possibility that Alfred Degiorgio was being compensated for his alleged involvement in that murder through cash collected from the casino.

But that time gap does not dilute the evidence that suggests that Yorgen Fenech's casino was willing to allow an unemployed person to wager close to half-a-million euro and walk away with most of it. That suggests there was or there had been a relationship between the two. Nothing more.

Once again, Alfred Degiorgio, his brother George Degiorgio, and Yorgen Fenech, in fact all concerned, deny any wrongdoing.

ROBBING LIBYA

Forty-eight hours after the killing of Daphne Caruana Galizia, on the small Italian island of Lampedusa, Catania law enforcement arrested a Maltese citizen on fuel smuggling charges. His name was Darren Debono.

Even before his arrest, Darren Debono was well-known in Malta. He had a great run with Malta's national football team and was a star of the Valletta Football Club. He also operated a restaurant on the Valletta waterfront, "Scoglitti", across from the Sliema ferry terminal. His restaurant was a favourite haunt of Malta's upper crust: ministers, MPs, professionals, bankers, iGaming executives. (Co-author Manuel Delia also ate there a few times.)

But Darren Debono's wealth was not made from footballing or catering. His money came from the sea and it was not caught in fishing nets. Not anymore, anyway.

Darren Debono went into the fishing business around the turn of the century. He started with a fleet of five boats – four trawlers and a service boat – berthed at Malta's fishing harbour of Marsaxlokk. He must have quickly realised that it takes a long time to become rich from fishing. Even if you go into business with the Sicilian fisheries Mafia of Acireale, which Darren Debono did.

As luck would have it – if luck is the right word – Mu'ammar Ghaddafi was shot after being dragged out of hiding in 2011. Libya fell into the abyss of an unending civil war and out of the chaos came Darren Debono's opportunity.

Debono crossed paths with a Libyan militiaman, Fahmi Ben Khalifa. He was the smuggling king of Zuwara, a north-eastern Libyan city and clearing house for the trafficking of two commodities: humans and fuel.

People were smuggled through Zuwara on their way to the Italian coast. Some 30% to 40% of the fuel pumped out of the refineries of the old Jamahiriya was siphoned through the same route.

Ben Khalifa and his militia's job was to oversee the security of the Zuwara refineries. That placed them in the best position to rob them. All they needed was an organisation that could transport the diesel to the buyers. Darren Debono's fleet fitted the bill.

Debono abandoned the fishing business and crammed his boats with fuel drums. Business was good. In no time his fleet grew to include two 60-metre fuel tankers – *Basbosa Star* and *Sea Master X* – big enough to increase volumes but still small enough to anchor at Hurd's Bank, the shallow bank 16 miles south-east of Malta where fuel coming from Libya is then pumped ship-to-ship onto the buyers' tankers.

But, without the proper certification, fuel drums on a fishing boat could very well be stolen goods. They'd never make it through customs. Enter another Maltese citizen: Gordon Debono, unrelated to Darren but with whom he shared more than a surname. They both loved a quick buck. He owned or controlled at least 20 companies with businesses ranging from real estate to yachting and motoring. But, more pertinently, he also owned a fuel trading company – Petroplus Ltd – that agreed to launder Darren Debono's smuggled fuel with some elegantly forged certificates.

Darren Debono and Ben Khalifa now had paperwork that said the Libyan fuel they were transporting was actually from Saudi Arabia, which, of course, it was not.

In Malta that sort of conjuring trick is child's play. Even beach pebbles had realised that a considerable chunk of the island's fishing fleet had switched from fish to fuel. And even beach pebbles preferred to look away.

If the paperwork looks right, no one, it seems, will ask questions.

Six kilometres from Valletta, at the office of the Libyan-Maltese Chamber of Commerce, it was possible to regularise anything exported from Libya to Malta on the back of a simple self-declaration of the points of origin and destination. It did not matter if your declaration was true or false; it was not the Chamber's job to check your claim. That was the arrangement designed by the Maltese authorities. The opportunity for misuse was glaring.

Job done. Fuel smuggled from Zuwara could now be transported with documents saying it came from Saudi Arabia and from Hurd's Bank it would be taken to Sicilian or Turkish harbours where it would be sold for stratospheric profits.

On the back of a single Italian buyer, the gang made €26 million in profits.

The fleet grew again. The *Vassilios XXI*, the *Santa Pawlina*, the *Portoria,* and the *Haci Telli* were added to this new maritime empire. In 2016, at the peak of the Debonos' and Ben Khalifa's huge swindle, they bought the *Temeteron*, an enormous oil tanker 110 metres long.

Gordon Debono purchased the *Temeteron* in partnership with Roderick Grech, another Maltese trader, who in the past had acquired experience in trafficking between grey Turkish, Russian, and Libyan markets.

But by the time the *Temeteron* joined the fleet, business had dried up. The partners fell out: Darren Debono and Ben Khalifa on one side, Gordon Debono and Roderick Grech on the other.

By autumn 2017 investigators in the Catania police and the Italian economic crimes agency had cracked the racket and both Debonos and Ben Khalifa ended up in handcuffs.

Darren Debono's arrest in Italy so soon after Daphne Caruana Galizia's murder created more than a little confusion. Not least because the government spokespeople that handled the tsunami of requests for information from press from all over the world, particularly the Italian press, hinted that Daphne's death was related to fuel smuggling.

Daphne had written about fuel smuggling. She had written about a whole lot more, but fuel smuggling was one way to distract journalists and prevent them from going down much more politically inconvenient paths. One would assume there would be some political fall-out from the assassination of a journalist in a democratic country. But if the murder could be pinned on some criminal conspiracy, politicians could avoid the heat.

There were two 'bases' for the PL government's spin. The first was that Daphne's killing was Mafia-style: a car bomb like all the ones used to kill or maim fuel smugglers with outstanding debts. The second was that preliminary analyses showed that the explosive used in Bidnija was likely Libyan army issue.

The past is the mirror for the present, they argued.

1 June 2014: Darren Degabriele was killed by a car bomb, detonated while he drove from Marsaxlokk to Żejtun.

16 June 2016: Martin Cachia was killed on the spot when a bomb exploded inside the Alfa Romeo he was driving to Marsaskala.

26 September 2016: A bomb studded with screws and ball-bearings exploded inside a van on Triq Aldo Moro in Marsa, seriously injuring its driver Josef Cassar.

31 October 2016: John Camilleri, known as *Ġanni tas-Sapun*, was killed when his Mitsubishi Pajero exploded in Triq Paderborn in San Pawl il-Baħar.

20 February 2017: Romeo Bone lost both legs in an explosion on Triq Marina in Msida.

29 June 2017: A car driven by Victor Calleja known as *iċ-Ċippu*, was blown up in Marsa.

The arrest of Darren Debono. Daphne. Maltese fuel smuggling of Libyan oil. From the web of possible motives, a single thread was pulled, leading public impression down a path it would have found difficult to imagine otherwise. There are very few degrees of separation between the underworld and above ground in Malta.

To realise just how short the chain is, here is an excerpt from Daphne's blog posted on 31 October 2016:

A man – John Camilleri, 67, known as Giovanni tas-Sapun, *of St Paul's Bay – has been killed in a car-bomb explosion in Buġibba. I woke to the sound of sirens blasting down Burmarrad hill and they didn't stop for half-an-hour. A major traffic accident perhaps, but there hasn't been one on that stretch of road for years, not since it was remade.*

And then the news: another bomb in another car and another man dead. And I thought, there goes another diesel smuggler. Because the discernible pattern in criminal assassinations over the last few years in Malta is that diesel smugglers are blown up by bombs in their cars, and drug smugglers are shot dead by hired hitmen.

And everybody pretends there's no pattern. The diesel smugglers are described as 'fishermen' or 'restaurateurs', and the drug smugglers are called long-distance lorry drivers or hauliers, or 'unemployed family men' or 'businessmen', though some of them are occasionally described as 'known to the police'.

There was one exception, last month: a haulier who was blown up by a car bomb rather than shot. But then the bomb was different to the ones used for diesel smugglers: it was packed with tacks, nails, and ball-bearings and didn't kill him, but led to his legs being amputated.

Today's dead man, too, is a 'businessman' who is 'known to the police'. The legitimate side of his business is tiles and bathroom fittings.

The National Statistics Office, in figures released five days ago, says that it calculates 'prostitution and illegal drugs' as making for €17.1 million of Malta's gross domestic product last year. Quite frankly, I think that's a conservative estimate.

Shortly after she published her post, there was a reaction. Daphne received a call with more information. She posted again:

This morning when I woke to the news that another man has been blown up by a bomb in his car, I wrote about an emerging pattern in which diesel-smugglers are blown up by bombs in their car while drug-traffickers are shot by hit-men.

There was one exception, last month, I wrote, a haulier who was blown up by a car bomb rather than shot. But then the bomb was different to the ones used for diesel smugglers: it was packed with tacks, nails, and ball-bearings and didn't kill him, but led to his legs being amputated. But I've now discovered that it was not an exception at all.

I am informed that the man in question, Josef Cassar, was also a diesel smuggler, and that he is linked to the MV Silverking, *a vessel owned by Silver*

King Ltd, whose only shareholders are Pierre Darmanin, black sheep of the well-respected Tan-Niksu family of Żurrieq, and his estranged wife Annabelle. The vessel was impounded by Customs three years ago and Darmanin was named in a police/customs investigation into a diesel-smuggling ring. Darmanin, who owns Darmanin Fisheries Ltd, had left his family for the Labour Party's Equal Opportunities Officer, Rachel Tua, and fathered a child by her.

When Martin Cachia, a notorious criminal and diesel-smuggler, was blown up by a bomb in his car last January, Malta Today *reported that it had seen a letter, signed by Pierre Darmanin and dated only four weeks earlier, asking 'an unspecified recipient to permit Cachia to travel with him to Egypt'.*

***UPDATE**/Pierre Darmanin has now contacted this website to say that his company has sold the MV* Silverking *when it was released from impound three years ago, but he doesn't remember to whom he sold it, though he thinks it was to a company owned by a certain Tony. He says that he was not charged with diesel-smuggling (he was investigated). When asked about his written request that Martin Cachia, who was murdered four weeks later, travel with him to Egypt, Darmanin said: 'My signature was forged. Martin used to do things like that.' When asked why a diesel-smuggler forging a travel request would pick out his name of all people's, Darmanin said: 'Those of us who own ships (vapuri) all know each other.'*

Smuggling diesel from Libya to Malta and Italy is a highly lucrative trade organised by networks of criminals in all three countries.

Officially Pierre Darmanin is a tuna fisherman. As Daphne wrote in her blog, he may have been suspected of smuggling but, if true, he has dodged the consequences. A boat he owns, the *Crystal Starlight*, was once impounded for cigarette smuggling. Nothing came of that either.

Co-author Manuel Delia briefly met Pierre Darmanin on a few occasions, a few years before Daphne Caruana Galizia was killed. Delia was a PN candidate in the constituency of Żurrieq in the 2013 elections. Darmanin lives in Żurrieq and attended a few public events held for that constituency campaign.

In December 2017, a few days after the suspected assassins were arrested in a hut on the Marsa waterfront, Manuel Delia visited the site of the arrest with a TV crew.

There he came across Pierre Darmanin who asked him to ensure the crew did not film him or his boats as any association with the arrests of the Degiorgios could damage his business.

Pierre Darmanin also told Manuel Delia he believed that one of the three suspects charged with Daphne Caruana Galizia's murder had had nothing to do with the case. He did not specify which one. Asked how he could be privy to such information, Pierre Darmanin again attributed his supposed knowledge to being plugged into the waterfront boat-owners network.

How could Pierre Darmanin rule out the responsibility of one of the three charged with Daphne's murder? The Degiorgios and Vincent Muscat deny killing Daphne. But the evidence pointing to their involvement in the murder is compelling. Does Darmanin perhaps know more about what the Degiorgios were doing? One thing is certain. Since the Degiorgios have been locked up, there have been no more explosions on the island. There have been attempted car bombs but none of them were successful.

Pending trials in Sicily, Darren Debono is back in circulation in Malta. A former football star who spent some time locked up for a multi-million euro smuggling racket cannot hide for long in an island of Malta's size. Which is why Darren Debono deals with that problem by staying firmly in plain sight. He is back on the football scene as a manager and has opened high-profile court cases against Malta's government to stop them taking away his money.

The Maltese authorities have asked the United Nations Security Council to issue sanctions against the Debonos and Ben Khalifa to get a hold on their profits from their smuggling years. That action has followed the initiative of the US who have blacklisted Darren Debono and marked his restaurant business for sanctions.

In court, Darren Debono's lawyers said US embassy staff asked him to give them information on Joseph Muscat and Keith Schembri in exchange for easing their sanctions. They also said Darren Debono fobbed off the Americans by telling them he would never spy on his prime minister.

A rare joint statement by the governments of the US and Malta dismissed the claim.

But interestingly, Darren Debono's lawyers did not say their client had nothing on Joseph Muscat and Keith Schembri. Rather, he implied that whatever he had on them he would not be telling the Americans.

Perhaps that was a message to Malta's prime minister and his chief of staff right there. Or perhaps not.

That is not all. A year after Daphne was killed, the murder investigation found that around the same time he called Daphne Caruana Galizia, Pierre Darmanin also called Alfred Degiorgio and Chris Cardona.

Was that a coincidence? Perhaps it was. Or perhaps not.

SEX, LIES, AND BURNER PHONES

On 30 January 2017, Daphne was having dinner with her stoic husband Peter. A gentle and thoughtful lawyer who loved his wife deeply, he felt that for the past few years Daphne's blog, *Running Commentary*, had taken over both their lives. She could not properly relax when on holiday, she could not go out very often because she was so dedicated to the blog. Every now and then he chided her over her obsession with documenting the latest horrors of her island home. He was worried about the personal price she was paying: the risks, the threats, the hours and hours spent on the blog, the loss of normal life.

That evening was unforgettable because she received a text message and their dinner was ruined. She gobbled up her food as fast as she could and the couple headed home, where Daphne hit the keyboard running.

This is what she typed:

Malta's Minister for the Economy, Chris Cardona, is currently at a brothel in the German town of Velbert, near Düsseldorf. He is accompanied by another Maltese man, described as 'short and bald', who my source at the brothel was unable to identify.

Daphne explained that Cardona was in the FKK Acapulco brothel and that its clients had to pay an €80 entry fee before going with the lady of their choice. Go to the FKK Acapulco website and you will see that it advertises itself as a 'sauna club', with services including stripteases, go-go girls, and '30 fully air-conditioned top suites'. The photographs on its site leave little to the imagination. It's a knocking shop.

Daphne's source described Cardona emerging naked from the shower at around 8pm and barking out in Maltese: '*Haqq Alla kemm hu kiesah l-ilma*' ("By God, the water's cold"). To anyone who knows Chris Cardona, the vulgarity is authentic.

The next morning at 10.27am Daphne was able to flesh out some more of the story she headlined BROTHELGATE:

> *More details arrive from my source at the FKK Acapulco, a whorehouse in Velbert, a small town outside Duesseldorf, where events of interest took place last night ...*
>
> *The Minister for the Economy and his friend got to the whorehouse at around 7pm. They had a sauna and a (cold) shower and then headed straight for the bar. They chose a prostitute and the Minister's companion went into a room with her. After a while, the Minister for the Economy followed them into the same room for three-way sex and some voyeurism. They were at the whorehouse for three to four hours in total.*

At a quarter past noon, a fresh update: 'Cardona's naked prancing in a German brothel last night reveals him to have a tattoed shoulder.' She added some more detail about his accomplice who she still had not properly identified: 'This morning, this man's Facebook page suddenly disappeared off-line and my calls to him on his mobile phone have gone unanswered. I have sent him a message, saying: "This is Daphne Caruana Galizia, trying to reach you for comment." He has not rung or messaged back yet.'

At 2.54pm she posted a screenshot of a press release from the government, denying her story: 'The Minister for the Economy categorically denies allegations published in the blog of Daphne Caruana Galizia ... this outright lie ... Minister Cardona is currently in Germany to participate in the first Stake Holder Forum on the digitisation of European industry as a speaker on the invitation of the German Ministry for Economic Affairs.'

She ran Cardona's denial under the headline: 'What is worse, that a government minister goes to a brothel while on official business in Germany, or that he lies about it?'

That evening, at 7.10pm, there was more: 'BROTHELGATE: Why is Chris Cardona in Germany?' Daphne blogged:

> *Chris Cardona is in Germany as a guest of the German government. He was invited as a guest speaker at a 'Stakeholder Forum' organised by the European*

Commission and Germany's Federal Ministry for Economic Affairs and Energy. The conference is called Futurium: Implementing the Digitising European Industry Actions, and it is held in Essen today and tomorrow.

Cardona, listed in the programme as 'Dr Christian Cardona, Minister for the Economy, Investment, and Small Business, Malta', was scheduled to give a 15-minute keynote speech at 2pm today, called Digitising European Industry: the View of the Maltese Presidency. The Economy Minister is accompanied by Joe Gerada, who has a law practice with former Labour Party television employees Charlon Gouder and Jonathan Attard. Gerada who worked at Malta Investment Management Co Ltd, the state corporation which manages state-owned companies and investments, is on secondment to the Economy Minister's private secretariat, as a consultant.

Essen, where the conference is being held, is just half an hour by car from Velbert, where FKK Acapulco, the brothel he visited, is located. Incidentally, FKK stands for Freikoerperkultur, which means 'nudism'. FKK Acapulco means 'Acapulco Nudie Club'.

Daphne was like a machine. At 8.17pm she had confirmed, to her satisfaction, the identity of Cardona's pal:

The man with whom Economy Minister Chris Cardona spent several hours at a brothel in Velbert, Germany, last night is Joe Gerada, a lawyer who Cardona has put on the state payroll in his private secretariat as a 'consultant', and who has now been given the role and title of 'policy coordinator for the EU presidency'...

Joe Gerada took down his Facebook page early this morning, in what appears to be a self-protective move following the story I uploaded last night. I have been trying to ring him all day, but my calls and messages have gone unanswered. He has now barred my number so that my calls are automatically rejected.

Gerada went to FKK Acapulco, a brothel, at around 7pm with the Economy Minister yesterday evening. The two took a sauna and shower, then went to the bar, where they negotiated with one of the prostitutes. Gerada went with her into a room, and after a couple more drinks at the bar, Cardona followed them in. They left at around 10.30pm.

Later that evening a fresh astonishing development: 'BREAKING BROTHELGATE: The Economy Minister and his consultant went to the same brothel again today.' She blogged:

The Minister for the Economy, Chris Cardona, accompanied by his consultant and 'Malta EU Presidency policy coordinator' Joe Gerada, went to the same brothel, FKK Acapulco, this afternoon that they went to last night. Cardona was scheduled to speak at a conference in Essen, as a guest of the German government, shortly after 2pm today. By 4pm he was at the brothel in Velbert, which is around half-an-hour away by car. On entering, Cardona called out to his consultant and policy coordinator, 'Joe, Joe, minn hawn' ('Joe, Joe, this way'). The patron who went to the locker-room to message me about it at 4pm said they 'looked jolly and rather pissed, like they came from a drunken lunch'. He asked me not to upload the information until he and his companion had left the place at 5pm, at which point Cardona and Gerada were still there. This means I have no information on what time the Minister and his consultant left the brothel today.

Then Daphne added the following update:

It's just occurred to me that the Minister and his consultant wouldn't have gone back for sex this afternoon, but for negotiation on making sure their backs are covered, given that the story had broken and the Minister had issued a press release of denial.

That evening Daphne blogged that the opposition leader, Simon Busuttil, 'has said, quite rightly, that the story about the Economy Minister and the Velbert brothel has left people shocked and disgusted. True, but I also hear a far more dangerous sound: the sound of loud, mocking, contemptuous laughter. Contempt spells the beginning of the end or the very end itself in any human relationship, including that between elector and elected.'

At 11.03pm, her blog carried the headline: 'The drunken idiot is going to sue me when he knows full well that he was at the brothel and that all my details were correct.'

All three co-authors of this book have been threatened with libel many times and also sued for libel. None of us would have had the mad courage to react in this way. Daphne's contempt for her adversaries takes one's breath away.

She wrote:

The Minister for the Economy has said that he is going to sue me for libel. This is the standard response of the cornered Maltese politician, particularly in sex-and-corruption cases. And not just Maltese – think Jeffrey Archer, one of the most notorious cases in political history. Archer, too, sued a newspaper for libel for reporting that he went with a prostitute. He won half-a-million pounds in damages, bankrupted the newspaper, ruined the editor's career – and was later imprisoned for four years for perjury, because he really had gone with the prostitute and lied about it under oath.

Suing for libel, or just announcing that you are, is a way of dealing with the immediate pressure of public opinion and your political bosses. Sue for libel – and then we'll see …

These are the facts. The Minister for the Economy was at a brothel called FKK Acapulco in Velbert, 30 minutes from Essen, where he had been invited to address a conference, between 7pm and around 10.30pm last night, accompanied by his ministerial consultant Joe Gerada. They had a sauna, then a shower, then they went to the bar where they negotiated with a prostitute. Gerada went into a room with the prostitute, and after a couple of drinks, Cardona followed. All three of them were in the room together.

They were there at the same brothel again this afternoon at 4pm, but I don't know what time they left because my source left before they did. Nor do I have any information on what they did there today, unlike yesterday night. I suspect it wasn't sex but an attempt at getting hold of any video footage which will compromise them, and/or making sure that their backs are covered in other ways as journalists are now bound to start ringing for information.

At 11.14pm she blogged: 'Sadly for Chris Cardona, his consultant is the weakest link.' Her story ran:

The Minister for the Economy has been tweeting madly in between issuing press statements calling me 'the queen of fake news'. Too bad for him that his aide, who was with him at the brothel, is the weakest link. Joe Gerada disabled his Facebook account early this morning, presumably immediately after reading my first 'German brothel' report. I hadn't even mentioned him at that stage. I just wrote that the Minister was with a bald man who looks a lot like Neville Gafà, and that my source had in fact mistaken him for Gafà. Boom! Gerada's Facebook page disappeared. He then spent the entire day not answering my calls or messages, and eventually set his phone to reject my number. Was that because he wasn't at the brothel? No, it was because he was at the brothel.

Her last blog of the day was to run a series of photographs with captions sent in by her readers, none of them complimentary to Chris Cardona.

All concerned deny any wrongdoing. Neither Chris Cardona nor his aide, Joe Gerada, went to a brothel, they say.

When the economy minister hit back, he hit back hard. He and his aide brought four libel suits against Daphne. The maximum penalty under Maltese law is €11,000. But for the first time in Maltese legal history, they applied for and got four seizure orders against her in advance of the cases being heard to the value of €44,000. Effectively, they froze Daphne's bank account. She became reliant on her husband writing cheques for her. She would go to the bank roughly once a week and cash one of Peter's cheques and that is where she was going when she was killed.

But Daphne was no fool. She was confident that her source was telling her the truth. Her source was willing to testify in court if necessary but Daphne found a better way to get to the bottom of Brothelgate. The answer lay in an acronym, TAP, which stands for transferred account procedure.

Daphne set out her magic trick in a post on 8 May 2017:

The Minister for the Economy, Chris Cardona, this morning filed an objection – on the final day permissible at law – to my request to the Court for an order to the mobile telephony companies to preserve evidence showing, through his phone TAP records, where he was on the night of January 30. I know for a fact, because a man I know was right there at the same time and looking directly at Cardona and his person of trust Joe Gerada, that they were at the FKK Acapulco in Velbert, Germany. Cardona and his person of trust are claiming that they were in their hotel room and in the hotel neighbourhood. Cardona has also spoken about his proof that he was in the hotel: a minibar bill. If Cardona and Gerada really wanted to prove that they were not at the FKK Acapulco, but in the town where their hotel is located, then they would have no objection to an order by the Court for the preservation of their phone TAP records. On the contrary, they would welcome this creative and incontrovertible manner of proving their whereabouts. But they have objected. And they have done so because they were at the FKK Acapulco and are now trapped because they never anticipated that my defence team would think of using their phone TAP records to prove conclusively where they were that night.

Phone TAPs do not mean phone tapping. This is the system that the mobile telephony companies use for billing you when you use your phone while you are away from Malta. When your phone is 'roaming', each time you make a call or send a text message, the system records exactly where you are, so as to be able to bill you. These records, which are available only to the phone companies, are accurate down to the street, and in some cases even the street corner. But they will only come into play if you use your phone. If the Minister for the Economy and his person of trust used their phones even once and incurred roaming charges while they were at the FKK Acapulco, the records would show they were in that location in Velbert. That is why they are objecting: they probably did use their phones, or can't remember whether they did.

Daphne applied to the court to get the phone TAP records of Chris Cardona which would pin-point his geo-location at the time to the brothel in Velbert – as her source asserted – or to the hotel room half-an-hour's drive away in Essen which was where Cardona said he was that night. Cardona's lawyers tried to knock that application out but failed. The phone company handed over the records in a sealed envelope but their contents could not be revealed until a witness from the company took the stand and that would only happen after the plaintiff had set out his case.

By the time Daphne was murdered on 16 October the libel case had not been heard – only the legal argument over whether the court would get the phone TAP records. Shortly after she died, her husband and two of her sons, Matthew and Andrew, turned up in court to defend the libel suit. Remember, under Maltese law, death is no defence in a libel suit. But Chris Cardona did not turn up for this hearing or any other.

In May 2018 Cardona failed to turn up yet again. Chris Cardona's lawyer, Pawlu Lia, tried to fend off the consequences of that by complaining that not all respondents were attending court. Daphne's husband, Peter, came to all court sittings in place of his wife. But his sons were working abroad. Pawlu Lia said he would ask the court to summarily close the case and award damages to his client. The lawyer for the Caruana Galizia family, Joseph Zammit Maempel would have none of that. He was reported in *The Times of Malta* as saying: 'Wouldn't it be better if the applicant were to stop playing hide-and-seek and just turn up in court to declare whether he ever left his hotel?'

It was a good question. After some argy-bargy, the Caruana Galizia family lawyer requested the *'liberatorja'*. *The Times of Malta* reported that this is a procedure whereby if the plaintiff, in this case Dr Cardona, is a no-show then the defendant can strike out the case at the expense of the defaulting plaintiff. Later that year his aide, Joe Gerada, dropped his case.

That suggests, of course, that Daphne's story stands, that Malta's economy minister did indeed go to a brothel in Germany and have a threesome while supposedly on official business.

The real issue here is not that a government minister went to a brothel. Think of that what you will. But if Daphne's story is right – and Chris Cardona's behaviour in court after her request for TAP records strongly suggests it is – then for him to consider lying on oath is a very serious matter indeed. It would disqualify him from politics and lead to his disbarment.

To understand the next phase of the story, it's necessary to go back in time to a series of bank heists, taped phone calls, and a former Maltese copper who was in no sense a Dixon of Dock Green. David Gatt was kicked out of Malta's police force in 2001 after former Police Commissioner George Grech asked then Prime Minister Eddie Fenech Adami to start proceedings before the public service commission.

Gatt was accused of links to crime after his name popped up in taped phone calls during an investigation into the hold-up of a Group 4 security van in 2000. No criminal action was ever taken against him but he was dismissed and then proceeded to sue the police commissioner and prime minister for unfair dismissal.

Transcripts of phone conversations which purported to reveal the familiarity between Gatt and the crooks allegedly responsible for the Group 4 heist were considered inadmissible in court because the police had not obtained warrants for the tapping operation.

The Group 4 heist led to the conviction of Alfred Degiorgio for armed robbery and handling stolen goods after his fingerprint was found on one of the bags of cash. In 2018, while in jail awaiting trial for the murder of Daphne Caruana Galizia, Degiorgio was acquitted of the robbery on appeal.

Meanwhile Gatt, who had since retrained as a lawyer, sought reinstatement into the police force in September 2010 but this was still being contested when, three months later, he found himself in bigger trouble.

Gatt was charged with complicity in four armed robberies: the 2007 hold-up of the Balzan HSBC branch, in which around €1 million had been stolen, the attempted hold-up of a security van carrying €2.8 million in Santa Venera in 2010, another failed hold-up at HSBC's Rużar Briffa Centre in Ħal Qormi that same year, and the attempted hold up of a jewellery shop in Ħ'Attard, also in 2010.

To paraphrase Oscar Wilde, to be accused of complicity in one armed robbery may be regarded as a misfortune; to be accused of complicity in four looks like carelessness.

Gatt was also accused of helping his accomplice Fabio Psaila escape from police custody and with attempting to prevent Dr John Zammit Montebello from contacting the police after treating Darren Debono, another accomplice who had suffered gunshot wounds in the failed Attard robbery.

Daphne blogged about Gatt in 2011:

This David Gatt appears to believe that he falls into the criminal mastermind category, at least if the current testimony is anything to go by. But that testimony reads like a film-script about small-town hooligans dreaming about the big-time and bungling their way to what they think is the top while modelling themselves on their Mafia heroes. With all that talk of initiation rites involving burnt holy pictures, drops of blood from pricked hands, candles, codes, and the use of Italian, it's like the story of a bunch of bored teenage boys trying to enact a fantasy in the garden shed before being called in for supper. The fantasy element is heightened by the use of the names of real Mafia people as code for the plotters in the shed. But the thing is that they're not teenage boys. They're grown men with connections in the police force, the law, and heaven knows what else, besides access to lethal weapons, so when they decide to act out their criminal fantasies they are in the ideal position to do so.

There is something hideously prophetic about this blog. Who carried out the failed hold-up of the HSBC Centre in 2010? One man was charged with firing more than 30 shots at the police. He was not convicted. His name was Vincent Muscat *'il-Koħħu'*. Alfred Degiorgio *'il-Fulu'* and George Degiorgio *'iċ-Ċiniż'* were never charged, but were implicated when their names cropped up in the evidence against David Gatt. These were the same men who would later be charged with Daphne's murder.

Before his arrest in 2017, Vincent Muscat had made the headlines in 2014 when he was shot in the head three times, losing sight in one eye and having a bullet fragment permanently lodged in his brain.

'Someone got out of the passenger's side and started shooting,' Muscat told a court. 'He was holding a large pistol in his right hand, and as soon as he got out of the car he rolled back his hood. At this point, I recognised the shooter as being Jonathan Pace,' he said.

On 20 August, 2014 Pace was shot dead in a spray of bullets from an automatic rifle as he smoked a cigarette on his balcony.

All the gangsters deny any wrongdoing.

The star witness against Gatt had been a police officer, Mario Portelli. He and other witnesses painted a grim picture of Gatt as the ultimate bent copper. Gatt had a poster of *The Godfather* in his office, and asked his cronies to kiss his hand like Don Corleone and call him *capo di tutti i capi* (boss of all bosses).

But the case collapsed, and Gatt walked out of court a free man.

Once free, Gatt joined the legal practice of one Chris Cardona. Cardona signed a letter recommending David Gatt be admitted to the bar.

The following is a free translation of the interrogation of George Degiorgio at police headquarters on 5 December 2017, edited only for clarity. The questions are asked by Inspector Keith Arnaud. Also in the room was Inspector Kurt Zahra.

— George, please, how old are you?

Silence.

— I'll ask you again. How old are you, George?

Silence.

— In that case, what's your father's name, George?

Silence.

— So, I shall read out the details from your identity card. George Degiorgio ... [personal details redacted]

— Some questions will be put to you George, you are not obliged to answer them unless you wish to do so, but what you say will be recorded, and can be used as evidence against you.

— As you know, yesterday the police arrested you in Marsa at 8.15am. You were in an area known as Lighters Wharf or the potato shed near the Marsa Regatta Club. You were given the usual police caution and your rights explained to you. Do we agree, George, that yesterday we asked if you wanted a lawyer before we start asking questions?

Silence.

— Let me ask you for the last time, George, do you want a lawyer? We have not asked you any questions yet. This is your right. We are obliged by law to ask if you want a lawyer present. What do you say to that? We have to start asking questions.

Silence.

— As we told you yesterday George, and as is written on the arrest warrant, we have arrested you on suspicion of the murder of the journalist Daphne Caruana Galizia. Do you have anything to say to this?

— Our work shows, George, the police work and the reports of the local and foreign experts show that the bomb was activated by SMS. The bomb had a circuit device, at least we are told it is called a circuit device, a GSM module, of the type which I am showing you now in document KK3.

— Exhibit KK3 is a photo of a reproduction of the device that triggered the bomb, an electronic circuit connected to a SIM card, with the card remotely activated by text message. This GSM module takes a SIM card, there is the slot, and the person activating it sent an SMS to the line at the moment they wanted the bomb to explode. We have the proof that you were the person who sent this SMS. Is this true?

Silence.

— So you don't want to tell us anything, do you? Then let me remind you how things went. The evidence shows that way back in November last year, two SIM cards were bought on the same day and activated on the same day, 10 January 2017 [...] somewhere near the Siġġiewi industrial estate [...] The SIM cards were placed into two mobile phones with these numbers: [...] 9968 3752 and 9968 4366. They were topped-up with some credit, 9968 4366 remained in the mobile phone, while 9968 3752 was placed in a device, a GSM module like the one I am showing you in the photo KK3. As a matter of fact, the GSM module carrying the SIM card ending in 3752 has an IMEI number, in other words its serial number is 861508036763140. This is the serial number of the apparatus linked to the explosives which killed Daphne Caruana Galizia. Have you ever seen anything like it George? Has SIM card 9968 3752 ever been in your possession?

— This SIM card was placed inside the device, then removed in August this year, topped up with credit and left inside it. On the other hand, 9968 4366 was placed in three different mobile phones. [The] last one had the [serial] number 356012089741510. I am saying the last one, as the last time it was used was actually on 16 October, a minute just before 3pm, when somebody sent a message to this device on line 3752 at the time Daphne was driving her car, so as to explode the bomb. Do you know anything about these two SIM cards, George? Doesn't this jog your memory at all?

Silence.

— Fine then, let me try to refresh your memory. It also means, George, that 4366 [is a] Vodafone number, used to send the SMS

[to] 3752 inside the bomb. The evidence shows the bomb was placed in Daphne's car, in the early morning of 16 October, at 1.40am. We are saying this because the evidence shows that this GSM module device with SIM card ending 3752 was switched on at 1.41am exactly, and remained active in the Bidnija area. It remained switched on, but idle without any activity, until 2.58.55pm. It left a signal every hour, indicating its location as Mosta, as Bidnija and so confirming to us that the device remained in Bidnija, which is clear proof of the time the bomb was placed. What do you answer to this, George?

Silence.

— But that's not all, George. Now let me tell you what happened to the other SIM card. The mobile phone with the SIM card ending in 4366 was switched on at 6.15am. It was turned on somewhere near that potato shed where you were arrested yesterday, that's where you folks hang out. [...] And at nearly 3pm an SMS was sent to the number ending 3752 and the bomb exploded [...] the message said *REL 1 = ON*, if you remember well, George. What do you say to this? If you like, I can help you. It means that you were the one who set off the bomb. Or am I wrong?

Silence.

— Let's continue, George. Last August, you, your brother Fred, and [...] Vincent Muscat acquired or bought three SIM cards and three mobiles. Your brother Fred had the number 9908 8820, Vince had number 9908 8823, and you had number 9908 8824. Is this true? These cards were all switched on 19 August this year. Where did you get these cards George? And what did you need them for, if you have a mobile phone registered in your name ending 3741, what did you need with another number 9908 8824? It clearly means to us, George, that the numbers acquired on 19 August were for you, your brother, and Vince to communicate. As a matter of fact, the records show that the calls made, were indeed between you three, there were no other calls on these numbers, incoming or outgoing except between you, your brother, and Vince. Is this true?

Silence.

— On 15 October, the number 8824 goes to Bidnija at 11.30pm. This was the day before Daphne was killed, the day before 16 October of this year. You went back home at 1.30am and returned to Bidnija at 1.40am, and while you were in Bidnija, the other line ending 37, 36, erm, 3752, 9968 3752 is switched on and the GSM module is turned on, at the same time you are in Bidnija. Is this true George? And not only were you there, but there was Vince and your brother Fred in Bidnija. Now the question is obvious, what were you all doing in Bidnija at that time, so early, on 16 October this year? In fact, we know you were in Bidnija because you received a phone call, eight seconds in all, the first at 1.30am and the second one 13 seconds later from 9908 8820. This is the number we know your brother Fred was using, so he phones you when he was in Bidnija. He was checking that it was safe for you, wasn't he? And it seems that it was you and Vince, you were the two who went to place the bomb inside Daphne's car. Is this true? Can you, for example, tell us how you opened the car, George? Perhaps you acquired a copy of the car key, or did you have some tools to help you open the car?

Silence.

— Now look here, George. Yesterday you were all there, these are the photos, document KK2. This is you, there is an 11-page set of photos taken on 28 November, a week ago, while you were at work. You, your brother Alfred, and Vince under the potato shed where Alfred's boat is moored, the one named *Maya*. The green shed, more photos, photo number 5, you have the boat with the fenders up front. This is your brother Alfred's boat. What would you all be doing there, George? No idea? Nothing? Then let me help you out.

— Document KK4 contains a series of stills from CCTV cameras at Grand Harbour.

— 16 October, 8am, you board your brother's boat and start heading out of Grand Harbour. At the same time, your brother is in Bidnija. He remains there from the moment the bomb is placed, all night, until the bomb explodes. Is this true? Let me show you photos in Document KK4; these are stills, taken from the CCTV cameras of Grand Harbour on 16 October at 7am and at 9.50am. There is your brother Fred's boat going out, but we know it was you who was on board, George. Maybe it is from far off, true. There, that's later. These are two stills taken from the video recording, they are more obvious, your boat leaving. You are an amateur fisherman, George, strictly speaking, but did you really go fishing that day? Tell me, can you confirm you went fishing that day?

— (Inspector Zahra) That's right, towards the sea, George. That morning you were looking towards the sea.

— (Inspector Arnaud resumes) And we know all this because you bought three numbers […] and maybe with good reason because you might have known we'd listen to your phone calls, our colleagues strictly speaking. So, you didn't want us to know what was going on and to a certain degree you succeeded. Luckily your credit expired, George, we know that while you were out at sea you had a little problem, your credit expired and you needed somebody to purchase a top-up and to send you the top-up voucher and [in fact] we have the phone call, I can let you hear it. You are talking to the [other] person, Ramon Gusman, asking him to buy you a credit voucher. Let me play the phone call for you, George.

A recording of a phone call which took place on 16 October at 8.58am is played.

— You tried but you didn't succeed, […] and here's where you phone your friend Miguel Caruana. This is the call you made from the same number 9962 3741 at 9.01am, practically two minutes after you spoke to the first person and you phoned [number] and this is the second phone call.

A recording of a second phone call is played.

— Why were you in such a hurry, George? Why did you need that top-up quickly? And after all, I'm sorry, if you were just out enjoying a quiet day of fishing, why couldn't you return to dry land and top up yourself? Malta is small. It wouldn't have been a problem to find a place where you could take care of it, right? But most importantly, George, do you remember what number you wanted to top up? The one that you used exclusively to communicate with your brother and with Vince. And do you know why? Because that morning you needed that SIM card, George. You needed it and how! And as you say, you needed it right away. Look here, after the top-up you started exchanging text messages with your brother. And do you know where your brother was? In Bidnija. And do you know what the cell phone signals tell us? That he had been there since the night before. He hadn't budged. Why not, George? What had poor Fred been doing there, since Sunday night?

— (Inspector Zahra) Indeed, George…

— (Inspector Arnaud resumes) All right, now, George, that morning you and your brother effed up again. You thought that, if you were out at sea, no one could track you. So you decided to get even smarter. Just to be safe, at 2.55pm you turned the boat around and started to steer the *Maya* towards Grand Harbour. Because, as your cell phone records show, your brother alerted you that Daphne had left the house and so you thought that, since you were soon going to have to send the text to trigger the bomb, it would be better to get to a point on the water where you couldn't be seen or caught by the TV cameras along the coast. But, instead, something unexpected happened. Daphne forgot her cheque book in the house. She went back in and then came back out. She wasted some time. And in the meantime, your brother called you. You talked for about 40 seconds. But in the meantime, the boat had been steered to a point that was visible to the security cameras. Under the Siege Bell. Where, at that point, you were forced to stop. Because you had to send that text message. Look, George, look at the photographs that I've just laid on the table. They were taken at 2.55.39pm on 16 October. The *Maya* was stationary under the Siege Bell. And you were there. On board.

Silence.

— And do you know, George, why the boat was stationary? Tell me, do you know? It was stationary because you had to stop it. Because in order to sail a boat, you need to have at least one hand free for the tiller. But instead, your hands were both occupied at that moment. In fact, take a look at what happened in those minutes,

George. Do you remember? At a little after 2.55pm your brother Fred called you on the SIM card you asked your friend to top up and the conversation lasted 107 seconds. Until the exact moment of the explosion. The time it took for Daphne to get back in her car and head out to the paved road. So think it over again, George. You were on the boat and, with one hand, you held the cell phone up to your ear so you could talk to Fredu, who was supposed to tell you the exact moment to blow up the car Daphne was driving. And with the other hand, you held the other phone you were using to send the text message to set off the bomb, *REL 1 = ON*. That's right. That's the way it went, George. Right? In fact, I'll tell you something else. I think you stayed on the phone to Alfred to hear the explosion, live. To be sure that your work was successful.

Silence.

— Now, here's where you made another mistake George [...] as you were going back in. When the SMS was sent and it was confirmed that Daphne had been killed, your brother Fredu threw away the mobile phone, and his mobile phone has not been found. Vince *il-Koħħu* threw away his mobile phone and his mobile phone has not been found. In fact the activity stops there, there is no further record of those two cell phones. You make the mistake of leaving yours on, 9908 8824, [...] and at 3.45pm, it sends a location update. You were at the potato shed, where you moored the boat. You were back on land. Where, on land? The Regatta Club, in Marsa, at Lighters' Wharf, where you moor the boat and [again] at 3.59pm. Earlier, at 3.30pm you send a message to your woman, your partner, what do you say to her? To open a bottle of wine so you could celebrate. Do you remember this, George? What was there to celebrate George, at 3.30pm, before you came in, or as you made it to shore, because you had probably made shore by that time. What did you want to celebrate, George, at 3.30pm? Were you so happy that Daphne was dead, tell me? Can you tell me what you wanted to celebrate? What's to celebrate with this, George? 'Open a bottle of wine' or something. 'Buy me wine, my love,' you told her.

Silence.

— 3.32pm, you send an SMS to 9991 7216, which was the mobile phone number written with a ballpen on your arm yesterday. That's what you yourself told me at the time of your arrest, that it was your woman's. [...] And the last mistake was made by you too, George, because you threw away the phone with the number 9908 8824, just like your brother and Vince did. But do you know where you ditched it? Underneath the boat, near the potato shed. You [made] all these mistakes George, nobody else made them and all I am telling you is what you did, that's why you are here, George. Thanks to the mistakes you [made]. Yesterday, as you can see, we sent in the army's divers and there under the boat you were steering on 16 October, under where you liked to fish. Thanks to the mistake you made [...] the army divers found a Nokia cell phone with IMEI number (serial number) 35601208473978. The same one which bore SIM card 9908 8824 on 16 October and the previous months, from 19 August. The same one which you used to call Mike, Miguel Caruana, on 16 October for a credit voucher. It was found yesterday, George, and it was not the only one. You throw so many phones away, and when I say 'you' I mean you and Vince because Vince's phone was found in the water as well, some eight mobile phones were found there. You 'lose' cell phones and you catch fish, and another one with IMEI number 35213407478104 bore the SIM card 9962 3741, which was yours.

Silence.

— As you can see, George, we're dealing with facts here. Incontrovertible technical evidence. The discovery of the *corpus delicti* in several feet of water, near your brother's boat, the boat you took out on the morning of 16 October. These facts aren't just hearsay. No one will ever be able to say, 'I must have been confused', 'I misremembered', 'Oh this actually means something else.' Eh, no. So I think you'd be wiser to tell me what you have to say about all this.

Silence.

— What do you have to say to all this George? All we've done is tell you the result (and what a result) of our investigation, George? These are records we are talking about, and not whether somebody saw you, maybe they were mistaken, maybe we have a doubt. These are facts we collected from the service providers, facts retrieved by the army divers yesterday. What was the reason, for example, that we did not find the keys to the room and your mobile phones, your mobile phone disappeared? Were you aware that we were coming for you?

— Why did you have the number of your girlfriend, your partner, written on your arm George, on your wrist? You knew, you all knew that we were coming, you went prepared, without a mobile phone and you had the number written on your arm. Is that what it means, because it isn't normal for anyone to write their partner's cell phone number, the number of his woman, on his arm, isn't that right? Because the cell phone number is on the mobile itself, right? Was it a coincidence George, that you had the number written on your arm? Or did some birdie come by and tell you?

— What about the dog? The dog you usually take to the potato shed, what happened to it? Why wasn't Maya, the dog Maya, tied up in her usual place, George? The place where we always saw her in all the weeks we've been watching you?

— George, we didn't come there yesterday by chance and you had known for a long time that we were coming. You had figured it out for a while, that you all made mistakes, George, and I think you did [most of all] because you were the one who [made] the most mistakes in this case. Probably, had it not been for your mistakes, it would have been more difficult. Did you know, yesterday, George that we were coming, tell us? Because even the mobile phone *il-Koḥḥu* uses ended up in the sea?

Silence.

— George, you have the chance here, if you want, to answer or rebut what we are saying. Is there anything with which you disagree, before steps are taken against you over this killing? Is there anything you want to respond to, George, instead of remaining silent?

— A question I want to ask, before my colleague does, as he may want to ask you something, is the most important question of all, George. Not who commissioned you, will I ask you, because that is a direct question. Why did you kill Daphne Caruana Galizia? George, that is the question we are asking you. What was the reason? Because we know what you did, we know what you and Vince and Fred did …

— …the call records …we would never finish this if we were to show you all the activity there was. We mentioned what was important. What you did, we know; why you did it, we do not know. Honestly, if we knew, we would tell you, it would not be a problem. What we have, we've told you, you can see it with your own eyes, you can check, we have not withheld anything, these are the facts. We've told you only facts, but there is one thing we still don't know. Why, George, did you kill her? What was the problem, that you had to kill a journalist in that manner? A reason surely exists, George and you three all know the reason. You, your brother; and Vince, there is no doubt about it.

[Inspector Arnaud concluded his questioning and Inspector Zahra went through all the evidence again, from the beginning, painstakingly thorough. He ended on the same question.]

— (Inspector Zahra) Why Daphne?

Silence.

— (Inspector Arnaud resumes) Here ends the interrogation of George Degiorgio, ID number … Present for this interrogation were Inspectors Keith Arnaud and Kurt Zahra.

— We agree George that remaining silent was your choice? Nobody threatened you or promised you anything. This was your choice of behaviour during the interrogation.

— Time now is 9.25pm, today 5 December 2017 …

— (Inspector Zahra) 9.20pm.

— Agreed. And the time is 21:20 hrs, and the interrogation ends here.

Three points arise from this interrogation. The first, Maltese, intelligence put the Degiorgio brothers under surveillance in June.

They should have been privy to an immense amount of information that would, one would think, have led them to the inescapable conclusion that the brothers were up to no good, that they were spying on Daphne, and that their operation might conceivably lead to her murder. And yet they never joined the dots.

Malta's intelligence service reports directly to the prime minister, Joseph Muscat.

The second point is that there were a series of car bombs in Malta, some fatal, some not, in the years leading up to the one that killed Daphne, yet the police failed to obtain a conviction for any of them.

The third point is that the police conducting the questioning seemed to suspect that the three had been tipped off that their arrest was imminent, which led them to throw away their phones and keep the dog out of the way, before the armed police arrived.

Who could that have been?

We, the authors, are aware that this is a very detailed rendering of the interrogation, but we are satisfied that the salient points have been extensively reported elsewhere.

And yet we find it astonishing that at the time of writing, 22 months after this interrogation took place, the trial date has not yet been set.

After the three men, the Degiorgio brothers and Muscat, were arrested for murder, reporters started digging. Who did they drink with? Where did they hang out? Did they know any senior politicians? What about Chris Cardona, the man Daphne had humiliated with Brothelgate? The critical path led to Ferdinand's Bar in Siġġiewi, a village a few miles southwest of Valletta. Two reporters, one from *Radio France* and the other from France 2 TV, working for the Daphne Project, struck gold.

— Is there a politician here who once went to a gentleman's club?

— Cardona. He drinks with us here.

— He comes here? Is he a regular?

— Yes. He comes on Saturdays and every Sunday. Chris Cardona. And there is the journalist who was killed in Malta, Caruana Galizia. Three persons have been arrested.

— And these men, they would come here as well?

— Yes, yes.

— In this very bar?

— In the same bar.

— And they knew the politician, Cardona?

— Yes.

— Did you see them together?

— Yes, yes.

— Frequently?

— Together having a drink.

— Was it before or after the murder?

— Before, yes.

A second witness was more precise.

— It was a November afternoon in 2017. And Cardona had been seen with Alfred Degiorgio. They talked for at least an hour. The cabinet minister looked worried. There must have been at least 20 customers in the bar and, at a certain point, Degiorgio and Cardona went for a stroll before heading home. I later learned from other regulars at the bar that the two men met frequently at Ferdinand's.

Cardona told the Daphne Project that he does not recall speaking to any of the three accused:

Like most seasoned criminal lawyers in Malta, I know who some of the suspects in the case are. The particular pub you mention welcomes patrons from all walks of life, including other politicians. I do not, however, recall having any discussions with any of these individuals, and have definitely never had any meetings with them. Anything else is baseless rumour and speculation.

Like much else Chris Cardona says, that statement is not quite true. Chris Cardona wasn't that much of a criminal lawyer. He mostly worked in commercial law but took time out to assist a very limited portfolio of clients in the criminal court. Cardona had been Vincent Muscat's lawyer when he was charged with – but not convicted for – the failed robbery of the HSBC centre in Malta in 2010. Hard to imagine how a lawyer can properly represent a client without ever having had a conversation with him.

Co-author Carlo Bonini and other journalists from the Daphne Project reported in October 2018 that Cardona and Alfred Degiorgio had attended a small bachelor's party in a secluded villa with a swimming pool on 29 June 2017, four months before Caruana Galizia was killed in a car bomb. Cardona told *La Repubblica* that he couldn't remember his whereabouts but did not deny the story. To the Maltese media, he said he had better things to do than entertain the curiosity of sensational journalists. In a statement issued by the Department of Information on his behalf, the minister said these smears on his character were highly damaging and false.

So Cardona gave three versions of the truth:

- I cannot remember.
- I am too busy.
- These are false smears.

Pick any one.

Far from never speaking to the accused, he'd represented one and had been seen with another twice, before and after the murder.

Cardona *did* tell the Maltese press: 'The assassination of Daphne Caruana Galizia was a horrible crime, possibly the worst of all, but so is character assassination.'

In April 2018, co-author John Sweeney rocked up at the Henley & Partners event in the City of London. When prime minister Joseph Muscat arrived to hear Malta's famous tenor, Joseph Calleja do his thing, Sweeney tried to doorstep Muscat. He asked: 'prime minister, do you stand by your economy minister, Chris Cardona?'

Sweeney was thumped in the chest by a member of Muscat's security team for his pains, so one can only assume the answer was yes.

On 16 October 2017 at 3.30pm, the news broke that Daphne Caruana Galizia had been killed. In Parliament, former PN leader Simon Busuttil and shadow justice minister Jason Azzopardi were sitting on the opposition benches. As they looked up, they saw Chris Cardona looking at his phone. His face was ashen.

Chris Cardona denies any wrongdoing.

BLOOD, SWEAT AND TEARS

5 June 2017. 7.03pm. Joseph Muscat has just been confirmed prime minister after calling a snap election 'because of unrest in the country caused by Daphne Caruana Galizia's lies'. The people have decided.

Daphne headlines her post: 'Right and wrong are not a popularity contest.'

It ran:

I know – you don't have to tell me; it's the reason I do it – that this website has over the last four years become a gathering-post or rallying-point for decent people who feel frightened and threatened at the rise, growth and spread of amorality (not by any means the same thing as immorality). I know why you come here, because lots of you tell me – but I knew it instinctively, even before you did.

You come here to feel normal in a sea of insanity where the crowd cheers the Commissioner of Police for failing to take action against a corrupt cabinet minister and the prime minister's chief of staff; where supporters of the party in power celebrate and have their picture taken on the steps of a bank which launders money for Azerbaijan's ruling elite, because it is linked to the politicians they support; where even educated people who have had all the advantages in life vote a corrupt political party into power for the narrow reason that they're renting out flats to buyers of Maltese citizenship who never set foot in them.

The electoral result shocked you (not me, for reasons that I will explain in another post on another day when I have more time) not because you see general elections as football matches in which the prize is unadulterated power for five years for 'your' team, but because it makes you feel like the only sane person in the asylum. Now you're hunting around for other sane people, temporarily blinded to the fact that 45% of the population made the same choice that you did, though 55% did not.

You want reassurance that it is not you who is in the wrong because you think people who do serious wrong should not be in government. No, you are not wrong because you think the police should act. No, you are not wrong to feel sick when the mob cheers a corrupt police officer. Of course you are not. You are right.

Four years ago, I wrote a piece calling out the incoming Nationalist Party leader for beginning a speech with '30,000 people can't be wrong'. Of course they can be, I wrote. A million people can be wrong. The rightness or wrongness of a fact, action or opinion is not established by the number of people who believe it, do it, or hold it.

Of course it is wrong to vote for corruption. Of course it is wrong to vote so as to put corrupt politicians into power. It is very wrong. And to do it for your own personal benefit, rather than simply to 'back your team' (which is bad enough), is worse than wrong. Winning and losing are not factors in deciding what is right and what is wrong. Winning and losing are about the power to prevent wrongdoing or the power to perpetrate it.

You would be surprised that the forces of darkness and corruption think themselves the decent ones, despite their necessarily intimate knowledge of what they themselves do. This self-delusion is a coping mechanism, nothing fancier than that. And part of that coping mechanism is using the media machines and other means at their disposal to go after their critics by portraying them as bad and evil, enemies of the people, who wish to harm the heroes of public largesse.

Why doesn't it get you down, somebody asked me the other day. How can you cope with an entire Labour Party machine going at you day and night, assaulting you from all angles? How do you deal with it?

My answer was what it always is: that the Labour Party, in all its different shapes and forms and under its different leaders, has hounded me irascibly since I was in my 20s. Yes, for a quarter of a century. The extent of it only became visible to the public with the internet. But it was there beforehand.

I can cope not only because I had the good example of my parents to follow, who had to contend with so much that was terrible in the years 1971 to 1987, and who always did so with dignity, correctly, and without moral compromise, but also because I read widely and know that this is a standard, textbook Fascist method that powerful people use for the public destruction of their critics, particularly when their critics stand alone.

Others have been there before me, in situations which require far more bravery and moral courage than has been required of me over the years in Malta. Others are there still, in horrendous situations as they are in Baku, Azerbaijan. What I am put through by the plots, conspiracies, and machinations of Joseph Muscat, Keith Schembri, ... their television station and radio, their internet trolls and the rest of them, is as nothing compared to the hellish nightmare that those brave people must endure in their far more dangerous battles.

The fight against corruption and [against] the decimation of the rule of law must continue. The temptation now will be for people to see no way out of this horrible mess and to leap on the bandwagon with the cry that if you can't beat them, then you might as well join them. It happened four years ago and has been happening systematically all along, which is why Muscat's party got the result it did (but more about this, again, when there is time).

The temptation, too, will be to round on the Nationalist Party and blame it for failing to deliver a victory that was well nigh impossible in the prevailing circumstances. Instead of holding the government to scrutiny as it ploughs on, railroading our already fragile democracy and collapsing institutions, we shall occupy ourselves ripping to shreds the party that was our only hope of deliverance.

And in doing so, we shall miss the point as we generally do: that it is people who vote for political parties, and not political parties which put themselves into power. Would Muscat's party have been returned to power in any other European Union member state outside Italy? That is the question we have got to address. And even in Italy corrupt politicians resign, are subjected to due process, or have coins thrown at them by angry crowds.

The problem that has to be addressed is the widespread and ever-increasing amorality among a sizeable percentage of the Maltese population of Malta (not all of Malta's population is Maltese; tens of thousands are not). It spans the entire socio-economic spectrum and has nothing at all to do with social class, privilege, or the lack of it. Thirty, forty years ago, this amorality could have been excused on the grounds of illiteracy and ignorance, of Malta's isolation from the world in a tightly controlled and insular environment.

Now, there is no such excuse and we have to face the brutal fact of what we are, and examine how it has come about and whether there are any solutions. I happen to think, right now, that there are probably none, because amoral familism, the root cause of it, is the result of centuries of social programming. But it may be possible.

One thing is certain: you are not going to change amoral familism by pandering to it, or by making its practitioners believe they are right. That simply perpetuates the situation, and the Nationalist Party has been guilty of this too, because the mentality is endemic.

Nobody can seek to understand Maltese politics or Maltese society without first understanding amoral familism, which shapes and drives both — and which, it has to be said, has ruined both too.

[...]

Malta is in a dangerous place, and now we can no longer say that it is corrupt politicians who have brought it to this point, for it can no longer be denied that those corrupt politicians are a reflection of society.

Daphne wrote her post on what must have been one of the toughest days of her professional life. After her death, the rallying cry in this post would become her legacy: 'the fight against corruption and [against] the decimation of the rule of law must continue'.

There is something else I should say before I go: when people taunt you or criticise you for being 'negative' or for failing to go with their flow, for not adopting an attitude of benign tolerance to their excesses, bear in mind always that they, and not you, are the ones who are in the wrong.

What they want most of all is for you to join in the chorus of approval, or at least shut up about it, so that they can feel better about themselves — because despite all that they say, and their cocky attitude, they struggle with their self-respect. They want people to admire them so that they can admire themselves, despite behaviour that is so far away from admirable that it isn't even on the horizon.

6 October 2017. 10 days before her assassination, Daphne sits down with Marilynn Clark, a University of Malta researcher

working on a project funded by the Council of Europe looking into threats faced by journalists.

From that interview:

I think that the biggest problems; in fact, all of the problems I encounter, stem from an exact parallel with what in psychology, and you'll be no stranger to this, is known as scapegoating. So, it's when you look at my story, it's a classic case of scapegoating on a nation-wide scale. When you have the scapegoat, there's an entity which is doing the scapegoating and encouraging others to scapegoat. And in my case, that became the Labour Party which was in opposition for many years but now has become more dangerous because the Labour Party is actually in government and so has a lot more power. But the greatest difficulties I encounter, come from the fact that they have made me into what in effect is a national scapegoat. And this has gone on for almost 30 years.

I am in a situation where people who can't even read English and therefore, have never read anything I've written, at the same time are aware of who I am, know that they are meant to hate me, or dislike me, or despise me, or disagree with me, or whatever, and react to me on that basis. Totally irrespective of what I write but as the figure that they are told to hate. So, this has become a massive problem and I have had cases, especially when the incitement is really high at times of political tension, where I have had problems even with people in the street and I look at them and I think, 'Okay, what's their problem with me? I don't think they've ever read anything I've written. They look like they can't even talk, let alone read.'

There was one case which had ended up in the papers, when I was in the car park at the hospital. I had spent all day there with my mother and by the time I went down to the car park, it was practically empty. It was after visiting hours, and I was trying to reverse out of my parking bay and I see this big car behind me.

My face had just been up on all the Labour Party billboards all round the island where they put me up in the same group as the prime minister, senior politicians, and I was totally the fish out of water; but I was there with these politicians, so I became instantly recognisable.

Now there was this car blocking me. I mean it was a really intense situation. I reversed out and this guy started shouting and blowing the horn and he went to file a report saying that I reversed into him which wasn't true at all. The police then did a conspiracy out of it because they happened to be supporters of the government. They took me to Court; it was headlines in all the papers. And when it came down to the crunch, the Magistrate said, 'she had no marks on her car, the police themselves confirmed this; the dried mud on the car wasn't disturbed and it's quite obvious that you conspired with the police for this whole thing'. And she just let me off.

Maybe you don't remember the newspaper environment in the 1990s when I started writing. There were just two English language newspapers: The Sunday Times *and* The Times. *The others were owned by the political parties. And* The Sunday Times *and* The Times *in those days were very drab. They had foreign news on the front pages, nothing like the news we have today. And there were no columns with the person's name, there was just one anonymous 'Roamer's Column'.*

Two things happened: Malta got its first named newspaper columnist and it was a 25-year-old woman. And this thing was a double shock. And I used to have people actually telling me, 'But does your husband write them for you? Does your father? Does your brother? Do you have a brother?' Which is really offensive.

The gender dimension was horrific. Because women were not allowed to have opinions.

I have advertising on my website. It's obvious I need the advertising since that's where the money comes from. A lot of my ads are Google but I also have the ability to sell advertising. I actually encounter situations where people are afraid. They recognise that it's their audience and it's a fantastic audience for them but they are actually afraid to advertise on it because they think they would get retribution from the government. I've actually been told this.

I can't even go to the beach! I can't! For four years I have not been able to go to the beach. The last time I went was four years ago. There was this group following me around taking photos of me and uploading me on Facebook. I said, 'Forget it, I'm not going to the beach anymore'.

I've been at it since I was 25 and experience hardens you and it just becomes your way of life. I know no other way of life. One of the wonders for me when leaving Malta, is knowing what normal life is like, because I can be invisible, I can go where I like, without people staring or nudging, or whatever. Because my whole life has been like … 25 is not much away from 18.

And so, I got used to it, like a scar forms around a wound. But, my biggest concern is that because people see what happened to me, they don't want to do it. It's scared others off. So, people keep asking, 'Why is there only one of her?' And the only reason, there's one of her is not because I do something unique or wonderful or my abilities are super special.

I really hate to give up. That's a personality trait. I've been doing it for a really long time. As they say, in for a penny, in for a pound now. What am I going to do? Give up now? Now I'm maybe a bit more secure but, can you imagine what happened to me earlier this year with Chris Cardona discovering that he can use that precautionary warrant for a libel suit that had never been done in Malta before? It was always legally possible, but it had never, ever been done before. Suppose that had happened to me when I was 25 or when I was 30. I wouldn't have had the resources to cope.

2006. I go home one day about three days before the fire and found that somebody had painted in big black letters 'Daphne sucks black cock' all over the road. Huge letters over the road. And luckily by the time I got home and phoned the police, somebody had come out with a paintbrush and had painted over them.

I said, 'Okay, they're coming next with a fire.' And they set fire to the house at about 3am. And, they didn't set fire to the front door because our house is isolated. They actually went to the back and put truck tyres packed with jerry cans full of petrol against a glass door.

They wanted to burst in the glass doors and behind there were rugs and so it was to set the whole house on fire. And we were really lucky because our bedroom is down on the ground floor. The house is built on a slope and they came up through the back and five days before we had changed those doors to security doors so even though they were glass, it was fire-proof. They took quite a long time to shatter and when they shattered, the glass stayed in place. But they didn't know because when they had come on the recce they found pine doors with normal glass which would have exploded. Also it was three o'clock in the morning when our son came home. He saw the fire reaching up to the roof and he started shouting.

It's a very primitive situation and I really don't feel I'm living in a European country. I can't say I do, I really can't. I used to have these arguments with people who used to tell me, 'But the Labour Party is so much more liberal than the Nationalist Party. You know, gay rights and whatever.' And I used to tell them, 'The true test of how liberal a society is or a person is, is not divorce and gay rights, it's their attitude, toleration of other people's opinions ...' They have divorce in Russia. It doesn't make it a liberal society. And what does it tell you if Malta has gay rights and gay marriage but then they literally decimate anybody with a different political opinion.

I'm quite sure women journalists are more harassed in more advanced societies than ours too. But, in Malta the form of harassment is really, really primitive. It's always what you look like, how fat you are, how overweight you are, and I remember that one of the very first columns I had written in the early 90s, I said 'I really can't accept the way a man can go into battle with dandruff on his shoulders, shabby suit, ugly hair, and nobody even mentions the fact that he looks like an unmade bed or he's really ugly or really messy, and why doesn't he wash his hair? Nobody! Because a man has a right to look like he's been dragged through a hedge backwards.' And God forbid you mention it because men are meant to look like that but then if a woman is going to be less than perfect, she's going to get trashed. And look at the efforts being made by the women in public life in Malta. I mean, look at them. I look at them and think, 'Why do you feel you have to fall out of bed in the morning at 6 a.m. and put on two inches of makeup on your face? Look at the men around you. Some of them haven't even washed their face.'

Intimidation is constant with me and it is absolutely terrible. And there have been periods where literally I would feel like, oh my God, I'm going to get a stomach ulcer; churning nerves all the time. Because you're living under it constantly. And it was bad enough, when the Labour Party was in opposition but now they're in government they have access to all my private information at the push of a button. The Nationalist Party in government also had access to that information. It also had journalists that it didn't like. But I can't imagine ever in a million years that anybody who was in government crossed the line and used any information about any journalist abusively or used it to threaten them or whatever. But it's happening now.

They have absolutely no red lines. For them, any information they have access to is fair. There have absolutely no boundaries. They can call up anything about anybody, even your children's exam results.

It's a climate of fear. People are afraid of consequences. For example, even when people send me information, they say 'Don't quote me.' And sometimes I feel like laughing. I say, 'All you've done is sent me a photo from Facebook, I mean, keep you anonymous? It's not like you're giving me a state secret.'

If you're writing an article talking about the banking sector and there are serious problems there, your article will be so much more powerful and more convincing if you could quote Mr X, chairman of X bank, not 'sources in the banking industry' and you know it's the chairman, but he doesn't want to be quoted. Your readers need to know it's the chairman.

16 October 2017. Evening. A sizeable crowd gathers on the waterfront in Sliema, Daphne's childhood town, carrying candles and flowers, stunned by the news of her cruel death. There is no plan, no speeches, no leaders. People just come together in shock and grief. At one point, someone starts singing the Maltese national anthem and others join in. Softly.

21 October 2017. The Maltese government offers a €1 million reward for information about Daphne Caruana Galizia's murder, conditional on the family's agreement. The family say the reward is for the government to decide and so the offer quietly sinks from public view.

22 October 2017. Some 15,000 people gather in Triq ir-Repubblika, Valletta in response to a call from civil society activists marching to demand the resignation of the police chief and the attorney general, and new appointments agreed by all parties, not just Labour.

Joseph Muscat and Adrian Delia are not present.

Across the street from the law courts, people leave flowers, candles, and protest messages at the foot of the Great Siege Memorial.

Over the next weeks and months, more marches will be held and the flowers, candles, and messages of protest replenished and refreshed. What starts as an impromptu memorial becomes a shrine to Daphne and a focal point for the calls for justice. This needles opponents into turning up in the dead of the night to try and stamp out the memorial but every day more protesters turn up to restore it.

23 October 2017. It's been a week since Daphne Caruana Galizia was killed. Hers is the first political assassination in Malta's history that killed its target.

Parliament convenes. On the agenda is the 2018 budget. But opposition leader Adrian Delia requests an urgent discussion of the assassination. Government MPs deny this is an urgent matter. Parliament proceeds with its regular agenda.

Four days later around 100 women gather on the steps of the Auberge de Castille just outside the closed door of the prime minister's office. They tell journalists they are protesting against the political class' outrageous behaviour in trying to imply that it was business as usual when Malta's democracy is under threat.

The protesting women said they intend to stay outside the prime minister's office until they get an appointment to see him and give him a piece of their mind.

Daphne's sons Matthew, Andrew, and Paul have pizza delivered to the protestors. One of the boxes is garnished with leaves from their mother's bay tree, and a note of thanks. In Greek mythology, the nymph Daphne turns into a laurel tree to protect herself from being raped.

The prime ministers's deputy press secretary is spotted taking photos of the protesters.

This evening a new protest movement in Malta is born. They brand themselves #occupyjustice and use the bay leaf as the symbol of their campaign.

14 November 2017. On the initiative of the President of the European Parliament Antonio Tajani, the press room of the European Parliament building in Strasbourg is renamed Salle Daphne Caruana Galizia.

4 December 2017. Maltese authorities release spectacular footage of the arrest of 10 people suspected of involvement in the killing of Daphne Caruana Galizia.

The next day, three of the 10, brothers Alfred and George Degiorgio and Vincent Muscat, are taken to court and formally charged with homicide. They plead not guilty.

21 February 2018. Ján Kuciak, a 28-year-old investigative journalist working for the Slovak online news site *Aktuality.sk*, and his girlfriend Martina Kušnírová are found dead at home. They have been shot multiple times. After Daphne, Kuciak becomes the second journalist to be killed in the European Union in as many years.

Tens of thousands of Slovak citizens take to the streets demanding justice.

Taking a leaf out of Joseph Muscat's handbook, Slovak Prime Minister Robert Fico also offers a €1 million reward for information. Fico outdoes Muscat, however, and with a remarkable flair of showmanship, plonks €1 million in cash on a table. It makes for a great photo op.

Within two days, Slovakia's Minister for Culture Marek Maďarič, a long-standing senior member of government, resigns. Marek Maďarič explains his decision: 'Plainly said, as culture minister, I cannot put up with a journalist being murdered during my tenure.'

Meanwhile, two public service officiails also resign, pending the outcome of the investigation into the murder. They deny all involvement but acknowledge that they are named in the last report Kuciak wrote. They are national security council secretary Viliam Jasaň and Mária Trošková, an aide to Prime Minister Robert Fico.

12 March 2018. Slovakia's Deputy Prime Minister, Robert Kalinak, resigns. He is responsible for the police force.

14 March 2018. Slovakia's Prime Minister Robert Fico loses the support of his coalition partners and resigns.

In Malta, activists are watching the story unfolding in Slovakia and cannot help comparing it unfavourably with the local scene. No one in Malta even offers to resign.

24 March 2018. The Maltese authorities refuse to grant former police inspector and former FIAU investigator Jonathan Ferris whistleblower status.

Jonathan Ferris was handpicked to join the FIAU by its director Manfred Galdes. He was reassigned from the police force, and lasted less than six months in the job before being fired summarily at the end of his probationary period. Galdes had just resigned. Ferris argues he should have been sent back to the police force if he was no longer needed at the FIAU, and sues for unfair dismissal.

Ferris says he became aware of 'corruption at the highest level' while at the FIAU but cannot say more because he can be imprisoned for breaching confidentiality. He is publicly reminded of this by government spokespeople including Labour MP Manuel Mallia, formerly a minister responsible for the police.

Ferris is also the police officer who arrested Maria Efimova for allegedly defrauding Pilatus Bank of less than €2,000 that had been alleged by her employer Pilatus Bank, and who was briefly investigated after she complained of police mistreatment.

In an interview with co-author Manuel Delia, Ferris says internal police investigators appeared keen to use Efimova's complaint to discredit her as a witness in other cases. Ferris says he was encouraged to embellish his testimony to achieve this aim but he refused to cooperate and stuck to his recollection of the facts.

Under Maltese legislation, an applicant for whistleblower status must first tell a government official from the office of the prime minister the gist of their complaint so that the government can assess whether the information they want to reveal meets the criteria established by law. In Ferris's case, this puts him in an awkward position. To be granted whistleblower status, he first needs to risk imprisonment and reveal official secrets, before he is granted the protection he needs to be able to reveal what he knows. If Joseph Heller had only lived long enough, he would have had enough material to write a sequel to Catch-22.

A month earlier, Ferris tells co-author John Sweeney that he fears for his life and wants full police protection in view of what he knows. While at the FIAU, Ferris worked on the investigation following on from the allegations made against Konrad Mizzi and Keith Schembri in the Panama Papers.

'We believe there was political interference (in my dismissal from the FIAU),' he tells the BBC's Newsnight programme. The FIAU denies this. The anti-money laundering agency claims Ferris's dismissal was based 'solely on an objective and comprehensive performance assessment'.

22 July 2018. The attorney general publishes a short extract, 49 pages, of a 1,500-page report prepared by Magistrate Aaron Bugeja, tasked with conducting a magisterial inquiry into the Egrant scandal. It has taken him 15 months. It has been nine months since Daphne was murdered.

The attorney general refuses to publish the report. The only people to see the full report are the prime minister (the subject of the inquiry) and Justice Minister Owen Bonnici. The prime minister says he shared the report with his lawyer Pawlu Lia and press secretary Kurt Farrugia.

The prime minister says it is not for him to publish the full report but for the attorney general.

The inquiry finds no evidence linking the Muscats to Egrant Inc.

Magistrate Aaron Bugeja finds no documentation linking the Muscat family to the allegations.

A UK-based forensic accounting firm, Harbinson Forensics, finds no evidence linking the Muscats to Egrant on Pilatus Bank servers. It finds no evidence that any of the Muscats had accounts at Pilatus Bank. It finds no evidence in the Pilatus Bank records of any bank accounts, or discussion about opening bank accounts for Egrant, Schembri's Tillgate, or Mizzi's Hearnville.

Muscat wheels in members of his cabinet to applaud at opportune moments as he holds a press conference and gloats. He tears into former Opposition leader Simon Busuttil and brands him the 'most irresponsible politician Malta has ever seen'. He also calls on him to resign from parliament.

Muscat cries on cue. He speaks of the emotional toll the allegations have taken on his family. 'We kept asking each other whether the truth would ever emerge. That day has come. I can tell my children that neither their mother nor their father is going to jail.'

Adrian Delia does not miss the opportunity to rise to the occasion as leader of the opposition, and acts as if on the instructions of the prime minister. He sacks his predecessor from the shadow cabinet. He calls on Simon Busuttil to resign the whip or face the consequences. Adrian Delia has been looking forward to some sort of resolution. His first 10 months in office have been overshadowed by Daphne, her allegations against him, and now her death. He wants to draw a line under the whole sorry affair. He wants to move on from the Egrant scandal.

He cannot have forgotten Daphne's words on 27 September 2017. As newly-minted PN leader, Adrian Delia paid a visit to

Joseph Muscat at the PL headquarters. The photo op showed two men who should have been at loggerheads but were apparently very pleased with each other. 'That gurgling sound?' Daphne's headline ran. 'Malta's future going down the plug-hole.'

Always on point, Daphne also wrote: 'Delia set the scene for the next five years by drawing a line under Egrant Inc.' But her death put paid to those plans. Magistrate Aaron Bugeja's failure to pin down the evidence is too good a second opportunity to miss.

Unfortunately for him and the motley crew of crooks, misfits and gangsters fingered in this book, 'absence of evidence is not evidence of absence'.

The point of the Panama companies registered by Mossack Fonseca on their behalf was to hide the evidence, to leave no trail of wrongdoing. And Ali Sadr Hashemi Nejad set up a bank to launder money for embezzlers from fabulously corrupt regimes. Ali Sadr was an expert at covering up his tracks, that is, until the FBI caught up with him.

Magistrate Aaron Bugeja decides that the certificates of ownership which indicate that Michelle Muscat is the owner of Egrant must have been forgeries. This appears to have been determined on the basis that the signatory, one Jacqueline Alexander of Mossack Fonseca, could not remember signing the documents or recognise her signature. A poorly-paid secretary who'd been employed by Mossack Fonseca purely to lend her name and signature to more than 10,000 companies could not single one out of the many companies she fronted.

Frame-up, cries the magistrate, not stopping to think how unrealistic his expectations are, in the circumstances, or to give weight to the fact that Alexander was herself under investigation in Panama and would want to keep her troubles to a minimum.

Less importance was given to the fact that Karl Cini, Brian Tonna's Number Two, asked Mossack Fonseca to explicitly deny that Egrant belonged to Michelle Muscat. Mossack Fonseca refused.

The motley crew have also conveniently ignored the fact that a magisterial inquiry is not a judicial process. The Muscats have not been tried and acquitted. A magistrate has simply ruled there is not enough evidence to support the claim, or even prosecute.

Magistrate Aaron Bugeja is promoted judge nine months later.

And in the meantime, the conlusions of the magisterial inquiry are being used to tar those blowing the whistle. It is open season on Daphne Caruana Galizia, Simon Busuttil, Jonathan Ferris, Maria Efimova …

And Adrian Delia conveniently joins in the tumult and tries to rid himself of a thorn in his side, a predecessor he can never hope to live up to. But he misjudges the strength of feeling with the PN and has to climb down. Simon Busuttil remains a member of the PN.

19 April 2018. #occupyjustice activists gather at the Valletta Police Station waving copies of international press reports claiming Economy Minister Chris Cardona was seen meeting one of the men charged with the assassination of Daphne Caruana Galizia.

They demand the police question Chris Cardona. The police do not. The minister provides a voluntary statement denying any wrongdoing and denying being in a Siġġiewi bar at the same time as any of the alleged assassins.

Inspector Keith Arnaud, one of the investigating officers, invites the activists to a meeting. Asked if the police have drawn up a list of suspects from Daphne's writings, as she must have made many enemies, Inspector Arnuad says the police do not consider Daphne's journalism a factor in the investigation of her murder.

25 June 2018. Joseph Muscat appoints Magistrate Anthony Vella to the bench of judges, meaning that, as the magistrate leading the inquiry into Daphne's death, he has to hand over the investigation to another magistrate. The magistrate having been the only public official willing to keep the family updated on the investigation, the family are thrown back into the dark.

8 September 2018. Today is a public holiday in Malta. Victory Day. It marks the anniversary of the ending of the Great Siege of 1565. The country's leaders usually partake in a sombre ceremony at the Great Siege Memorial in Valletta involving the laying of wreaths. In preparation, city cleaners scrub it clean and remove all flowers, pictures, and mementos laid in memory of Daphne. The ceremony is held, and no soon is it over than the memorial is boarded up 'for restoration'. It had been restored only eight years earlier.

Today marks the start of a concerted campaign by the government to erase Daphne from memory. Every day activists, relatives, mourners, friends build a memorial and every night the government sends cleaners to clear it up.

Fights occasionally break out.

Justice minister Owen Bonnici confirms that the cleaning is happening on his instructions.

In Leeuwarden-Fryslân on official business, Owen Bonnici tries to justify to his Dutch hosts the removal of protest banners demanding justice for Daphne Caruana Galizia. Leeuwarden officials are unimpressed. They boycott their scheduled attendance at all Valletta Capital of Culture events and withdraw their invitation to the Maltese officials to attend the Leeuwarden Capital of Culture events. Instead, they decide to screen the film *Daphne: The Execution* as part of the Leeuwarden official programme. The film is the work of co-author Carlo Bonini and others.

Meanwhile, the chairman of Valletta 2018 is none other than former secretary general of the PL, Jason Micallef. He makes his antipathy towards Daphne clear, calls on supporters to remove Daphne memorials or banners and mocks Daphne's last words by captioning a street party celebration with the words: 'The situation is desperate. There is [sic] happy people every where you look.'

Daphne's last words have become haunting. 24 minutes before she died, she ended her last blog post: 'There are crooks everywhere you look now. The situation is desperate.'

Across the world, writers (including Salman Rushdie, Margaret Atwood, Neill Gaiman and several others) petition the government to remove Jason Micallef. Their pleas are ignored.

Co-author Manuel Delia files a human rights case against Malta's government claiming that the government's repeated and assiduous removal of Daphne's memorial amounts to a breach of freedom of expression. The case is ongoing.

5 October 2018. The constitutional court rules that the police and the attorney general have breached the fundamental human rights of the Daphne Caruana Galizia family. The case was brought over the deputy police chief's refusal to step down from the investigating team. The deputy, Silvio Valletta, is also the head of the criminal investigation department (CID) and is married to Justyne Caruana, a minister in Joseph Muscat's cabinet. Testifying in court, Valletta says the police are not ruling out the possible involvement of a cabinet minister in the murder. 'We're ruling out nothing.' The courts agree with the family that Silvio Valletta has a conflict of interest. Twice.

It is nearly a year since the murder and investigations have failed to produce a motive for the murder or the identity of the person or persons who ordered the killing.

Silvio Valletta stays on as head of the CID. He and his team are still the police officers responsible for investigating allegations of corruption and money-laundering against his wife's friends and colleagues: Konrad Mizzi, Keith Schembri, Chris Cardona and Joseph Muscat. Up to the time of writing, no one has been prosecuted.

9 October 2018. Drama in Parliament. The prime minister sees red and accuses Simon Busuttil, sitting across from him on the PN backbenches, of being a fraudster. It is one of the most vicious parliamentary sessions in living memory. The session has to be

suspended when a furious prime minister lashes out at Busuttil. When the session resumes, Busuttil tells parliament that Muscat threatened him. 'I will make you carry the can, and you will not even be able to set foot in Malta again.' Busuttil says it is his understanding that the prime minister is accusing him of forging the signature on the Egrant Inc certificates of ownership.

18 November 2018. The minister responsible for the police force, Michael Farrugia, gives an interview to the Italian TV news channel Rai Tre. He confirms a story in *The Sunday Times of Malta* that the masterminds in the assassination have been identified and arrests are expected shortly.

The news spreads around the world. The case appeares to be nearing its conclusion.

Michael Farrugia takes back his statement to Rai Tre.

13 December 2018. It is a public holiday in Malta and a traditional Christmas shopping day. The streets in Valletta are chockful of people and the flickering candles at Daphne's memorial are dimmed by the gaudy city decorations.

At a café across from the Great Siege Memorial, Clémence Dujardin sits with her son. She is an #occupyjustice activist and the wife of co-author Manuel Delia. She is in Valletta to meet fellow activists to finalise plans for their monthly vigil for Daphne three days later.

Activists lay fresh flowers and candles. She hears shouts and knows it is a common occurrence for activists to be verbally abused. She decides to film the altercation just in case it turns ugly.

Clémence crosses Triq ir-Repubblika, camera in hand. A woman charges at her, shouting abuse and insults. A man attacks Clémence from behind and her phone goes flying and smashes on the ground.

It turned out the two are PL activists from Santa Luċija and the man runs the southern town's PL club. The police charge them with assault. The couple plead guilty, agree to pay for the broken phone and are slapped with a three-year restraining order and ordered to stay away from Clémence and her husband. The court interprets the incident as an assault on free speech.

Christmas 2018. Tony, the 10-year-old Staffordshire Bull Terrier that Daphne nursed from the brink of death after he was poisoned in July 2017, dies.

16 January 2019. The Australia-based NGO, Blueprint for Free Speech, gives Maria Efimova its Special Recognition Award. Previous awardees include Chelsea Manning, John Kiriakou, Raj Mattu, Ari Danikas, Howard Shaw, and Visnja Marilovic. She is in excellent company.

28 March 2019. The European Parliament approves a resolution condemning corruption in Malta and the lack of judicial independence. The resolution attracts the backing of all political shades in the chamber including the PL's Socialist sister-parties in Europe. The only detractors are, significantly, far-right parties.

The resolution follows several reports and country visits by MEPs including Socialist MEP Ana Gomes, Green MEP Sven Giegold, Conservative MEP Monica Macovei, and left-wing MEP Stelios Kolouglou. They are supported by Maltese PN MEPs David Casa and Roberta Metsola.

The European Parliament calls on other EU institutions and member states 'to initiate an independent international public inquiry into the murder of Daphne Caruana Galizia and the alleged cases of corruption, financial crimes, money laundering, fraud and tax evasion reported by her, which involve Maltese high-ranking current and former public officials'.

7 April 2019. *The Times of Malta* reports that two PN frontbench members held a private meeting with Yorgen Fenech at his Tumas

Group office. PN president Kristy Debono initially denies meeting the owner of 17 Black. She later admits to a meeting two days earlier and says she and Herman Schiavone wanted to 'ask for a sponsorship for a conference'.

Debono and Schiavone are part of PN leader Adrian Delia's inner circle. They insisted the meeting was entirely innocent but the fallout is considerable. Six months previously, the PN had called on Konrad Mizzi and Keith Schembri to resign after fresh revelations that the owner of 17 Black was Yorgen Fenech and 17 Black was a 'target client' of Mizzi and Schembri's Panama companies.

Herman Schiavone 'suspends himself' from the PN Parliamentary Group pending an internal investigation. The investigation subsequently clears him and he is reinstated.

8 April 2019. The family of Daphne Caruana Galizia file a judicial protest calling on the Maltese government to order an independent and public inquiry into the assassination. The letter follows months of failed attempts by the family to persuade the government to order a public inquiry run by 'suitable, independent, and impartial' members. The family say the inquiry should determine whether:

- the fundamental right to life is being safeguarded by the state
- Daphne's murder could have been avoided
- the state had taken all the necessary precuations to protect her life
- there had been a lack of 'procedures, processes and administrative structures'
- these could be strengthened to protect other journalists at risk.

6 June 2019. The magistrates' court continues hearing the compilation of evidence against the three men charged with the murder. The Degiorgio brothers' lawyer William Cuschieri makes an odd request. He asks the magistrate to give his clients permission

to meet visiting MEPs Ana Gomes and David Casa. Both have been strongly critical of the Maltese authorities over their failings to enforce the rule of law. The MEPs decline the invitation, saying they have no role to play in a criminal investigation. The court eventually also turns down their request.

26 June 2019. The parliamentary assembly of the Council of Europe joins the calls for a public and independent inquiry into the killing of Daphne Caruana Galizia. It echoes other calls made by several international free-speech NGOs, including RSF Reporters Without Borders, the Committee to Protect Journalists, PEN International, the European Centre for Press and Media Freedom, the International Press Institute, and Article 19.

The Council of Europe's resolution follows a report by Dutch MP Pieter Omtzigt, entrusted to look into the Maltese situation. Investigations of this sort are not everyday occurrences at the Council of Europe. There have only been two, both into murders in Russia. An investigation into the killing of Boris Nemtsov. And an investigation into the killing of Anna Politkovskaya.

The PL's delegation in the Council of Europe attempts to stop the investigation from occurring. They then attempt to remove Pieter Omtzigt from the job of rapporteur because they perceive him as hostile. Then they attempt to force him to make more than 50 amendments to his draft report to tone down its impact. Then they attempt to persuade the parliamentary assembly to reject his report. They fail. Every time.

One of the authors interviews Pieter Omtzigt, who has a nose for corruption and is nicknamed (in Dutch) 'The Bloodhound'.

Malta has serious problems with the rule of law. There is, for example, a culture of overstatement. After she was killed, Daphne's family, her widower, and sons, faced multiple libel suits. These libel actions stifle debate. It's a small country but it's really like a town. The problem of enforcing checks and balances is higher. Set against that, the history of being besieged means that they are very good at defending themselves. But Malta and the government of Malta are not synonyms.

The primary problem is the lack of the rule of the law. And then there are a series of secondary problems: very weak financial controls. A banking licence in Malta is enough to move capital anywhere inside the European Union. Crypto-currencies are booming in Malta but they can be used to launder dirty money. They have been selling passports. Visas have been given to all sorts of people, including a good number of Libyans who would not pass elementary security checks. In the past, Malta has been too small to look at. But you can undermine the rule of law from a small or a big jurisdiction.

Omtzigt's report is damning. His conclusions are set out in a series of recommendations adopted by the Council of Europe. 'The Assembly notes that these fundamental weaknesses have allowed numerous major scandals to arise and go unchecked in Malta in recent years, including the following.'

He lists eight scandals.

One: *The Panama Papers revelations concerning several senior government figures and their associates, which have still not been investigated, other than by a magisterial inquiry primarily into the prime minister and his wife whose full results have not been made public.*

Two: *The Electrogas affair, in which the energy minister, Dr Konrad Mizzi, supervised a highly irregular procedure whereby a major public contract was awarded to a consortium. The consortium included the Azerbaijani state energy company which also made large profits from a related contract to supply liquid natural gas at a price well above the market rate. Another member of the consortium owned a secret Panama company, 17 Black, that was expected to make large monthly payments to secret Panama companies owned by Dr Mizzi and Mr Schembri, chief of staff of the prime minister. 17 Black received large sums of money from an Azerbaijani national and a company owned by a third member of the consortium. Despite being officially informed about the case by the FIAU, the police have taken no action against Dr Mizzi or Mr Schembri.*

Three: *The Egrant affair, in which, nine months after presenting a report said to exculpate the prime minister, the inquiring magistrate, who had been appointed by the prime minister, was promoted to judge by the prime minister. The assembly calls on the prime minister to make good on his promise to publish the full inquiry report without further delay.*

Four: *The Hillman affair, in which Mr Schembri was allegedly involved in money laundering with Adrian Hillman, then managing director of Allied Newspapers. The police failed to act, despite an FIAU report, and a magisterial inquiry is still ongoing after two years.*

Five: *The 'golden passports' affair, in which Mr Schembri received €100,000 from his long-standing associate Brian Tonna, owner of accountancy firm Nexia BT, an agent for 'golden passports' applicants. The FIAU found that Mr Tonna had received this money from three applicants for golden passports. The police have declined to investigate and a magisterial inquiry is still ongoing after two years.*

Six: *The Vitals Global Healthcare (VGH) affair, in which the health minister, Dr Konrad Mizzi, awarded a major hospitals contract to a consortium with no prior experience in the field and to which the government had allegedly promised the contract before the bidding process began. VGH may have received as much as €150 million from the government, yet made negligible progress with promised investments in the hospitals, before being sold to a US healthcare company. The auditor general is currently investigating this affair.*

Seven: *The fact that Mr Tonna and his firm Nexia BT, who played key roles in the Panama Papers, Electrogas, Egrant, Hillman, and 'golden passports' affairs, both received numerous lucrative government contracts, including after Mr Tonna came under investigation. The accountancy board has declined to take disciplinary action against them.*

Eight: *The role of Pilatus Bank, which was rapidly licensed by the Maltese Financial Services Authority (MFSA), leading to significant concerns on the part of the European Banking Authority; whose clients included mainly 'politically exposed persons', including Mr Schembri and companies owned by the daughters of the president of Azerbaijan; whose owner was connected to the prime minister and Mr Schembri, and was arrested by the US authorities and charged with violating sanctions against Iran; and which was subsequently closed by the MFSA and the European Central Bank.*

Omtzigt concludes: *The rule of law in Malta is seriously undermined by the extreme weakness of its system of checks and balances ... If Malta cannot or will not correct its weaknesses, European institutions must intervene.*

The Council of Europe report is no less disapproving of the investigation into Daphne's assassination. Omtzigt notes 'the weaknesses of the rule of law in general and the criminal justice system in particular are also directly relevant to its analysis of the authorities' response to the assassination of Daphne Caruana Galizia ... No one has been arrested for ordering the assassination. A magisterial inquiry is still ongoing, with no news on its progress.'

The rapporteur identified 10 serious concerns over the investigations into the murder.

One: *The need to recuse a series of magistrates from various roles because of conflicts of interest*

Two: *The need to remove the investigating police officer because of a conflict of interest*

Three: *The prime minister's removal of the inquiring magistrate after months of work*

Four: *The failure of the authorities to request possible evidence from the German police*

Five: *The failure of the police to interrogate economy minister Chris Cardona, despite claims that he had had contacts with the suspects*

Six: *The allegation that a police officer warned the suspects before they were arrested*

Seven: *False claims by the interior minister about progress in the investigation*

Eight: *Inflammatory and misleading statements by persons close to the prime minister*

Nine: *The possibility that the Maltese security service may have had prior intelligence about the murder plot*

Ten: *The director of Europol's complaint about co-operation with the Maltese police on the case.*

Omtzigt calls on Malta to comply with a deadline set by the parliamentary assembly of the Council of Europe to launch a public inquiry not later than 26 September 2019. At the time of writing, 10 days before the expiry of this deadline, the government of Malta has not yet done so.

The report condemns Malta's culture of impunity. Omtzigt has sharp words for prime minister Joseph Muscat's advisers, including John Dalli. Dalli writes a letter, attacking Omtzigt's report. Here are some of the choicer cuts from Omtzigt's reply which starts with a reference to Dalli's exit from the EU Commission and the smokeless cigarette scandal.

In these circumstances, I feel that my use of the word 'disgraced', whilst succinct as a description of your situation, was well within the bounds of fair comment.

... you mention my report's reference to your Pilatus Bank account. I note that you do not deny the truth of this statement but rather assume that it was included at the request of the anonymous alleged 'prompter', with the aim of implying certain connotations. In this case, not only are you imagining the existence of a 'prompter', you are also reading more into the text than it was intended to convey. Since you mention these possible connotations, however, I would agree that it seems peculiar for a person in your position to engage with a bank such as Pilatus, whose business model and operations have since been exposed as highly dubious to say the least, entrusting it with the not insignificant sum of €1000 merely in order to 'see what services they offer', when a simple enquiry would surely have provided the same information for free.

In light of the foregoing, I consider that I have nothing for which to apologise to you. I am, however, prepared to overlook for now the accusations and insults against me in your published letter.

16 July 2019. The constitutional court rules in favour of Daphne Caruana Galizia's family and finds a breach of their right to freedom of expression.

The family hung a banner against their property in Valletta in April 2017, six months after Daphne's death, with the questions:

- Why aren't Keith Schembri and Konrad Mizzi in prison, Police Commissioner?
- Why isn't your wife being investigated by the Police, Joseph Muscat?
- Who paid for Daphne Caruana Galizia to be blown up after she asked these questions?

It was taken down by planning enforcement officers within hours.

Two weeks later, Daphne's family put up another poster. 'This is our second banner. Our first got stolen.' It went the way of the first.

The court ordered the planning authority to compensate the family for suppressing their right to freedom of speech.

Other protest banners or posters get the similar treatment.

In the wake of the Oscar-winning film *Three Billboards Outside Ebbing, Missouri*, #occupyjustice activists hire three billboards from a private contractor in February 2018. Their billboards read:

- No Resignations. No Justice
- A Country Robbed. No Justice
- A Journalist Killed. No Justice.

No sooner were they put up, then planning enforcement officers were taking them down, and fining the contractor for erecting illegal structures, despite the fact that the billboards used existing infrastructure.

It was a case of using a minor administrative law to crush the higher fundamental right to freedom of expression.

23 July 2019. Adrian Delia demands to see a full copy of the Egrant inquiry report, all 1,500 pages of it. After all, the attorney general had provided the prime minister with a copy, so why not the leader of the opposition as well? When the AG refuses, Adrian Delia sues and his lawyers push the AG, Peter Grech, to list the recipients of the full inquiry report.

The list is short but telling. Peter Grech says he felt Joseph Muscat should get a copy of the inquiry report because after all it was about him and he had requested the inquiry in the first place. He also gave a copy to the justice minister. Why? In administrative matters, the minister may well be seen as the AG's boss. But Malta's constitution clearly states that in criminal matters the AG reports to no one. Especially not to a government minister.

Peter Grech explains that the justice minister, Owen Bonnici, had requested a copy in his capacity as personal legal adviser to Joseph Muscat and he could only assume he was acting on his client's instructions.

The court turns down Adrian Delia's request.

9 September 2019. The second anniversary of Daphne's death is upon us. At the time of writing, the Maltese authorities have yet to set a date for the trial of Alfred and George Degiorgio and Vincent Muscat.

The Maltese authorities have yet to open a public and independent inquiry into the killing of Daphne Caruana Galizia.

The Maltese authorities have yet to apprehend the masterminds.

The Maltese authorities have yet to investigate John Dalli, Konrad Mizzi, Chris Cardona, Keith Schembri, Brian Tonna, Adrian Delia, and others whose misdeeds were revealed by Daphne Caruana Galizia.

The Maltese authorities have yet to prosecute anyone on the back of the evidence unearthed by the Panama Papers.

The Maltese authorities were forced to close Pilatus Bank under pressure from the European Central Bank. But they have yet to take any criminal action in relation to Pilatus Bank for money laundering.

The international arrest warrant against Maria Efimova is still in place. She remains under the protection of the Greek authorities.

The attorney general, Peter Grech, and the chief of police, Lawrence Cutajar are still in office.

Keith Schembri is still the prime minister's chief of staff.

Konrad Mizzi is still a senior cabinet minister and is pitching to succeed Joseph Muscat as party leader and prime minister.

The magisterial inquiry into the assassination of Daphne Caruana Galizia is still open.

MALTA'S SHAME

Two days before Daphne Caruana Galizia was assassinated, prime minister Joseph Muscat was at a small shindig celebrating 30 years of a manufacturing company at the Meridien Hotel. Economy minister Chris Cardona was present and there is a photo of Muscat twinkling at the audience. Muscat is a politician to his fingertips, seriously good at the small change of politics: the easy smile, meeting and greeting, pressing the flesh. *The Shift News* team, led by reporter and founder Caroline Muscat (no relation), broke the story of what happened next.

The prime minister fainted.

There is, of course, no suggestion that the prime minister had prior knowledge of what was going to happen to his archenemy within 48 hours.

In January 2018, co-author John Sweeney, then working for BBC Newsnight, interviewed Muscat. It was the last time Muscat would give a major interview to a member of the international media, as at September 2019.

The interview took place inside the prime minister's office, a magnificent palazzo called Auberge de Castille overlooking the Grand Harbour. It was originally built to house the Knights of the Order of St John in the 1570s. The present building is a Baroque pearl, dating back to the 1740s. Inside, hushed courtiers and minions move hither and yon behind gloomy curtains. The furniture is spindly and French, elegant once, but now with a touch of woodworm.

After the camera team had set up, Muscat entered the room. He's a small, compact man, elegantly dressed, smooth, smiling frequently, a little too smiley perhaps, as if there might be something wrong within. He sat down, smiled, and battle commenced.

Where was the PM when he heard of Daphne Caruana Galizia's assassination?

Right in this office. The security services informed me that there was a bomb. First information I got that it was in the town where I lived and then it got corrected to the town where Daphne Caruana Galizia lived which is basically next door. And then within minutes I got an unofficial confirmation that it was probably her car.

What had been the effect of the assassination on Malta's standing in the world?

Well I think it's been very bad. I think it's the worst nightmare I ever had coming through having such a horrific act taking place under my watch. So I feel the responsibility for it. Given our judicial system I really cannot comment on what's taking place since then but I am comforted that our security services have put forward and have prosecuted people who have allegedly made this bomb. What I want to see is that justice is done fully. So I know that there are people who will ask whether it was them who planned the whole thing, who were the commissioners of the whole thing or that they were just the executive arm of this whole plot ...

What was the effect of her assassination on his own standing?

Well, bad. Definitely because that's not something that any prime minister would want. She was a very fierce critic of many people. I might have been the top of that list and this doesn't look good on me. I'm very realistic on this ...

Daphne's fiercest criticisms were that the Panama Papers revealed that two of his closest political associates, his chief of

staff Keith Schembri and minister Konrad Mizzi had opened shell companies in Panama. When that came out, what did he do?

Well I removed a minister from his post as deputy leader of my party. I removed his portfolio, put him directly under my supervision, and then there were elections in which these people, the minister went to the people and I went to the people with my judgment and the people judged us on this.

So Konrad Mizzi is still in government?

Well he has a different portfolio now but I think that people judged both what he did and what I did. I have gone on record saying that I think that, they, it was a misjudgment from their side to do those things. They came up with, they explained their reasoning. Mr Schembri is a businessman who gave up his positions in business to enter politics on the executive arm. He gave his reasons for opening companies, he had companies before entering politics. Mr Mizzi gave his reasons too. I said that it was lack of good judgment. I made my decisions on their regard. And then people made their decisions on me.

Why is it OK for these two guys who are still in government to have opened secretive companies on the far side ...

(interrupting) I'm not saying it's okay and I'm not here to give their version of facts. I'm here just to say that they gave a very open account of what they did. They subjected themselves to open audits. They published those audits. Mr. Schembri, my chief of staff, was in business and had companies before entering politics. They gave their answers and people judged us on those answers. I said that's something I wouldn't have done. [Daphne] also said that my wife or myself had such companies something which is totally false and I went to the judiciary. I asked for those allegations against me, against my wife to be investigated and I said quite clearly and I stand by my word that, if there is even a whiff of evidence on what Mrs Caruana Galizia had said in my regard, I would resign on the spot. And I still, I still, I will keep my word. That's something that would be unacceptable.

Daphne Caruana Galizia had many enemies. You'd expect the police to interview them, wouldn't you? Have the police interviewed your wife?

(taken aback) *I am not … well, I don't know what the police have done. I know that my wife wasn't called in because she's my wife. I am pretty sure that the security services know what they're doing. We're not intruding in all this for sure. What I can tell you is that we're not that sort of people and what I can tell you is that this goes beyond politics. Besides her family, I think if there is one person that has suffered from this assassination, it's us. Just because this long shadow has been cast on us.*

Sorry, one person is us? That doesn't make sense.

Me and my wife, well, two people. It has cast a long shadow on us when we have nothing to do with all these things and you know yes she made allegations on my wife, on me, on my family. [Daphne] *hasn't produced one shred of evidence on this. She had all the time and I am informed that, before the assassination took place, she went to testify in front of the inquiring magistrate on the case relating to me on an inquiry that I called myself through the independent, an independent magistrate, so she said what she had to do and I await with trepidation the day in which the results of this investigation comes out which I am sure will prove that there was nothing in all this. I think Mrs Daphne Caruana Galizia, you couldn't box her really in one type of journalism. On the one hand she produced some cutting-edge world-class pieces of journalism where she uncovered things both locally and on all sides of the political spectrum and also internationally. On the other hand, some parts of her blog were purely gossip, were purely unsubstantiated stories that she put forward and which I think no other journalist would put forward without evidence. So in the case of what she said about me, that's one of the latter.*

Have the police interviewed you?

No they haven't.

Have the police interviewed your wife?

No, they haven't and I know …

So how good an investigation is that? Because there was evidence, she said, she had a whistleblower inside Pilatus Bank and this whistleblower said that your wife had a shell company.

OK. I think I think we're now confusing things. I submitted myself and my wife submitted herself to answering questions by the investigating magistrate on the allegations you have mentioned. We have been subjected to a long interrogation. We went there quite some time ago. We produced all the evidence that was asked by us. We answered all the questions. We went into the interrogation separately without the help of any lawyer and we have not availed ourselves to the right of not answering. We have fully collaborated, both of us.

No lawyer?

No lawyer because we have absolutely nothing to hide. That we have done fully. Where the police have not called us in is in interrogating us on the assassination of Mrs Caruana Galizia. So if you're referring on whether we were interrogated on the claims that she made, yes, because we subjected ourselves and I myself asked for that investigation. On the latter, no...

But while you are being investigated and while members of the government are being investigated, they're still in power, they're still in office?

Well I wouldn't say that we are, I am being investigated. I asked for investigations on allegations that have been made. God forbid that we are in a situation where if someone were aware of this and this does not, in anyway, I don't want to be seen, I know I am in a quite uncomfortable situation having to criticise someone who has been killed brutally. But I hope we're not in a situation where in any democracy situations are such where if someone writes something on social media it's taken as a fact.

But you're doing exactly that, though, aren't you? She was killed brutally and you are saying at least some of the time she was running gossip?

Yes she did.

And as far as you're concerned and your wife is concerned, she had no evidence?

Yes, she didn't have any evidence because what she said was totally incorrect.

That doesn't follow, sir. She had evidence. You don't agree with it, you don't think it's right but she did have evidence. She had a whistleblower.

Have you seen the evidence?

... some of this stuff is difficult because it's been deliberately placed in an opaque and difficult-to-read place. The allegation that she makes ...

I think that you were coming from the wrong place. So you're saying you coming here with questions saying you have seen no evidence ... that you've just read a blog.

No, I'm aware of what she said but critically what she said in the most compelling blog was that your wife had a company in Panama and a million dollars was paid to that company by the daughter of the president of Azerbaijan. Is that true?

It's totally false.

She said that and she said she had evidence.

OK, OK, so have you seen that evidence? You haven't?

I've seen her description of it. But there's a problem here, isn't there, because in this area of dirty money, slush money, the evidence is hard to come by.

No, I totally disagree because I read exactly what she said. So first of all there isn't a shred, not only a proof, of truth, of what she said on all this. She based herself on a person calling herself a whistleblower and the account of this whistleblower is dubious to say the least. But apart from that, if there exists a document somewhere, it would come out, for the simple reason she's saying that money was wired in from somewhere to an account which my wife had somewhere in the world, she said here in Malta, owned this account by a company in Panama. Now I think you will agree with me that in this modern world there is no way in which money can be wired from one place to another without leaving a trace. What the inquiring magistrate has the power to do is to see all the transfers of money made in my name, in the name of any company in this bank in whichever bank in the world and see if there is one shred of truth in that money has been transferred to me, to my wife, or to anyone else. I think you will agree with me that it is impossible. To have money transferred from one account to another without leaving even a single trace. What I am saying is that not only there is no evidence, if even there is a whiff of any evidence to this, I would resign on the spot.

[Sweeney pulled a face.]

I think no politician would put out his neck in such a clear and unequivocal manner if he wasn't sure about what he's saying. And yes I'm sorry, the issue with Mrs Caruana Galizia is that she said things that were facts. She wrote stories that were cutting edge. But then these were coupled by things that were false. I don't know whether she knew that what she was saying against me or about me was false, whether she was party to this invention. Or whether she was fed the story by this whistleblower or someone else and maybe it looked too true, too good not to be true. Let's put that way because it fitted the narrative that some people wanted to put in. What I am saying is that even she had you know placed her faith in this magistrate. She went to testify in front of this magistrate. As far as I know she gave him all the evidence and so we just, I will just be waiting for the results of this inquiry and will make all the necessary decisions. And I do this in a serene manner because I know that not only, I didn't do anything which is wrong, but I didn't do anything, my wife or anything, anyone else that is wrong in all this so I must tell you because maybe you know not you know but maybe you were briefed on the latter part of the story in the beginning. The ... the ... the ... the ... rumour was that she and other people were putting forward that I owned this account. And then when it was crystal clear that I didn't own any account well it's his wife who owns this account, then it's his kids. You know I have given, I have asked myself for the judiciary to investigate, not only me, not only my wife but all the members of my family, anyone, who they thought might be holding any monies in my name.

And this investigation continues?
Yes, of course.

At the moment there is no result?
I cannot hold the judiciary to …

You can't say definitively there is no evidence.
I'm saying what I read in the papers would say that to date no evidence has been produced. In the papers that was reported.

So what about your family's relationship with the first family of Azerbaijan?
Well I met President Aliyev, I believe twice, in Baku. A number of times when we were at the EU Eastern Partnership summits. Mrs Aliyeva came here once, she met with my wife. That's it. That's the relationship.

Nothing more?
Nothing more.

Daphne said there was a lot more.
The prime minister laughs.

A million dollars?
You know I don't think you can hide $1,000,000. I don't think you can hide $100. Definitely not in a bank. Definitely not anywhere else.
[This may not be true. If the bank account is owned by a shell company in Panama and the name of the true owner is not directly written on the paperwork you can hide $100. You can hide $1,000,000.]

The flight of the files, the suitcases being removed from Pilatus Bank in the middle of the night from Malta to Azerbaijan? There are pictures of them being removed.
Well, I've seen so many pictures. I can surely tell you because I also happen to have a background on banking and due diligence and all the rest that there

is no way in which you can wire money, transfer money from one account to another in the world without that leaving one trace. And that's not governed by one single bank it's governed by an international system ...

Our judiciary is looking at the international databases, they're getting all the necessary help from all jurisdictions from the international assistance. And I'm sure there is even one cent transfer not one million dollars but one cent of transfer, they will get to the bottom of this. The problem is that all this, it's not ... simply not true and I find myself having to fight for my reputation because of some blogs that have been written and because other things that she's written were substantiated on various people, then by association, 'what you wrote about Joseph Muscat must be true'.

I find myself in the unfortunate situation where you know without even one shred of evidence being produced about me I need each and every week to fight this thing that has been said about me. So if there is one person who wants this inquiry to be out as soon as possible, it's me.

One week after Daphne's assassination: where were you and what were you doing?
I wouldn't know. Honestly.

You were in Dubai selling passports.
[Muscat's laugh did not reach his eyes.]
I was. We don't sell it. We have, as other European jurisdictions, other European countries, systems by which and programmes, and ours is the most open programme. People can invest in our country, can have residence and even citizenship ... We're the only country in the European Union where we have an agreement with the European Commission on how such a programme works. Other countries have such residence and citizenship programmes but the spotlight is on us for reasons which I don't know.

Daphne said you were selling passports effectively with this company called Henley & Partners?
It's not about selling them ... It's about investment ... We're not the only European Union country that does that. We're not the only country in the

world that does that. And Henley & Partners were given the concession after an open call.

Who's buying these passports?
Well, various people, wealthy people. But wealth doesn't buy you the right to citizenship.

It helps if you've got €650,000 though?
It helps but it doesn't mean that you can get access to our programme. I had some of the wealthiest people in the world in this office complaining to me that they were not given citizenship even though they were very wealthy. It's because our sponsor, Reuters said, our due diligence system, our four-tier system is the most advanced in the world.

[Reuters, the world-famous news agency, said no such thing. Muscat was referring to comments by an American lawyer, Peter Vincent, who worked for Thomson Reuters Special Services which is a management consultancy arm, not part of Reuters' journalism empire. Vincent has left the consultancy and is now a member of the group executive committee at Henley & Partners.]

The law says the minister responsible – and I believe that's you – can override a problem for example if somebody has got a criminal record or is being under criminal investigation?
This system has never been overridden …

If that's the case why don't you list the names?
There was there was an article yesterday saying who these people are.

[The names and true identities of the passport buyers are not clearly given in Malta's system. Muscat expanded on his defence of opacity.]

No, I think first of all, we don't distinguish between one citizen and the other. We're not saying, this is not a list of hundreds of thousands of people as in other countries. It's a list of hundreds of people that is published regularly and I think simple Google search will give you a simple database I think will give you the backgrounds of people with names. The names are public. So I cannot understand all this hullabaloo because the lists are not listed in the right manner or that sort of thing. The lists are there and I don't think that any journalist would stop because of some database.

People on the island say that you're selling passports to dodgy Russians?

Well, people on the island say also that since the inception of our programme we have had the attention of people with networks that would have never given attention to our country and because of that our economy is benefiting because these people are investing even more in our country. You know the problem with some people is that they think they can box more with this sort of dodgy tax haven definition.

So it's not a dodgy tax haven?

Definitely not. And I'll tell you why. First of all our economy is hugely diversified. Do you know what our main export is? Semiconductors, microchips. That's our main export. That doesn't really suit the narrative of a tax haven.

[Microchips are indeed the biggest single manufacturing export from Malta. But the manufacturing sector is dwarfed by finance, services, and banking – and a part of that could indeed fit inside the narrative of a dodgy tax haven.]

Secondly, there are no tax havens in the European Union for a simple reason tax haven means you have banking secrecy. We don't. [Tax havens] *don't give information to other jurisdictions. We do. Thirdly,* [tax havens] *don't share information. We do share information so all these facts show that we are not a tax haven. If we wanted to be a tax haven we would go out of the European Union but we are very happy with the European Union.*

[The subject changed, somewhat.]

Tony Blair supported you in the last general election.

Yes, he did.

Describe your relationship with Tony Blair.

A relationship of the like-minded. I have a lot of time for Mr Blair. I take in many of his policies as a role model for me when it comes to and for us when it comes to the way he introduced minimum wage in the UK and the way he put forward civil liberties and the way in which he showed that a Labour government could grow an economy and put forward socially just policies. I don't agree with him obviously on the Iraq war. That's the type of relationship we have.

Does Malta have a problem with money laundering?

Well … we have a financial services industry that is thriving, that is growing. And it's growing also because we are a serious jurisdiction. Reports have always suggested that we need to do more when it comes to enforcement. That is what we are doing. So I don't feel comfortable in saying no, we don't have any problems or yes we have problems. I'd say we have as many problems as any other jurisdiction, be it the city of London, be it Luxembourg be it in the Netherlands, when it comes to making sure that we comply with the rules.

Two members of the anti-money-laundering Agency FIAU were sacked last summer. Are you comfortable with what happened?

Well, first of all, the anti-money-laundering agency is an independent agency. Those same two people were hired during my term in office so no one says, 'Oh you hired them'. They say 'you sacked them'. I didn't hire them, I didn't sack them. It was the agency that hired them. The agency that sacked them. You'd have to ask them why they did so.

Do you stand by your economy minister, Chris Cardona?

Definitely. I stand by all my ministers.

Daphne alleged while on official business in Germany he went to a brothel.

And he put forward a libel suit in her regard and as far as I know that libel suit is still ongoing.

Why are you letting your ministers sue a dead woman?

I think it's a bit of a Catch-22 situation. So, on one side, if he does not sue ... we will never know the truth. On the other hand, if he continues this case, people say he is suing that woman. So really and truly I think it's a bit of a Catch-22 situation. My point is that he has given me his word that this hasn't happened. Mrs Caruana Galizia wrote that she is basing her article on an anonymous source ... And I do believe that her sons can put forward any evidence they have.

Do you think it's seemly to have somebody in your cabinet suing the estate of an assassinated journalist?

That is a decision that he needs to make.

Surely, you're the boss though?

No, I'm OK, but I must tell you I must tell you I must tell you again but I must tell you again it's a bit of a Catch-22 situation where I'll give you another example.

[Muscat seemed rattled. His normal fluency had departed, for a moment or two.]

Does this look good for the integrity of the Maltese government? One of your ministers ...

It will not look good either way. I'll give you another ...

It's worse this way, some would say.

Well, let me give you another example. Daphne Caruana Galizia just before she was killed alleged that the leader of the opposition was a cover for a money-laundering operation. As soon as she was killed, he rushed to court to drop the case as the criticism over here was that it was a convenient thing to do because now no one will really know what she could produce on the case. And the case is now dead and buried. And is that a worst-case scenario or a best-case scenario? I think that's a decision that the minister needs to take. It's not good either way.

You could say that. If your minister Chris Cardona wins, then he'll take money from the estate?

I don't think it's an issue of money. I think you know, I, I, really don't think it's an issue of how much money and I think if the issue is simply a monetary issue that can be resolved very easily. I think no one is after money here. I think it's about clearing someone's name.

Members of the European Parliament came here and they said that there was perception of impunity in Malta on your watch. Malta hasn't got a good reputation in Europe.

Well it depends on the MEPs that make such statements. You know the thing I know is that under my watch we had introduced party financing rules. We were the only country in Europe with no such rules. We've introduced a law by means of which we give protection to whistleblowers. We've removed time-barring on cases of corruption for politicians. So until we came to office there was a situation where after ten years any politician could not be prosecuted on corruption simply because the cases would be time-barred. We moved and we have put in legislation where in my lifetime in any politician's lifetime, past, present, or future. Once there is any evidence of a case of corruption time-barring would not come into effect and that the person can be prosecuted. So that's what happened during my time in office so far.

Yes but when the MEPs came they didn't go clap, clap, well done. They said there's a perception of impunity. Too many people in your government appear to do bad things and get away with it.

You know I'm not here to do a tit-for-tat with some MEPs. There is a political agenda for some of those members of the European Parliament. I was a member of the European Parliament myself. I know that we've been caught into some sort of political crossfire with some groups wanting to take their pound of flesh from the other group and we were caught in that crossfire.

One of those MEPs who made that criticism of impunity was a Portuguese Socialist?

She's one of the very few Socialist MEPs who criticise me. I think that in the larger narrative is that of a centre-right versus centre-left political battle.

The charge in a nutshell is that you are the artful dodger of Europe?

[laughing] I, well ... if that is the charge, I am I am definitely not guilty of that. It's preposterous. I do believe that our success story as a country might not go down well with others but is this a success story that will continue for a long time.

After Daphne's assassination her son Matthew wrote: 'If institutions were already working, there would be no assassination to investigate and my brothers and I would still have a mother.' What do you say to that?

Well, I have made this very clear. I would never take issue with people who have lost their mother in such a brutal assassination. I've said that, that if my mother was killed in such instances I would say much worse things than that.

On the other hand, you called her a gossip-monger and you said that she reported stuff with no evidence?

Yes. I don't think that I have a situation where because of her brutal assassination ... I can just say that anything she wrote in her life was true and that I subscribed to that. You know in my case I reaffirmed the fact that what [she] wrote about me was totally false. I think I am entitled to do that.

Interview ends.

Prime minister Joseph Muscat denies any wrongdoing.

WHO KILLED DAPHNE
CARUANA GALIZIA?

The authors advise the reader to resist the temptation of starting this book by first reading this chapter. Do not board this train thinking it has reached its destination. Go back to the beginning and read it properly as you know you should.

At the start of this book, we described Malta as a dirty money locomotive hurtling through the night. On board, a cast of dodgy characters, with Daphne Caruana Galizia in the role of detective.

You can imagine our suspects on the train, Poirot twiddling his moustaches, every eye on the great detective. He coughs, revelling in the moment, then asks: 'Who ordered the killing of Daphne Caruana Galizia?'

The camera pans on the faces of all present, smiling, impassive, neurotic, twitching. All concerned deny any wrongdoing.

Was it the Artful Dodger himself, Malta's sleek, smooth-tongued yet blatantly dishonest prime minister, Joseph Muscat?

Or the woman who denies receiving a €1 million bung from the family of the fabulously corrupt President of Azerbaijan, who just so happens to be the prime minister's wife?

Was it the prime minister's consigliere, Keith Schembri, who had a shell company in Panama?

Or the only minister in the democratic world with a shell company in Panama who didn't get sacked, Konrad Mizzi?

Or the third man who had a desk outside the prime minister's office, accountant Brian Tonna?

Was it Yorgen Fenech, the casino boss whose Dubai shell company 17 Black was supposed to pay big money to Schembri and Mizzi? Remember Fenech's casino, some years before the assassination, had handed €440,000 to one of the men accused of killing Daphne – evidence, one would have thought, of an unhealthy relationship?

Was it the brothel-creeper Chris Cardona?

Or his pal who laundered the dosh from the Soho brothel, Opposition Leader Adrian Delia?

Was it John Dalli, the man 'let go' by the European Commission five years to the dot before Daphne was murdered?

The dirty fuel king, Darren Debono?

Was it Ali Sadr, the litigious owner of Pilatus Bank, busted by the FBI and waiting for trial in the United States?

The people Ali Sadr banked for, the fabulously corrupt 'royal family' of Azerbaijan?

The Passport King?

His clients?

The Italian Mafia?

Or all of them together?

The screen goes black.

This isn't fiction. This is not make-believe. This is real life and what really happened was that Malta's brilliant detective was blown up in the most hideous way.

The authors stand aghast at the depth of corruption Daphne Caruana Galizia managed to unearth on her island home. We have turned over some stones and seen creatures wriggling away from the light but have elected not to tell everything we know for reasons we cannot, for the moment, explain.

There is fresh information about the men who have been charged with her execution. One of them is afraid of being poisoned, and is refusing prison food. He eats only what his family bring him and deliberately shares his food with other prisoners. All three men face spending the rest of their lives in prison. In Malta, life imprisonment means life. The pressure to reveal all must be strong. One day, perhaps, one of them might roll the dice and gamble on the fact that telling the world what he knows may be the least dangerous way out.

Perhaps.

What is certain is that the culture of impunity in Malta helped create the conditions in which its greatest and most fearless journalist could be murdered. But the dodgy characters listed above are not alone. The people of Malta, too, bear some responsibility for her murder. For too long they have turned a blind eye to the corruption of the government of Joseph Muscat. And if you ignore corruption for too long, you end up with innocent blood being spilt.

Casting the net still wider, across Europe and the western world those shifty politicians and PR smooth-sayers, rickety lawyers, bent coppers, dodgy bankers, and tricksy estate agents who look the other way when dirty money is flashed in their faces, bear some responsibility too.

Corruption stinks. We can all smell it. It is time that we did something about it.

For a new reader, Daphne's blog is a thing of wonder. In between the shocking revelations, the scandals and the tightly-documented unveiling of wrongdoing, there is wisdom, anger, insight, humour, passion, contempt, frustration, sympathy, impatience, kindness, fury, and shock.

There are some things in her blog we would not have written. There is a lot more we wish we had. Her autonomy gave her the freedom to ask questions that news organisations would be afraid or unable to ask. It also allowed her to make her own mistakes. She owes no one an apology. The only journalists who make no mistakes are the ones who write nothing worth reading. Journalists must not be jellyfish.

As we read the work she wrote in the last months of her life, we see an air of melancholy creep in. She knew what she meant to her readers. Her *Running Commentary* was pretty much the only way they could understand what was happening to Malta. No one could explain it as well as she did. She knew that. She carried that burden with pride.

As we seek to understand the context in which she wrote, we share her frustration at the unanswered questions, the obfuscation, the double-speak.

Malta is part of the modern, open, globalised economy. But we can see that it is also being used by criminals for whom laws and national borders are trivial occupational hazards.

The people of Malta do not always acknowledge the victims of these crimes. They do not see the suffering caused by embezzlement and corruption in other countries; they do not see the blood on the floor left by smugglers, racketeers, extortionists, and drug traffickers.

Money-laundering is not a victimless crime. People suffer.

We worry for Malta, a home to one of the co-authors and a place the other two authors admire for its sad, threatened beauty.

Like Daphne, we worry that an oligarchy of interests — in politics, in business, in crime — has made Malta its private fiefdom. And the Maltese live in a country possessed by men, with some faces they recognise, others they do not because they know to stay hidden.

In this book, we write about Italian organised crime, the Russian state, Azerbaijani oligarchs, Iranian sanctions-dodgers, oil-smugglers, casino-operators, corrupt politicians, bent cops, and sleazy judges. They come from all over the world and use Malta as their backdoor to Europe; they use Malta as their clearing house, caring nothing for those they harm if they get in their way.

With time, we started to feel Daphne's anger as if it was our own.

We wrote her story. But we also wrote the story of Malta.

Daphne deserves justice and this can only be had through the truth. Her husband, her sons, her parents, and her sisters deserve it too. We wish it for them.

But truth and justice for Daphne are truth and justice for Malta too. For as long as this train hurtles on, Daphne will not be the only victim.

In a dark hour, when many told Daphne they could see no hope, she wrote, 'the fight against corruption and [against] the decimation of the rule of law must continue'.

Indeed, it must.

In Valletta, every night city cleaners remove flowers, photos, candles, and messages of support for Daphne's family at the Great Siege Memorial in Valletta. In the morning, supporters and activists start again.

And the battle continues. As it must.

ALL CONCERNED DENY
ANY WRONGDOING

The authors have attempted to present a fair account, including the points of view of people who might feel criticised by this book. We have, as far as practicable, included in our account, comments made by these persons and took pains to make sure that, wherever we are aware that this is indeed the case, we have made it abundantly clear that the persons concerned deny any wrongdoing.

In the cases of the following persons, we have informed them ahead of time of what we intended to publish and invited them to send us any response they wished us to include: Joseph Muscat, Michelle Muscat, Keith Schembri, Konrad Mizzi, Chris Cardona, John Dalli, Christian Kälin, Alexander Nix, attorneys for the directors of Pilatus Bank, Brian Tonna, Karl Cini, Stephan Roh in respect of himself and his client Joseph Mifsud, Adrian Delia, Anthony Axisa, attorneys for Darren Debono, Yorgen Fenech, and lawyers for Alfred Degiorgio, George Degiorgio, and Vincent Muscat.

We have not received responses by the time of publishing from all these persons. Here are the responses we have received. Any errors contained in the responses have not been corrected.

JOSEPH MUSCAT, MICHELLE MUSCAT, KEITH SCHEMBRI, KONRAD MIZZI AND CHRIS CARDONA

The authors put a series of questions to Malta's prime minister, Joseph Muscat, his wife, Michelle Muscat, economy minister Chris Cardona, tourism minister Konrad Mizzi, and Keith Schrembi, the PM's adviser. We received a letter from London law firm Carter-Ruck marked private and confidential. The authors are placed in a bind. If we print the Carter-Ruck letter, we breach their request for confidentiality. If we leave it out, it might appear that we have not offered Joseph Muscat, Michelle Muscat, Chris Cardona, Konrad Mizzi, and Keith Schrembi a right of reply which is not the case. Below, we set out the points made in Carter-Ruck's letter.

Carter-Ruck says it is instructed by the government of Malta ('the Government') in connection with the authors' communication on 2 September to the prime minister, his wife, and three government ministers [sic].

Carter-Ruck says that the authors have given no indication of the identity of the co-authors or the publishers of the proposed book. Carter-Ruck invites the authors to tell Carter-Ruck who the authors are.

Carter-Ruck says that although the authors say the book will be published in the 'next few weeks', and it must have been in development for some time, the authors have stipulated that a response will need to be given within a week of receipt of the authors' email, by 9 September, after which time 'the commitment to print deadline will have expired'. Carter-Ruck says that given the serious nature of the allegations that the authors raise, and the complexity of the background, this is an unreasonably short timeframe in which meaningfully to address the claims.

Carter-Ruck says that the authors will appreciate that, whilst the allegations put to each individual differ, each is highly defamatory. Carter-Ruck says that all of the matters put to the individuals in the authors' correspondence are expressed, by implication, to be linked to the murder of Daphne Caruana Galizia as 'the circumstances prior to and the aftermath of the assassination' is said to be the overall subject of the book. Carter-Ruck says the individuals concerned reserve all their rights in relation to the publication and repetition of any allegation that is defamatory and untrue.

Carter-Ruck notes the authors' assurance that the book takes into account the public comments, statements, and responses to criticism that the subjects of the allegations have made. Carter-Ruck says that its client (the government of Malta) would expect that, in so far as investigations have reached a conclusion, the public findings are reported faithfully and comprehensively, and that the public statements made on behalf of the government or individual ministers about these matters should be fairly reflected in any published book or other material.

Carter-Ruck understands that the matters the authors raise in the authors' correspondence are either the subject of ongoing court proceedings or investigation in Malta, or have already been the subject of magisterial investigation. Carter-Ruck says the Egrant inquiry, for example, found signatures had been falsified on documents, inconsistent testimonies, and nothing linking the prime minister's family to the offshore company.

Carter-Ruck says its client is engaging with the Council of Europe concerning the establishment of a public inquiry into Ms Caruana Galizia's death, with a view to having a full and independent inquiry that will not interfere with ongoing criminal proceedings.

Carter-Ruck says, as the authors know, criminal proceedings are ongoing against three individuals charged in December 2017 in connection with Ms Galizia's death and further investigations are being conducted by a magistrate in relation to potential involvement by other individuals. Carter-Ruck says its client has been clear that Ms Caruana Galizia's death, and other allegations, should be investigated properly through the appropriate channels.

Carter-Ruck says yours faithfully, Carter-Ruck.

JOHN DALLI

John Dalli sent us an 84-page, 28,000-word monograph. This is our edited extract of his response.

Daphne Caruana Galizia directed an aggressive campaign of character assassination against me. I was called a crook and had to endure a whole litany of *ad hominem* insinuations. She joined forces with all those who, for one reason or another, had an axe to grind …

Caruana Galizia, in one of her articles, gives a good description of her mindset. It's the sort of mind that resorts to crude stereotyping of other people. It is also obsessive and inflexible in its judgements. The article makes interesting reading and offers some fascinating psychological insights.

It will come as no surprise, therefore, that over the years Caruana Galizia invented all sorts of lurid fantasies about me. She placed me, strategically, in the middle of many untoward events – indeed anything that suited her own spurious narratives and vindictive agendas. She effectively demonised me. The comments under her articles, mostly written by organised psychos hidden behind nom de plumes …

I have endured fifteen years of vitriolic abuse from this warped and obsessive individual.

This spate of harassing blogs shows not only the obsessive mindset of Daphne Caruana Galizia but also her unceasing and malicious determination to destroy my reputation, my health, my peace of mind, my social existence, and my economic wellbeing …

On the smokeless tobacco scandal

Daphne Caruana Galizia continually referred to me as 'the disgraced former European Commissioner'. This denigrating designation is copied by the poison pens in Malta who are still running a hate campaign against me. I am in all this the fall-guy: the victim of a set-up…

On his bank account at Pilatus

A bank account is a fact of life for most people. Our accounts and their confidentiality are protected by legislation. My own

Pilatus account never showed any kind of suspicious transaction. I opened it with a €1000 deposit and closed it after the balance had been depleted by bank charges associated with the account's inactivity. My reason for making this public statement is to counter the perception that I was one of the villains in Daphne Caruana Galizia's Pilatus narrative.

On the Ponzi scheme allegations

I did not inform my EU colleagues that I was leaving Cyprus. And I had no need to inform them, let alone resort to a trumped-up excuse: I left simply because the meetings there had come to an end.

My reason for attending the Bahamas meeting was to learn about the possibility of a long-term solution to the refugee problem in the Mediterranean – a solution, I believed, that could only come about by creating viable domestic economies in the refugees' own countries.

CHRISTIAN KÄLIN

The following was received from the Group Public Relations Director of Henley & Partners UK Ltd in response to our communication with Christian Kälin:

Thank you for your contact through the electronic portal. As Henley & Partners Group Director of Public Relations, please feel free to come to me direct should you need any further assistance from now on.

We appreciate your giving us the opportunity to provide input before you publish, and we will try to respond as fully as possible in order to prevent any misconceptions or even false statements.

We respect the efforts of serious and in-depth journalism, and it is in this spirit that we have welcomed the numerous media enquiries we have received on previous occasions, and responded to them in detail — even when we are often given very little time to reply because of the tight deadlines imposed by journalists and media houses.

As long as the media's work remains factual, neutral, and balanced towards the reader, we believe it can truly make a difference, not only in helping correct general misconceptions but also hopefully in uncovering the truth behind the brutal murder of Daphne Caruana Galizia.

It is on this point that I wish to start. You have referred in a generalised and non-specific manner to multiple defamatory and factually incorrect allegations made about both Henley & Partners and its Chairman Dr Christian Kälin. We have – as you note and are well aware – refuted all of these in multiple public sources and made our position very clear in the past.

We have always been transparent with the global media; any suggestion of wrong-doing on our part, or even any reference to different facts in a misleading way (for example, failing to provide the proper context to an uninitiated reader not intimately familiar with the situation in Malta, or elsewhere). It is likely that such reporting will be defamatory.

We are sure you will understand that it is entirely wrong to report (undisputed) facts in a way that leaves the uninitiated reader with an impression of improper conduct on the part of particular persons or entities, let alone to make statements that are simply false.

It is unfortunate that despite our best efforts to provide clear and open answers to media enquiries, factually incorrect information is still quite frequently being (mis)reported.

We therefore request that instead of referring to a series of unsubstantiated and libellous, defamatory allegations, you ask direct questions that we can answer equally directly. This is a prerequisite for us to be able to respond adequately.

In the past we have been more than happy to engage with the international media consortium that investigated the tragic circumstances of Daphne Caruana Galizia's death. They were always strictly professional, giving us full details of whom they worked for, but also where any pieces they wrote would be published.

In the case of this engagement, assuming that you are part of the same international media consortium, we would be grateful for the same professional courtesy. We note that you appear to have contacted the Chairman of Henley & Partners through his personal website only and at a (very) late stage, and have only given a week to respond in circumstances where the book has presumably been written over an extended period of time and where it would have been possible to contact us at a far earlier stage to ask any questions that you may have regarding Henley & Partners and/or Dr Christian Kälin. As you will be aware, this is far from best journalistic practice should you wish to be objective in your analysis and conclusions.

We therefore request the following information so that we can engage with you in good faith. As soon as possible, please provide us with details of any print deadline, the publisher, the co-authors, where the book is to be published, and in what medium.

We make these requests in order to try to prevent any possible misunderstanding (whether caused by other false and misleading reports, or otherwise), and to support more balanced reporting on the subject at hand, while at the same time reducing your own possible legal exposure. You should be aware that, if required to do so, we will protect our reputation against the publication of any false and damaging allegations to the full extent of the law. We hope that by entering into a constructive dialogue no such action becomes necessary.

Please understand that while we fully support and believe in open, in-depth, and serious journalistic work, we also have a legal right to object to false or misleading reporting in order to protect our good name and reputation.

We hope that by providing these responses we can contribute to an objective, factually correct, and balanced report in this instance. We remain open to receiving further questions should you need more information or details or if anything remains unclear.

Kind regards
Paddy Blewer

Group Public Relations Director
Henley & Partners UK Ltd

ALEXANDER NIX

This was the response received from Alexander Nix:

I am very sorry about the death of Daphne Caruana Galizia in Malta in 2017; it was a tragedy that never should have happened. That said, it is wrong of you to try and connect me, or SCL/Cambridge Analytica, in anyway whatsoever with her assassination.

Your letter to me is premised on false allegations and mis-reporting, the majority of which has been investigated and proven to be untrue. Specifically:

- As I explained to the UK Parliamentary Select Committee, I (or any of my former companies) have not had any involvement with Mr Kälin or Henley & Partners for almost a decade.

- Neither I personally, nor SCL/Cambridge Analytica, have ever undertaken any work in Malta. This includes political campaigning or electioneering in any form for any political party. This position was corroborated directly by the High Commissionaire of Malta and by the Chelgate PR company (acting on behalf of the Government of Malta).

- Political campaigning is a legitimate business undertaken by companies all over the world. There is nothing illegal or unlawful about working in political campaigning. To suggest otherwise, especially in the absence of any evidence of wrongdoing, is defamatory.

- The tragic death of my very good friend and colleague, Dan Muresan, in Kenya was thoroughly investigated at the time by the local police and the Romanian Embassy (Dan was a Romanian National) and there was no suggestion that his death was anything other than a terrible accident. In the independent report following an investigation into SCL/CA, Julian Malins, QC concluded, 'His death was certainly unexpected, but I have found nothing in the circumstances to suggest that he was murdered. None of those closely involved at the time (the police and family and embassy staff) thought that he was murdered. The autopsy findings did not suggest murder. His death was in fact the kind of very sad event that can happen to a young man on a Saturday night, who has been drinking. To suggest to the world's press that he was murdered was an irresponsible act, no doubt causing pain to his loved ones.'

I reiterate, that I am very sorry about the death of Daphne Caruana Galizia, but any attempt to connect me with events surrounding this tragedy will be met in the strongest terms, where all my rights are reserved in this matter.

Kind regards,
Alexander Nix

cc:
Alex Deal, Esq. – Messrs RIAA Barker Gillette (UK) LLP
Vinay Verma, Esq. – Messrs RIAA Barker Gillette (UK) LLP

THE DIRECTORS OF PILATUS BANK

We wrote to the lawyers who represented the Directors of Pilatus Bank in a court case seeking damages from the government following the bank's closure. This was their response:

I write with reference to your earlier email in relation to the upcoming publication of a book which will feature Pilatus Bank.

We started representing the interests of the directors of Pilatus Bank on the 5th of April 2018 following the administrative actions taken by the MFSA against the Bank and its Board of Directors – namely the directives issued on the 21st and 22nd of March 2018. In this regard, our involvement has been limited to seeking out those remedies afforded by law to a party that feels aggrieved by an administrative action. The actions that we, as a law firm, have taken in the interests of our client are in the public domain. Consequently, we are unable to provide any comments or statements in relation to the allegations listed in your email since we had not yet commenced representing our clients at the time that the alleged activities concerned, we were not engaged to assist or advise with any matters related to the listed allegations and we are unaware of the facts and circumstances related to and connected with the said allegations.

Whilst wishing you the best of success with the upcoming publication, do not hesitate to contact the undersigned should you require.

Regards,
Jonathan Thompson
DF Advocates
Partner

BRIAN TONNA

We received the following from Brian Tonna:

I have already replied to the allegation that I am 'aware and have sought to conceal the ownership of Egrant Inc' and, without having had sight of the actual text that you intend to publish, I can only refer you to the facts as I have set them out, and deny the allegation.

I also deny, more broadly, the implication of wrongdoing, both from a legal and also from a conduct perspective in all the instances you refer to in your email below.

Finally I would remind you that I co-operated to the fullest extent with all official inquiries and investigations that have taken place, and in relation to the entity Egrant Inc, of the conclusions reached in those processes.

Additionally I must reserve my position, my rights, and my remedies at law in relation to any reference to myself in your upcoming publication.

Brian Tonna

KARL CINI

An almost identical response was sent by Karl Cini:

I have already replied to the allegation that I am 'aware and have sought to conceal the ownership of Egrant Inc' and, without having had sight of the actual text that you intend to publish, I can only refer you to the facts as I have set them out, and deny the allegation. I also deny, more broadly, the implication of wrongdoing, both from a legal and also from a conduct perspective. Finally, I would remind you that I co-operated to the fullest extent with all official inquiries and investigations that have taken place in relation to the entity Egrant Inc, and of the conclusions reached in those processes.

Additionally I must reserve my position, my rights and my remedies at law in relation to any reference to myself in your upcoming publication.

Regards
Karl Cini
Partner, Tax and International Client Services Department
Nexia BT

STEPHAN ROH

We asked Stephan Roh to comment on his behalf and on behalf of Joseph Mifsud since we had no way of contacting his client:

I herewith inform and notify you about a formal cease and desist instruction not to mention my name, or the name of our client Prof. Mifsud, in a book dedicated to the Maltese high-profile murder case which you mentioned hereunder. The matter is highly sensible, of international attention, politically charged and used for many political actions and propaganda and any such relationship (between myself, Prof. Mifsud, and the case) insinuated in your book is of a nature to severely damage reputation, business, etc. to the extend that it must be considered a civil and criminal liability of an author, publisher. There is no reason to do so, and we will, as soon as we understand place of publishing, sale, distribution etc. intervene to prohibit the printing, production and distribution of such a book with all legal means and recover our costs and damages from all persons involved and review all possibilities of criminal laws in any jurisdiction available.

I understand you are asking the following questions in form of an interview: Please find my prelim comments in red as follows:

1. *That you have purchased and own a stake in Link Campus or University and that you have done so using your ownership of Drake Global Limited registered in the UK;*

    My 5% investment in LINK Campus is on public record and shall not be put in relation to the above-mentioned murder case. This would be highly damageable to my investment and to the University and I will need to recover losses by legal means available, from authors, publishers, etc., while the cease and desist instruction shall govern this aspect, too.

2. *The suggestion that your participation in Link served Russian interests;*
    This is not true and my cease and desist instruction shall cover this as well. It is highly damageable to my investment and to the University to insinuate that my investment serves Russian interests and I will recover losses by all legal means available, from authors, publishers, etc. for such untrue allegations.

3. *Your interest and takeover of Severnvale Nuclear Services Ltd and its exponential growth under your tutelage especially in view of the suggestion that you are linked to Russian interests.*

    This is not true and my cease and desist instruction shall cover this as well – any public insinuation of me being linked to Russian interests re. my private, exclusively Western European entrepreneurial business incl Severnvale, LINK Campus, etc. will expose you and your publisher to direct claims for damages – and the cease and desist instruction shall govern this aspect, too.

In respect of Professor Mifsud:

4. *The fact that he left the University of Malta and EMUNI with suggestions of financial mismanagement, overspending, and wrongdoing;*
    This has been disputed by Prof. Mifsud as highly defamatory and any repetition of same will allow for claims for damages etc. I herewith instruct formally to cease and desist from any such allegation.

5. *The suggestion that he allowed himself to be known or to be introduced as a Professor before he was granted the title by an academic institution;*
    Prof. Mifsud has been allowed by divers higher education institutions and Universities to be called 'Professor' – any dispute or allegation contrary would certainly trigger Prof Mifsud's claims for damages.

6. *The suggestion that his association with you and other persons indicate that he represents interests of the Russian state;*
    Myself, I am not representing the interests of the Russian state, but am fully cooperating with divers US investigators re Spygate. There is no indication that Prof. Mifsud was or is representing the interests of the Russian state and in case you intend to make such allegation in public, about Prof. Mifsud, or about myself, it is herewith instructed a formal cease and desist and, if you may contravene, Prof. Mifsud and myself will certainly claim for damages.

7. *The allegation that he offered to provide persons connected with the Donald Trump presidential campaign 'dirt' on Hilary Clinton acquired from thousands of emails hacked from her computer servers by Russian activity.*
    This statement is untrue, and based on the sole declaration of Mr George Papadopoulos (without any other supporting proof) and the cease and desist instruction does extend to it, as well.

I hope that the above is satisfactory.

Best regards,
Stephan Roh

ADRIAN DELIA

The PN leader sent us these comments in response to our questions:

1. *Your reaction and behaviour in public at the time of and since the assassination;*

   Shocked, then angry. Now perturbed that government, repeatedly, refuses to launch an independent inquiry on Daphne Carana Galizia's resignation (sic). I spoke about and acted upon Mrs Caruana Galizia's assassination on numerous occasions, and reiterated how this was, by far, Malta's darkest moment in decades. Justice must be done. The mastermind of Caruana Galizia's murder is still at large.

2. *The allegation that you facilitated the laundering of proceeds of crime from a prostitution ring in Soho, London;*

   I was never involved directly or indirectly in any criminal activity including money laundering. During over 25 years of private practice as a lawyer I never tendered advice in this sense or assisted clients in any manner towards this end. I built my whole career and reputation on ethical professional counsel. Over a decade and more before I entered politics, I had assisted a client in acquiring property in London using legitimate funds deriving from a leading Maltese bank.

   The client rented out the property and in turn there were other sub-rentals. I never appeared for or assisted any of the tenants, sub-tenants or any other third parties. For a short limited time period I was also a director on the owning company. All transactions that I knew about were above board and completely within the parameters of the law. The client also hired professional counsel in London.

3. *The allegation that you lied about never having a bank account in an offshore jurisdiction;*

   I never lied. Not about this nor about anything else.

I was first asked about the bank account in question in the context of my personal assets, that is in relation to assets belonging to me personally. This, within the wider context of a country having politicians in government who had been exposed by the Panama papers as having opened accounts overseas for evidently illicit purpose. I replied clearly and adamantly that I did not have and had never held funds, accounts, shares, property, or any other assets overseas. Of course, I was referring to my own or family funds. I stand by what I said then that I personally never had bank accounts abroad.

I have also repeatedly said that I would not divulge matters pertaining to clients' advice. When I had requested information from the bank abroad pertaining to information in the public domain about an account allegedly held in my name, the bank had replied in the negative stating that there was no such account, there was no account/s at all in my name and this even as far as their records went back.

4. *Your association with Dr Chris Cardona in the structures involved in the services provided to the owners of the Greek Street, London property raided by the British police because of illegal activities therein, including prostitution and human trafficking;*

I have and never had any association with Dr Chris Cardona. In private practice I held several directorships. Sitting on the same board at any given time with other directors does not mean that you have an association with them. At the time I was not a public figure and unless I am mistaken neither was he.

Having said that, today I do not hold records in my hand and do not specifically recall whether we were directors on the same board at all, and if so, for how long. Documents which I cannot verify as being original or truthful in the public domain however, show, that if this was the case it was for a very short time indeed.

I once again rebut forcefully any preposterous and absurd allegations that I was ever involved directly, indirectly, or even remotely in any prostitution or human trafficking activity. You must be aware that the British police had investigated the matter and proceeded to prosecute foreign nationals – not the sub-tenants, not the tenants, not the owners, not my client, certainly not me. Several degrees of separation removed, which has one defy logic to make even fantastic connections with me, let alone attributions of guilt.

5.   *Your reaction and behaviour in public at the time of and since the publication of an extract of the Egrant inquiry report.*

I have, time and again, insisted that Government must publish the inquiry in its entirety. I have also taken the matter to Court. It is unacceptable that the PM, his aides, the Justice Minister, and his lawyer, and God knows who else, are privy to the Magistrate's inquiry and the Leader of the Opposition is not. We respect the conclusions of Magistrate Aaron Bugeja's inquiry – the Nationalist Party publicly declared its willingness to accept its conclusions, long before I became party leader, but we – the country, must know the entire findings of the inquiry.

ANTHONY AXISA

This is the response we received from Anthony Axisa:

I do believe that I have been mentioned in this context several times, albeit I am somewhat disappointed that although I have always provided an adequate context, no one has ever bothered to include same.

Keeping in mind that I cannot comment specifically on what you wrote in your book, because you have not provided me with the relevant sections, I will still endeavour, with a healthy dose of optimism, to provide you with some key facts that you may want to consider and hopefully reproduce:

1.   The implication that there is something sinister in moving on in one's career is unwarranted. It is something that many of us have done, including you.

I have left my job with the Lotteries and Gaming Authority (now the Malta Gaming Authority). Ever since, as a matter of prudence and policy, I have never been on the MGA's books in any capacity, nor have I ever expressed an interest in offering any services for which RFPs have been issued over the years.

2. Cybergaming Consultants provides its services to several gaming clients. Under the regulations in force at the time, a key official was mandated by law to also be a director. My job as key official was to be the point of contact between the licensee and the Authority. The law mandated me to ensure ongoing compliance with each and all obligations emanating from the gaming licence. During my tenure, Centurionbet Ltd was always fully compliant with its obligations.

Obviously, I am well aware of our obligations when onboarding a client. There was nothing to suggest that the shareholders of the company at that time had any connection with criminal activities or that they were acting on behalf of third parties. In good faith and using our best endeavours, we could ascertain this and I am sure that with its resources and access to other regulatory bodies, the LGA also ascertained same when carrying out its due diligence exercise prior to issuing of the gaming licence.

3. I have to clarify that I resigned from director and key official of Centurionbet Ltd on the 14th August, 2015. Allegations about the company's possible links to the criminal world were made years later. Indeed, the MGA only revoked the licence in question towards the end of 2017.

On the 13th August, 2015 I was informed that the company was being investigated by the executive police of Malta. I duly delivered to them all the files and informed the MGA that I was resigning for these reasons. Albeit, I could only attest that the client was in good standing in terms of its adherence to obligations under the licence, I am not an investigator and had to assume that the police had information which I did not have. For the sake of completeness, I am attaching a copy of both the form K and my email to the MGA at the time.

In the light of the above, I do trust that we can rise above sensationalism which unfortunately has tainted most articles that I have read on the matter, and that if you still deem it fit that I deserve an honourable mention in your book, the facts above are reproduced by way of factual context.

Given that in my replies, I am referring to the MGA, I am copying in the CEO of the Authority, so that the Authority will have the opportunity to make any clarifications that it deems necessary.

Wishing you every success with your book and journalistic endeavours.

Best regards,
Tony

Dr Tony Axisa
CEO
Cybergaming Consultants

DARREN DEBONO

We received the following from Darren Debono's Maltese lawyer:
I refer to your email of the 5th September 2019 wherein you state that you are co-authoring a book examining the circumstances prior to and the aftermath of the assassination of Daphne Caruana Galizia in Malta in 2017, and also refer to our short telecommunication earlier on this morning.

You state that my client will feature in the book.

My client fails to understand how he could possibly feature in a book about the circumstances mentioned above and nor do you give any indication of the circumstances or the manner in which.

You are therefore kindly requested to make available the extracts that will refer to my client and explain how a connection will be created between the allegations mentioned in your email and the murder of Daphne Caruana Galizia.

In the circumstances, please note the following:

1. My client is facing charges in Italy regarding alleged participation in a smuggling activity of oil out of Libya, which charges are being denied. The case is ongoing and he has the right to be presumed innocent. However, your publication may prejudice his right of fair trial.

2. My client has no connection with the Mafia of Acireale or anywhere else and is not being charged with such activity. Any mention of such fictitious connection is pure conjecture and will damage his legitimate fishing business.

3. Your email fails to refer to how your publication will create a connection between the two allegations above and the murder of Ms Caruana Galizia. This failure is evidence that your email sent on the eve of publication is only intended to pay lip service to your duty to give my client the right to respond without actually giving him an adequate opportunity to make effective representations.

Please be advised, so as to avoid any unnecessary actions for libel and damages in any of the jurisdictions in which the book is distributed.

Regards
Dr. Victor J. Bugeja LL.D, B.A.,LP.,
Dip. Not. Pub., AMRSH., DSS
Advocate

YORGEN FENECH

We received the following from Yorgen Fenech's lawyers:

We write on behalf of Yorgen Fenech and the Tumas Group Company Limited and refer to your email of the 2nd September 2019 addressed to the attention of Mr Fenech requesting comments on a number of unsubstantiated statements ahead of the publication of a book you intend publishing together with other undefined authors.

Firstly Mr Fenech categorically rejects any allegations, assertions, and/or suggestions made in his regard as completely baseless and unfounded. In this respect reference is made to numerous public statements made by our client denying the said allegations, and therefore it is indeed unethical and unlawful that you seem intended in persisting with the reiteration of such falsities, despite the absence of any shred of evidence corroborating the veracity of such allegations.

Furthermore, we note from your email that you may be implying some form of association in illicit activity by the Tumas Group with third parties. Any statement, suggestions, and/or insinuation to that effect is entirely baseless, gratuitous, and speculative and is herewith rejected in the strongest manner possible as totally unfounded both in fact and at law.

The Tumas Group conducts its operations in full compliance with all its obligations at law. You are well aware that the Company is not in a position to divulge any specific details in respect of any patrons or clients, including of the casinos operated by the Group, but rest assured that such casinos apply strict compliance procedures and take all required actions at law whenever there may be suspicion of any illicit activity, and indeed has been the case when such action was required.

In the light of the above, you are herewith reminded of your duty and obligation to duly verify the veracity and accuracy of any statements you may wish to publish and not to misrepresent any facts by colouring them with innuendos, insinuations, and/or suggestions purposely intended to twist such facts and/or provoke false inferences.

Finally you are solicited to desist from making and/or publishing any allegations and/or make any insinuations referred to in your email public, and are herewith holding you responsible for any damages which may be sustained as a result of any such publication.

Yours
Karl Briffa
Joseph J. Vella
GVZH Advocates

We went back to lawyers Briffa and Vella and asked them to comment on
Alfred Degiorgio's lucky turn at casinos owned by the group run by Yorgen
Fenech. We asked them if it seemed odd to them that Alfred Degiorgio could
walk away from the Portomaso casino with €440,000 over a period of
time; whether his gambling was flagged as suspicious; whether they checked
the provenance of the money that was gambled; and whether Yorgen Fenech
thought this money was a cloak payment for services Alfred Degiorgio carried
out for a third party while Yorgen Fenech was aware of the transaction. This
was their response:

The matter to which you make reference once again regarding
the running of the Tumas Group Casinos has already been
comprehensively addressed in our previous email, but since
you keep returning to this subject we would only add that our
clients are strictly precluded by law from providing you with any
information in addition to what has been already stated in the said
email such that your repeated requests are therefore being done
with an ulterior motive.

For the record, however, we refer you to the evidence tendered
by a representative of the casinos operated by Tumas Group in July
2018 in the ongoing proceedings before the criminal court against
Alfred Degiorgio and others relating to money laundering charges,
which evidence had clearly established that Alfred Degiorgio's last
visit to the said casinos goes back to 2012 in the case of one casino
and 2013 in the case of the second casino.

Consequently, the inferences and insinuations made in your last
paragraph are so spurious, false and contrived that they do not
merit any consideration whatsoever.

Yours
Joseph J Vella
Karl Briffa
GVZH Advocates

To be absolutely sure, we asked the lawyers to categorically state whether Alfred Degiorgio had gambled in Yorgen Fenech's casino after 2013. This was their response:

Dear Mr Delia,

Please refer to our earlier email of today which is very clear on this matter.

Regards,
Joseph J Vella

ALFRED DEGIORGIO, GEORGE DEGIORGIO, VINCENT MUSCAT

We have contacted the lawyers for the three men charged with murder for Daphne Caruana Galizia with a request for their comment. The lawyers said they would ask their clients to see if they had any comment. None was forthcoming by the deadline.

The three men are awaiting trial. All their requests for bail have so far been denied. They have pleaded not guilty to all charges.

INDEX OF NAMES

Printed in Great Britain
by Amazon